"An excellent book for every idea person, whether inventor or entrepreneur. In fact, this is the book I wish I'd written when inventing Rollerblades— and I recommend it to all who dream of starting the next Rollerblade Company."

—Scott Olson, inventor and founder, Rollerblades

"*The Great American Idea Book* is a great idea! Not only is the information valuable and complete, but it is presented in an enjoyable and understandable way . . . [This is] one of the few "how to" books that is actually fun to read! Who knows? I wouldn't be shocked if this book led the next person with a great concept every step of the way to the next blockbuster movie!"

—Roger Corman, producer/director, *Little Shop of Horrors* and president, Concorde–New Horizon Films

"With luck, I turned my idea into a best-selling book. *The Great American Idea Book* can give you the guidance and direction to replace luck with step-by-step logic. Got an idea? Get this book!"

—Robert Kowalski, author of *The 8-Week Cholesterol Cure*

"This is the reference book I wish I had had when I started up my business in 1951. It's filled with good advice . . . not only for struggling artists or inventors, but for anyone who has ever wrestled with an idea they wanted to see work."

—Lillian Vernon, founder and CEO, Lillian Vernon mail order company

"Provides a unique perspective on how to turn an idea into a profitable commodity. The authors' five-step approach is simple and transforms the emotional, inventive, and creative reader into an analytical, business-minded person ready for the challenges of the competitive business world. . . . Every creative reader will gain something of value from reading *The Great American Idea Book*."

—*San Diego Union-Tribune*

By Bob Coleman

NONFICTION

The Small Business Survival Guide
The New Small Business Survival Guide

NOVELS

The Later Adventures of Tom Jones

The
GREAT
AMERICAN
IDEA
BOOK

———

The GREAT AMERICAN IDEA BOOK

Bob Coleman

Deborah Neville

W · W · NORTON & COMPANY

NEW YORK / LONDON

The text of this book is composed in Times Roman with the display set in Garamond Oldstyle and Galliard. Composition and manufacturing by the Maple-Vail Book Manufacturing Group. Book design by Marjorie J. Flock.

First published as a Norton paperback 1995

Library of Congress Cataloging–in–Publication Data
Coleman, Bob.
    The great American idea book / by Bob Coleman and Deborah
Neville.
        p.   cm.
    Includes index.
        1. Inventions—United States.   2. Patents—United States.
3. Intellectual property—United States.   I. Neville, Deborah.
II. Title.
T212.C59   1993
609.73—dc20   92–13144

ISBN 0-393-31211-9

W. W. Norton & Company, Inc., 500 Fifth Avenue, New York, N.Y. 10110
W. W. Norton & Company Ltd., 10 Coptic Street, London WC1A 1PU

3 4 5 6 7 8 9 0

*For our parents, who treated children
as a wonderful idea*

Contents

Part One
THE BASICS OF *IDEAS*

___

WHAT EVERYBODY NEEDS TO KNOW

Part Two

THE ART OF *IDEAS*

BOOKS, MOVIES, SONGS, AND THE VISUAL ARTS

Part Three

THE MACHINERY OF *IDEAS*

YOU AND YOUR INVENTIONS

Part Four

THE BUSINESS OF *IDEAS*

TRADEMARKS, TRADE SECRETS, AND
FRANCHISING YOUR GREAT BUSINESS IDEA

Acknowledgments

IT IS IMPOSSIBLE TO ACKNOWLEDGE BY NAME all the hundreds of people who contributed to this project, but we are grateful to them all. In addition to the book's interviewees, named and unnamed, we are grateful to the many authors and journalists whose work we cite and most heartily recommend.

In addition, we owe special thanks to our agent, Peter Ginsberg of Curtis Brown, and our editor, Starling Lawrence, both of whom contributed to the project from its earliest days.

Lastly, special thanks to our colleagues and teachers, and especially to that most remarkable of teachers, Peter Guber.

Authors' Note

WHILE WE HAVE TRIED in this book to give accurate and up-to-date information, laws and customs change constantly, even in the time that elapses between writing and publication. Moreover, this book contains authors' opinions based upon their own experiences; your idea, whatever it is, will certainly involve special circumstances. Therefore, the authors and publisher assume no responsibility for any actions readers may take based upon material offered within this book. Please consult with competent professionals before taking any action concerning your specific situation. Ideas are valuable. Take the time and trouble to protect them!

Part One

THE BASICS OF *IDEAS*

———

WHAT EVERYBODY NEEDS TO KNOW

Introduction:
You and Your Great Idea

IF YOU'RE AN AMERICAN WITH AN IDEA and want to make money from it—congratulations! You're part of a great and honorable tradition. That tradition, in fact, is embedded in our founding document:

The Congress shall have Power . . . To promote the Progress of Science and useful Arts, by securing for limited Times to Authors and Inventors the exclusive Right to their respective Writings and Discoveries. —*U.S. Constitution, Article I, Section 8*

In plain English, progress depends on people knowing they'll be able to profit from their ideas. The American system has turned that simple truth into two centuries of unbroken creativity in science, engineering, business, and the arts.

This is a great country for creativity. But if you're an average person just setting out to profit from your idea, the trip can look overwhelmingly long and hard.

You need a guidebook. That's what this book is—a guide to turning ideas into money.

What kinds of ideas? Almost any kind, but especially:

Inventions	Films	Visual Arts and Animation
Books	Music	Businesses

That may seem a wide range for anyone, but why narrow yourself? If you're creative by nature, why start out with restrictions? You may have one idea now, but it's another great American tradition, dating from Franklin and Jefferson, to be creative in many fields.

Get the habit of having ideas, taking them seriously, and following through on them, and you can create and succeed in more areas than you'd ever imagine.

Who succeeds with ideas? Anyone with the courage to pursue them.

• Eileen Goudge was a welfare mother when she borrowed a friend's typewriter and banged out a "true confessions" story. Then she wrote— and sold—twenty-five teen novels, and when she turned to adult fiction, her first two novels both hit the *New York Times* best-seller list.

• North Carolina dirt farmer Marsh Williams was in prison when he hand-made the mechanism for what ultimately became the M-1 carbine. Paroled because of his inventive genius, he led Winchester's design efforts during World War II and ultimately won more than seventy patents.

No handicap matters, you see, if you have the idea—and the heart.

Writing this book allowed us to meet creative people of every sort. Rich and famous or still working on their first big idea, they all taught us that life offers few rewards greater than following through on whatever idea most excites your imagination.

We want to give you your shot. Will you make a million dollars? We can't promise that. But we can promise that you'll have a better chance if you pay attention to this book, and that, win or lose, you'll feel better about yourself for having believed in yourself enough to try to make your ideas real.

The choice is yours. You can work to make your great idea a reality and so reap the money and the glory. Or you can sit back and do nothing, then snap on the TV one day, see somebody else getting rich, and know, in your aching heart, that he or she is making it with "your" idea.

The Romans used to say, *"Dum vivimus, vivamus"*—while we live, let's *live*.

If that appeals to you, turn the page and let's get started.

1

How to Use This Book

AS FAR AS WE KNOW, nobody's ever before tried writing a guidebook to all kinds of ideas. So it might be worth about one minute to explain how we think you can use this book best.

The book divides into four parts:

Part One is meant for everyone. It covers both the basic rules of improving, protecting, and selling your ideas, and a lot of basic psychology for sticking with the process, dealing with your problems, and having the maximum amount of fun.

(Don't laugh! If making money from your ideas isn't fun, you're going about it the wrong way.)

Part Two is for ideas in the arts. If the arts (movies, books, music) interest you, you'll probably want to read the section straight through, for two reasons:

First, many art forms today are multimedia—your creation may not fall into any neat category.

Second (and this is far more important), nowadays you aren't getting full value from your idea unless you think about how all the different media interrelate. Today, after all, a comic book can become a film, which inspires a "novelization," which leads to a video game, which grows into a television series. Remember, you artists, think big!

Part Three is for inventions. Some of this is fairly technical, but the whole legal system surrounding patents and the tremendous amounts of money at stake make that inevitable.

We'll take a step-by-step approach to the entire process, from finding an idea to commercializing and defending it. As an inventor, you will have a lot of options (whether or not to patent, whether to make the product yourself or to license someone else, and so on). We'll try to discuss all those options, so you can make the choices that suit you best.

If your idea is an invention, you'll probably also want to read:

Part Four is for business ideas. This isn't a day-to-day business operations book, although we list several such books in our Recommended Reading section. We're covering the areas books neglect: how to protect and exploit the *ideas* within your business. We'll show how to use trademarks and trade names, trade secrets, franchising. This is for you if you're either thinking about a business idea or eager to protect and expand a business already in existence.

The Case Studies. Concrete examples are better than abstract theories. Included in this book are many short examples of the ways people have succeeded with their ideas. But also included are longer studies of three unusually successful people: one entrepreneur, one inventor, and one artist. Their stories can teach you a lot.

Summing Up. This book is action-oriented. We want to give you the tools and the confidence to put your ideas into action. If some of it reads like a pep talk, forgive us. Mood matters, and winners have a certain attitude. That attitude can be yours.

2

Getting Started

IF YOU'RE LIKE MOST PEOPLE, you're going to spend the first few days after getting your idea just walking around (maybe bumping into a few walls), and thinking: "Wow! This is great!"

Soon, though, the thrill dims and you find yourself facing the creative person's oldest question: "Now what?!" How do you make the idea into something real?

The Five Tasks of Profiting from an Idea

Whatever your idea, whether it's a song or a rocket engine, you have five tasks to accomplish to turn it into income:

Securing   Developing   Promoting   Defending   Profiting

Note that these five tasks don't occur in any fixed order. If you sell a screenplay, for example, you may get paid immediately—and then spend the next year or more developing it into something that can actually be filmed.

What do the five elements entail?

Securing means securing the legal rights to an idea.

Before you can secure the legal rights, you need to know two things: does anyone already own the rights, and is my idea the kind that can be legally secured?

You obviously can't trademark the business name Xerox, for example, because somebody already owns it. But you can't patent a rosewood baseball bat because (even if nobody's ever built one) it's an obvious extension of existing art, and you can't secure any title to a literary work, because titles aren't legally protectable.

Don't worry, we'll show you how you can secure the greatest possible protection for any idea and when in the process you need to do it.

Developing means getting your idea into a form where somebody will invest in it. It may also mean the continuing process of improving the product until the investors feel it's ready for the wider market.

Promoting means persuading people to spend money (or time) on your idea. It can mean everything from finding your first agent or investor to hitting the talk shows after your product's on the market.

Defending, while it may never be a factor for you, is taking legal action to protect your legal and financial rights to your idea. This normally happens only after your idea has proved valuable enough to be worth stealing—but it can occur at any time.

Profiting is what it's all about: cutting deals, getting checks—in short, all the good stuff.

Now here's the real point:

Nearly all of us find sooner or later that we're good at some parts of the process, less good at others. Whether by nature or training, some of us are great at inventing; others are terrific promoters; and so on.

It's human nature to concentrate on our strengths and to duck our weaknesses. Unfortunately, that won't get the job done. You need to pay attention to all five parts of the process.

Meanwhile, your goal at this point should be threefold:

1. Make sure everything you do in connection with your idea (even thinking about it in the shower!) advances at least one of the five goals.

2. Be honest with yourself about the areas where you need to improve. Do you have twenty well-polished short stories sitting at home, but none out in the mail to publishers? You need to learn how to promote

and profit. Have you been out trying to raise money for an invention you secretly know needs a redesigned main switch? You're weak on development.

3. Improve your skills wherever you're weak—or, at least, find the right people to help you. Don't worry! We're going to teach you skills— and show you how to get great people to help you.

If all that seems daunting, cheer up. We're going to talk next about where you get the mental energy and the discipline to stick to the job.

3

Think Like a Winner

Enthusiasm: You've Got to Have It

WE ASKED VIRTUALLY EVERYONE we interviewed for this book—designers, attorneys, film directors, entrepreneurs—to name the single most important factor in making an idea succeed. What was their most common answer?

Enthusiasm.

Sounds corny? Maybe—but think about it. For some businesses the role of emotion is obvious. Columbia Pictures (or any other film studio), for example, isn't in the film business. Kodak is in the film business; studios are in the emotions business. If their product doesn't make an audience laugh or cry, gasp or cheer, they haven't got a movie; they've got a lot of expensive junk in a can.

But think a little more. Almost nothing you're likely to create or invent is going to be a necessity in the average person's life; at most, it's going to be an option. Getting people to buy means making them feel enthusiasm.

Who's going to believe your idea will create an exciting product if you, the creator, are vague or tentative about it? Nobody!

Remember, enthusiasm isn't egotism. Most people are interested in hearing how great your idea is; they aren't interested in hearing how great *you* are. You can be personally modest and still push your idea.

But if you're reading this in the first flush of inspiration, you're probably chomping at the bit. Why give you a lecture on enthusiasm?

Because we're talking about enthusiasm over the long haul, enthusiasm after you've gotten ten rejections—when agents don't return your calls, when investors back out and the banks turn down your loan. How do you stay enthusiastic then?

Rule Number One: Trust Yourself About 1980 a friend of ours, an electronics engineer, had a great idea: He'd write a computer program to help people do their taxes without a CPA's help. He asked his co-workers, all Ph.D.s working on a top-secret missile project, what they thought of it. Their answer? "No way. Any moron can figure his taxes."

Now, these rocket-scientist pals certainly could figure their taxes without help. So our friend took their advice. Even though he could have pounded out a computerized tax program in short order, he dropped his plan.

Was he right?

No! About 249 million of us in this country aren't rocket scientists. For us, taxes are confoundedly complicated, and a computer program to do them is so tempting a product that during the 1980s several people became millionaires from selling those programs.

To this day, our friend still kicks himself because he let an easy fortune slip through his fingers.

Our point?

People will always be happy to tell you why you can't make it. They'll have more reasons than you can imagine. *Your job is to believe in yourself.*

Rule Number Two: If You Believe in Yourself, Be Stubborn Winning a patent or selling a screenplay or publishing a novel may be tough, but it's definitely doable if you're stubborn enough.

What do we mean by "stubborn"? Well, Robert Pirsig sent *Zen and the Art of Motorcycle Maintenance* to 121 publishers. They all bounced it. Number 122 bought it—and at last count had sold more than three million copies.

Another friend of ours went through UCLA film school, won some awards, then set out to be a screenwriter. She wrote—and aggressively promoted—ten screenplays. She didn't sell anything.

Did she quit? No! She told herself that she was not "the world's best-trained, unsold screenwriter"—and wrote screenplay number eleven.

Number eleven sold. So did twelve, thirteen, and fourteen.

Today she both writes and produces movies—and divides her time between a home in Bel Air and a home in Wyoming. Not bad for somebody who failed to sell ten straight scripts.

Not a bad story to remember. And remember this: You're the world's greatest authority on your own idea. There's an excellent chance you'll see its true strengths when other people haven't.

Obviously, you want to be rational as well as stubborn. Just because you have an idea doesn't mean it's automatically worthwhile. Listen to other people, especially those with solid track records. Sometimes you have to drop an idea entirely; sometimes you revise it; sometimes you set it aside for a few years until the technology or public tastes catch up with you. But never quit on an idea you still believe in.

How long is reasonable stubbornness?

In the late 1930s a young woman named Gertrude Elion thought she had some interesting ideas for cancer research. She also had a chemistry degree from a university and a master's on top of that.

But for seven years she couldn't get a job in research. She bounced from place to place, mostly as a glorified lab tech. Things got so bad that, according to *Scientific American,* she thought about giving up and going to secretarial school.

Finally, with most male scientists pressed into defense work for World War II, she got a grudging shot at a research job, even though the head of the lab said she'd probably just distract her male colleagues.

A pretty sad beginning, but she stuck to her guns. During the next forty years she put one of her ideas after another into action.

It seems her ideas weren't too bad, after all. In 1990 Gertrude Elion became the first woman admitted to the American Inventors Hall of Fame. But that was small potatoes, because in 1988 she's already been awarded the Nobel Prize for Medicine and Physiology.

Whenever you think you've got it too tough, remember Gertrude Elion and keep plugging.

4

An Even Keel

YOU MAY BE one of those rare lucky people whose ideas go almost effortlessly from conception to success. For most of us, though, there are going to be glitches along the way. When you have setbacks or problems, what (aside from just gritting your teeth) can give you the courage or the energy to go on?

Here are five devices you might consider. None is magical, but any of them might help you.

Have Heroes You can sometimes model your efforts, or understand your own situation, in terms of what other people have done or endured. In other words, you can help yourself by learning about people you admire, either for the way they lived or for what they created or, if you're lucky, for both.

Most of us, for example, can identify with stories of adversity overcome.

Thomas Carlyle spent seven years writing his history of the French Revolution, only to lend the sole copy to a friend whose maid, thinking it was scrap paper, threw it in the fire. Carlyle, true to his philosophy, simply told his friend the setback was God's will, sat back down, and wrote the book anew—and it proved to be a Victorian classic.

You may rather pick your hero for the quality of his or her work. According to the *New York Times,* Director Martin Scorsese spent much of his youth watching old movies on television. At some point he realized his favorite films were all produced by the British Archers studio, whose heads, Michael Powell and Emeric Pressburger, became his heroes. Their lively work inspired his own bold early career.

(The story has a nice ending. In the 1970s, after Pressburger's death, Powell fell on hard times. Scorsese, then a rising young film maker, traveled to London to thank Powell for the inspiration—but, finding him neglected, brought him to the United States and helped revitalize his career. Powell, in turn, served as key adviser on Scorsese's *Raging Bull,* sometimes ranked as the finest film of the 1980s.)

Heroes can teach you what modern education neglects: such virtues as courage, honesty, endurance, and loyalty. When you're in the crush of trying to get your book published, your gadget on the market, or your film made, those virtues can slip from view. Yet they can serve you better than a dozen hot tips or a hundred connections.

Take Breaks One of the enduring images of inventors and artists is of unwavering, fanatical devotion to the work. As a practical matter, that's a good way to end up in the loony bin at worst and as an unsuccessful person at best.

The problem is probably worst for people pushing for their first break. You try one idea, then another and another. If nothing sells, you may find yourself banging your head against a wall but unable to come up with anything new. The harder you push, the worse it gets.

UCLA teacher and screenwriter Cynthia Whitcomb uses the interesting example of Hindu philosophy: Rama, Vishnu, and Shiva, three gods, representing, respectively, the creator, the preserver, and the destroyer. The idea (and this may be playing free and easy with the religious significance) is that life proceeds through a cycle, and that to create, you need times not only to have great ideas and to develop them, but to recharge the system, to get away from your old habits. In simple terms, to take a break.

This idea may not mean much to you now, but think about it if you ever get really stuck, unable to advance your idea or to move beyond it to something better. Sometimes you do need to get away, rather than simply to become obsessive about the same points.

And here's one more great Cynthia Whitcomb idea:

Cheer Yourself Up: Try the Manhattan Method No, we're not talking about the drink called the Manhattan. (Trying to cheer yourself up with drugs or alcohol is the single stupidest thing you can do.)

We're talking about something Woody Allen mentions at the end of his film, *Manhattan.* Basically, the idea is this: You make up a list of all the things in the world that make life worth living. Throw in all your heroes, the best things you've ever done, your favorite music—whatever. Make the list as eccentric and personal as you can (Woody's list includes the Marx Brothers and Louis Armstrong's "Potato Head Blues"). Then give the list to a friend, and if you ever get really down, call that friend and have him or her read the list back to you. Weird as this sounds, it really seems to work.*

Don't Fall into Envy If you're in a major center for whatever business interests you, you're probably going to know people who are doing tremendously well. If they started out on your level and hit it big before you do, you're likely to begin envying them—even to the point where it spoils not only your relationship with them, but all your pleasure in your work. Cut it out! By envying people, you're a) wasting time, b) making yourself miserable, and c) isolating yourself from people who may very well still consider themselves your friends and may be eager to do you a good turn. Above all, remember that no industry is so small that only one person is going to succeed, and the fact that someone you know has succeeded improves the probability that you'll succeed, too, if you stick with it.

Enjoy the Process One successful writer has this definition of a real writer: "A real writer is anybody who, when he spent a day where he wrote ten good pages, but the car blew up, the kitchen caught fire, and the dog bit a lawyer's kid, thinks he had a great day—but when he spent a day where he won the lottery and found a long-lost love, but didn't write anything good, thinks the day stank."

If you aren't enjoying the process, you probably aren't going to enjoy the rewards. When film producer Peter Guber won his first Academy Award, he put a stopwatch on the process and found that his crowning glory lasted almost exactly one minute. You can't make a life out of that. Enjoy what millionaire inventor Peter Norton calls the "frosting in the work"—then, when you finally collect the cake, you can enjoy that, too.

We probably haven't told you anything you haven't heard before. Maybe you'll never have use for it. Still, it's here if you need it.

Now let's move on to some ways to focus your ideas and your energy and to move your ideas toward reality.

---

*We're talking about the ordinary gloom that can come with temporary difficulties. Remember there is also clinical depression, a relatively common and, increasingly, easily treatable medical condition. If simple measures don't cheer you up or if unhappiness is seriously affecting your life, by all means get professional help.

5

Know Your "Dot"

YOU BELIEVE IN YOURSELF. You have enthusiasm, and you know a few tricks for keeping your mood steady in case it takes time before you succeed. How do you begin channeling your enthusiasm into a workable plan?

Start by creating a clear and powerful mental image of exactly what you want to achieve—of what we're going to call your "dot."

When Peter Guber, the producer of *Batman, Rainman, The Color Purple,* and other megahit movies, teaches his UCLA classes on making a Hollywood movie, he often starts by drawing a dot at the top of the blackboard. "That," he'll say in a fine New York accent, "is your dot— your goal, your dream."

Then he'll draw three more lines, so that the dot becomes the apex of a broad-based triangle.

"Down here," he'll say, filling in the triangle's broad bottom, "are all the people who *think* they want to make movies. Most of them are really going nowhere, because what they really care about is having a nice office, going to Hollywood parties, or telling everyone they've got a deal with Paramount.

"But you never lose sight of that dot. The ones who lose sight will never get there. Keep your eye on your 'dot,' and you'll make it."

Focus, in short, is crucial. Between now and the final victory, you may meet all sorts of problems, from fatigue to missing skills. Just keep your eye on the dot—and remember to aim high. Make that dot something worthy of your dream. "I want to sell my book" isn't enough. "I want to sell my book, see it on the best-seller list, and win the Pulitzer Prize," is probably more like it. You may not get all that, of course, but why start out expecting to achieve little?

Visualization If you'd like to try it, you can even turn your "dot" into an interesting psychological motivator.

Peter Guber takes his "dot" method one step further by devoting his energies to visualizing exactly what he wants to accomplish, even if he doesn't yet know how to accomplish it. His favorite example is how he became involved in the Olympics. He'd always wanted to participate, but by the time he got serious (when he was about forty), it was pretty clear he wasn't going there as an athlete. For most of us that would have pushed the idea out of mind, but Peter Guber took a different approach.

"Every night I'd take a moment before bed and picture myself standing in the Olympic stadium. I'd have the image fixed in my mind, with all the attendant success and glory. I wouldn't dwell on the idea, but at least once a day, with regularity, I'd call it to mind."

For a long time nothing came of this—he simply pursued the film career that ultimately made him chairman of Columbia Pictures. But one evening:

"I was in a busy restaurant, with so many conversations going on around me I couldn't hear anything clearly. Then suddenly one phrase came through with crystalline clarity:

" 'I always wanted to write the theme music for the Olympic Games.' "

Mr. Guber turned around—and saw that the remark had been made by John Williams, conductor of the Boston Pops and composer of the soundtracks for (among other things) the films *Jaws, Raiders of the Lost Ark,* and *Star Wars.*

Mr. Guber saw this as his chance. He introduced himself, explained he'd overheard the remark, and said that, as a film and record producer, he might be able to arrange for Mr. Williams to write the Olympic fanfare.

So Peter Guber became the music producer for the 1984 Olympic Games, and—you guessed it—made his way to the floor of the Los Angeles Coliseum for the opening ceremonies. And he credits the habit of visualization for helping him pick John Williams's one key remark out of all the noise of that restaurant.

Now, if most of us had gone up to John Williams and asked if he'd like to help us coproduce the Olympic Games, we'd have gotten the bum's rush by three burly waiters; we don't have the credentials (at least at this point) to make the idea plausible. But before you dismiss the whole notion, ask yourself this: How did Peter Guber get to the point where he could plausibly approach the country's most successful symphonic composer with an idea to help stage the world's most famous games?

Visualization, obviously, isn't going to take the place of genius, luck, or—especially—years of hard work. If nothing else, though, it should help you cheer up when your prospects seem gloomy. And it seems to be so widespread a trick among successful people that we couldn't resist mentioning it. If it helps you, fine; if not, forget it.*

*Interestingly, the *Wall Street Journal* profiled a woman who hit the best-seller lists after working seven years on a biography of poet Anne Sexton. Asked whether her success surprised her, the author said it didn't. During the seven years of writing, she pictured herself making the front page of the *New York Times Book Review,* alongside a review of her book by another major poet. And that was exactly what happened.

6

Priorities

Give One Project Priority Many people complain, "My problem isn't a lack of ideas—it's too *many* ideas. I start on one, and another one hits me."

The simple solution is to keep an idea journal (or better, a computer file, with backups). Jot down ideas as they occur to you, even devote some time to refining and expanding them in your spare time, but always return your focus to the one idea you most want to succeed.† Only drop your primary idea if a) the idea's absolutely dead, or b) the new idea is demonstrably better.

If you still can't focus, you're probably using the multitude of ideas simply as an excuse to keep you from what scares you: actually making one idea sell. In that case, pick your one best idea, lock the others in a drawer, and *focus*. You can do it!

†There are disciplines, of course, where one project won't do it. For instance, you need at least a small portfolio to promote yourself as a visual artist; you probably don't want to try selling screenplays unless you've got at least three to show. Still, the point stands: Get one piece in shape before you move on to the next.

7

Start Thinking about Business

HAVING A "DOT"—a goal, even a vision, of success—is fine, but it's still in the realm of the imagination. Now it's time to get down to work.

If you want to make money from your idea, you have to think of it as a business proposition.

We understand that some people, especially artists, find this tough. And we sympathize. Still, this is a good time to be honest with yourself. If you're pursuing an idea for pure intellectual pleasure, that's great; but if you want to make money from it, begin thinking like a businessperson now.

For businesspeople and inventors, the matter is simple. Before you've put more than a week into an invention or a business idea, you should be able to answer the question: "Who's going to buy this thing?"

For artists, of course, the question is more complicated. Your idea can involve not merely cleverness but your deepest feelings and beliefs. Is it wrong to try to give them a market orientation?

We think not—if you approach the matter correctly. You should use a sense of the market, not to corrupt yourself, but to improve the chances that what you want to create will actually succeed.

Suppose your dream is to make movies about the great events in American history. If you know that major studios almost never make historical epics today because of the costs, you might plan early to solve the problem; you might turn to documentaries or choose subjects that don't need elaborate outdoor action scenes.

On the other hand, you might just say, "To hell with it," and write whatever screenplay you want. (After all, *Glory* got made, and most pros in the business wouldn't have given that a chance.) The risk you run, in short, should be up to you, but there's really no excuse for working in blind ignorance of the market.

We'll talk about specific markets in later chapters; for now, just pay attention to this:

Early Stage Action List

Even as you begin working on your idea, begin defining your market—that is, your potential buyer. Learn everything you can about that buyer, because his or her preferences can help you further focus your product. You want to know:

a. Marketplaces where the products are bought and sold (inventors' fairs, Hollywood offices, or whatever).

b. The main centers, the main ways in. Are some few cities the centers of the action, and do you need to be there? Are there contests you can enter? Do certain schools provide useful prestige?

c. The major players—and the agents or intermediaries who can reach them.

d. The products that are selling. (Artists, be careful about this one. If you spend time chasing current fashions, you'll betray your talent and always run behind the times—because by the time you start on what's currently fashionable, the next fashion will be taking shape out of sight.)

e. The money being offered. Get a sense of what you can realistically hope to make. First, you want to be able to recognize a fair offer when someone makes it. Second, it can be downright inspiring to know there's a big pile of loot waiting at the end of your rainbow.

8

From a "Dot" to a Schedule

YOU'VE PICKED ONE IDEA. You're excited and prepared to work hard. You're starting to learn the business side of things.

What do you need next?

The Anthony Trollope Story One of the most successful, admired, and productive novelists of the nineteenth century was a fellow named Anthony Trollope. He published half a dozen long novels before his career was far enough along for him to quit his regular job—and then he *really* started turning out the books. As he succeeded, he became extraordinarily well-connected, with friends in publishing, in society, in government.

Whom did he most credit for his success?

The "old valet" who used to wake him several hours before dawn, so he could get in a full day's writing before breakfast.

Skill Number One: Discipline!

Even if you have your "dot" firmly in mind and think about it night and day, you're still just thinking. How do you make yourself actually create?

There are probably as many methods as there are creative people. Balzac used to chain himself to his bed until he'd written his pages for the day. Some people set themselves work quotas, then find partners who call them, perhaps twice a day, to make sure they're on schedule. They merely check in, then sign off—no chat, just a way of bench-marking work.

Still, here are a few basic rules:

Lay Out the Scope of Your Project: Get the "Dot" Down on Paper
Write down what you want to accomplish. Do you want to publish a "literary" book—or make the best-seller list? Sell an invention—or own your own company? Whatever your "dot" is, getting it down on paper is a great start. If you can't articulate something clearly, in a few words, you probably don't understand it very well yet.

Break the Project into Steps If a "dot" is worth its salt, it's probably looking pretty huge. How do you tackle it?

First, break it into steps. This is where you go from the dream stage to reality; most people find it automatically gives them a boost of excitement. Suddenly you realize there's a first step you need to take to make your dream real and that it's a step you can manage.

For example, writing a screenplay has certain widely recognized stages:

a. Treatment. A one-page summary of your story.

b. Character sketches. Usually three or four paragraphs about each main character.

c. Three-act outline. Roughly five pages, with a page or two devoted to the main events of each of your movie's three acts.

d. Step outline. A list describing, usually in one or two sentences, where each of the movie's forty to sixty main scenes is set and what happens during it.

e. First draft. The complete screenplay.

f. Second draft. The complete screenplay.

Don't worry if you aren't interested in writing screenplays—for now, let's say that's your goal. The next step is simple:

Block Out the Work How and when you work is up to you. Voltaire wrote *Candide* in one sitting. Lawyer Ken Ludwig rose every morning at 4 A.M. and wrote plays for four hours. By 1992 (when he was forty-one), he had hit plays running on both coasts, had sold the screenplay for one, and had been hired to write a film for Steve Martin and Michael Caine.

Whatever method you use, define a time period for each step. If you can't estimate it yourself, simply ask someone in the field. Then set a demanding but doable schedule. For a screenplay, you might allow one week for the treatment, one day for sketching each main character, and so on. Don't set yourself up to fail by using too rough a schedule, but do push yourself. Then:

Tie the Schedule to a Calendar Too many people give themselves a week for the treatment, but somehow never decide *which* week. So much for writing a screenplay! Set fixed dates for everything you need to do— and above all:

Start Today! All the weapons ever sold haven't killed as many good ideas as the word "tomorrow"—as in, "I'll start it tomorrow." (Or "the day after tomorrow," . . . or . . . you name it!)

Sure, Mark Twain made the famous crack, "I never put off for tomorrow what I can put off for the day after tomorrow"—but he could afford to make a joke like that: He was one of the hardest-working creative people of the nineteenth century.

Want a sample calendar? Something like this works as well as anything else:

Day	Date	Goal	Done
Mon.	2 / 17	Treatment	√
Tues.	2 / 18	Name all characters	√
Thurs.	2 / 20	Character sketch: Rick	√
Fri.	2 / 21	Character sketch: Anne	____

And so on. The day lets you match the project against the other demands on your time (schedule more work on the weekends, for example); the date will show you how much you'll have done after a week (or month) of work. The goal should be simple, clear, and doable, and checking off "Done" as you finish each task gives you the satisfaction of confirming your schedule.

If you're serious about your idea, you'll find the time to work on it, even if it means taking an ax to the TV or sacrificing something else. Ten minutes on the project today is worth two hours you promise to devote tomorrow—because most often tomorrow never gets here.

One last note: If your schedule runs more than 90 days, you've probably taken on too big a project. Set yourself a task for 90 days, finish it, then sketch out the next phase.

Case Study: What People Can Do
When It Counts

If you want to cite the one organization that traditionally represents gold-plated, bureaucratic slowness, it's probably the Pentagon, which has sometimes taken a decade to develop a single weapon. Yet during the otherwise brilliant success of Operation Desert Storm, Allied military planners found themselves with a terrible problem: Our own fire, principally from aircraft, was causing many friendly casualties.

In New Hampshire an engineering technician named Robert Walleston of Test Systems, Inc., "sketched out an idea of building a battery-powered infrared 'beacon' that could be easily spotted by combat pilots peering through their night-vision goggles."

Partly by luck, the Pentagon's Defense Advance Research Projects Agency heard about Walleston's idea and asked his company to send a prototype the next day.

TSI delivered—by being flexible enough to use lots of off-the-shelf components.

The Pentagon tried the prototype—and within a week gave TSI a $3.2 million contract to build 10,000 AFIDs (Anti-Fratricide Identification Device). Within another week a joint team from TSI, DARPA, and an Army research lab had built and tested seven further prototypes, collectively incorporating some one hundred improvements—and eighteen days after the first contact between TSI and DARPA, TSI began shipping units to the Gulf. (*Los Angeles Times,* June 13, 1991)

You certainly see our point: With enough motivation you can do things you never dreamed possible.

You'll never, let's hope, have the pressure of a war to make you work. In fact, unless you go out and create the pressure, you'll never be forced to do anything, and that's why so many projects drift off to that fantasy land where good ideas go to die.

Working Schedule Action Plan

1. Chart out the steps needed to get your project "reduced to method."

2. Break those steps into workable subunits—ideally, day-length tasks, but nothing over week-length.

3. Convert the subunits to a schedule.

4. Attach dates to each part of the schedule.

5. Don't count passive activities (like going to lectures or taking classes) as working. Orson Welles spent three hours studying film making, then went out and shot *Citizen Kane*, by many accounts the greatest film of all time. Don't take classes—take action! Classes should only augment what you're doing. Above all:

6. Start working today—and push yourself! The real fun doesn't begin until you have a product to show.

9

Going Public

AS YOUR SCHEDULE TAKES SHAPE, your project may start looking both huge and discouraging, especially if you have limited time or money. Before you quit, answer this:

Do you think a nineteen-year-old black man, from a rough neighborhood and a broken home, could bring out a feature film? Especially given that the average U.S. feature film made the year his came out (1991) cost over $18 million—in fact, over $25 million when promotional costs were included?

Well, a young fellow named Matt Rich did it—and here's how:

First, he wrote a story based on his own life, set in an area he knew. Next, he and his sister financed the first $13,000 of the production on credit cards. That got them about fifteen minutes of edited story, which is in itself remarkable, since a major studio will usually budget about $100,000 a day for shooting, and would normally consider about three minutes of usable film time a fine day's work.

Okay—they had fifteen minutes of film, and they couldn't beg or borrow any more money. What did they do?

They leveraged their work. They persuaded the largest black-owned radio station in New York to hold screenings of their fifteen minutes of movie, and invited everyone they could think of with the ability to help them finance the rest.

This took immense nerve; inviting media hotshots to watch a snippet of your homemade movie is almost beyond fantasy. But people showed up. And some of them were impressed enough to provide another $40,000 in production money.

Among the people who eventually saw the fragment was director Jonathan Demme, who was impressed enough to find $250,000 to turn the snippet into a finished film. While $250,000 is spare change for Hollywood, for Matty Rich it was a fortune. He entered the finished film in festivals; a distributor picked it up. Titled *Out of Brooklyn*, it was shown in limited national release. (*Los Angeles Times*, January 26, 1991)

Matty Rich had launched his career.

That brings up one of the most useful tips of all: *Take your dream at least to the first tangible stage.*

Books are sold on outlines and sample chapters; demo tapes done at home get record contracts; venture capitalists will invest in well-done business plans. Once you've got something solid, you've got a shot at attracting the money you need for completion.

Even better, your self-esteem will skyrocket. Most people get a boost from discovering that the process can be shortened and that they can attract help without a completed project. But they also get a bigger boost from actually starting to work.

Once you get your first solid piece of work completed, you can protect it legally, show it safely, and (perhaps) get paid for it. Even if you don't make a sale right away, with real work in hand, you can call yourself a pro.

Action Plan

1. Learn (from this book or simply by asking around) the minimum amount of work people in your field expect to see before they'll take you seriously.

2. Decide how long you can afford to advance your project on your own funds. If you can possibly finish the project on your own, do it—as we'll show next chapter, the more you achieve on your own, the more control you'll have and the more money you'll make. Still, if there's no possible way you can stretch your resources—

3. Push to get your work to the first presentable stage, then polish it as much as you can and begin promoting it.

10

Rip-offs

HERE'S THE COUNTERPOINT to trying to win early support for your work:

As long as your idea stays in your head or in a notebook you show to nobody, you can probably develop it without a care in the world. But once you begin thinking about showing it to possible buyers or investors, you're sure to be hit by a scary thought: "What if somebody rips me off?"

Theft of ideas at a very early stage is rare, Still, since worrying about it is common and basic precautions are easy to take, let's cover those basics, just to set your mind at ease.

As an idea person, you have two conflicting objectives: You want somebody to invest in you, which means people have to know about your idea, and you want to keep your idea secret, so nobody can steal it.

How do you strike a balance?

Protecting Your Idea: The Basic Rules

1. You Can't Protect an Idea. You Can Protect a Method This is the crucial point. What's the difference? In simple terms, an idea is an abstract notion; a method shows us how the notion can be achieved in the real world.

In this context, "It would be neat if people could fly" is an idea; the working design for a jet engine is a method. Similarly, "Let's make a movie about a little guy from outer space who gets stranded on earth" is an idea; the screenplay for *E.T.* is a method. If you have a method, the law will probably help you protect it. If you have an idea, it's usually "*Adios, amigo.*"*

If you're concerned about getting ripped off, reduce your idea to method.

Once you have your method (your rough draft, design drawings, or whatever):

2. Documentation Is Crucial Keep records of your work, including dates, and convert those records to a form which will, if needed, have legal weight.

One of the simplest devices is still one of the best: Once you have your idea reduced to method, put a copy of it in an envelope, address it to yourself, and mail it to yourself registered mail.

Registered mail is postmarked all over its surface, so that it will be absolutely clear when the package was mailed and whether or not it's been opened. When the copy arrives, simply put it away unopened, in a safe-deposit box for maximum security, for example. If you ever anticipate a legal dispute over origins, you can present the envelope unopened to your attorney.

Any number of professional organizations, such as the Writers Guild, archive materials for a fee. They're fine, but more expensive than the mail-it-to-yourself method.

3. Don't Rush to Engage Attorneys An attorney can help you with a lot of formal protection for your materials, but attorneys are very expensive. If your money's limited, you're probably better off spending it to promote your materials than to protect them prematurely. (If you're well-heeled, however, by all means seek competent legal advice as soon as you can—and if you see a dispute over ownership brewing, go to an attorney at once.)

4. Use Responsible Agents Some of the best protection you can get will be through finding reputable people to represent your work. Good

---

*Remember, "method" is our term, not standard legal usage. Patent lawyers, for example, talk about an idea being "reduced to practice," but the basic idea remains the same: What can be protected is the concrete, workable expression of your idea.

agents protect you in several ways. They know who in the business is honorable and who isn't; they let you devote time to developing your ideas instead of promoting them; and they give you credibility. They also protect you in another way: Even truly rotten people avoid crossing reputable agents, because their long-term interest is in getting a shot at future projects represented by those agents.

5. *As Your Property Grows More Valuable, Step Up the Level of Your Protection* Legal protection, which means both securing rights and *enforcing them,* is expensive. To protect a simple mechanical patent worldwide over its patent life will cost you roughly $100,000. And that's just for routine costs—if you ever have to sue anybody for infringement, you can probably multiply that by four or five, for starters.

Obviously, you wouldn't think of spending $100,000 on worldwide rights to a little gadget that's only going to make you, say, $50,000 in royalties. You'd be better off making that quick $50,000 and walking.

But right now the idea is to follow a few simple steps to protect your ideas, so you can clear your mind of anxieties and get on to developing your product and beginning to promote it.

Action List: Securing Your Rights

1. Before you discuss your idea, reduce it to a method.
2. Document your work correctly.
3. So far as possible, work through reputable agents.
4. Don't overspend on legal services. Get an initial opinion, then engage more legal help and more complex legal protection only as the potential of your idea justifies it.

11

Keeping Quiet

YOU SHOULDN'T WORRY TOO MUCH about theft of your ideas once they're reduced to method. On the other hand:

Patent attorney Coe Bloomberg uses this fascinating example of how ideas can be spread by casual chat. Here's a small map:

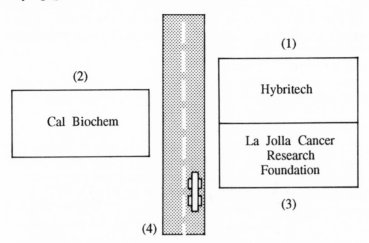

Researchers at a San Diego company called Hybritech (1) invented a very valuable biotech assay called the "monoclonal sandwich"; it involved blending two recently proven technologies in one of the world's hottest-breaking fields. Scientists all over the world were working in the area, and when Hybritech had the technique nailed down, it rushed to file its patent—only to find that three other groups were filing for the same technique.

So of all the world's scientific groups—from England to Australia to Japan—pursuing this field, whence did the three competing patent applications emerge?

A fellow from Cal Biochem (2) said he walked over to Hybritech for lunch, and the idea hit him on the way back. Oddly enough, the same thought struck someone (3) at the La Jolla Cancer Research Foundation, which shared lab space with Hybritech. And, son of a gun, a guy who car-pooled (4) with Hybritech workers said he came up with the notion, too.

Get the picture?

Now, the competing people were clearly honorable; nobody was accused of pilfering lab notebooks or anything of that sort. All that happened, apparently, was that somebody at Hybritech liked to talk— and people at three other companies liked the ideas well enough to pursue them. Maybe it wasn't even that dramatic; maybe just a passing hint sparked the ideas in the heads of these competitors.

The point is, *keep your mouth shut!* Yes, legal protection is often relatively easy to come by, but legal protection works only when your ideas are in a fairly advanced stage. And even when it works, it's slow and costly.

You need to share ideas with people—but with the right people and at the right time.

Loose lips sink deals as well as ships!

12

Keeping Control

YOU CAN SELL AN IDEA at a surprisingly early stage of its development, and as long as you've properly documented your work and used reasonable caution in the people you approach, you can feel fairly safe in showing it to others. But whatever your idea may be, try to keep control of it for as long as possible. There are two main reasons for this:

1. Maximum economic gain,
2. Maximum intellectual control.

The more developed your project is when you offer it to the market, the more valuable it is. Lots of things can go wrong with an idea that looks good on paper, and even people willing to invest in you will expect a big discount for the risks they're assuming.

Why Selling Early Can Be Expensive

Dr. Jonas Salk, who invented the polio vaccine, thought he could do the same thing with an AIDS vaccine. The medical community thought his ideas were old hat. So, to start his company, he sold people close to him stock for $1,000 a block.

Four years later a tiny test of his vaccine (nineteen patients) seemed to show positive results. And those $1,000 blocks of stock?

Suddenly they were worth $12 million apiece. (*San Diego Union,* October 1, 1991)

Yes, that's obviously an extreme case, but you get the picture—and it holds for the arts as well as business and inventions. Consider this parable of risk and reward: An advance on a first novel (and very few people get them) might be for no more than $7,500; an option on a screenplay in its early stages might be only $1,000 (and plenty of people will want *free* options). On the other hand, completed first novels have sold to publishers for well over $500,000, and completed first screenplays for nearly $1 million.

Publishers and studios, in short, are like every other investor; they want big discounts for assuming the risk of developing your ideas.

And, equally to the point, if they want your finished product badly enough, they'll be far more willing to agree not to make any changes in it without your approval—and to artists, that can mean as much as the money.

Obviously, if you're living in a cold-water flat, buried in unpaid bills, you're probably not going to hold out till the very last day just to keep control. Still, you don't want to be in such a great rush to deal that you sell today for $5,000 something that might be worth half a million to-morrow.

Of course, you are going to face two different sorts of pressure to cut a quick deal: financial pressure and psychological pressure.

So our next topic is another psychological one: how to keep pressures under control.

13

Dealing with Pressure

AS WE HAVE SEEN, there can be big profits in holding on to your ideas as long as possible. On the other hand, there is going to be pressure to cut a deal quickly, no matter what it costs you.

Economic pressure is obvious enough: You need money, either to keep developing your idea or to live on. You can deal with this in a number of ways:

1. Pursue your idea(s) strictly in your spare time, while earning your living elsewhere. Thus, Lawrence Kasdan spent a long time writing in the evenings while working days in an advertising agency. He went on to co-write the screenplays for *Star Wars* and *Raiders of the Lost Ark,* and to direct such films as *Body Heat, The Accidental Tourist,* and *Silverado.* (Interestingly, he optioned his first screenplay only a few days after his first agent, having tried everything to sell it, returned it to him as unsalable. Kasdan says he later made a nice income optioning and reoptioning that story, before it finally became a movie—fifteen years after the first option.)

2. *Borrow money from friends and/or family.* It's sad but true: Statistically, the most common source of start-up capital in the United States is personal savings. Next in line are loans from friends and family.

3. *Sell resources.* Barneys New York, the smart clothing store chain, was launched with $500 the founder's wife raised by pawning her engagement ring. Now that's love—and it's also a way to get a grubstake.

4. *Simplify your life.* Pretty obvious—but lots of people either never think of it or are too proud to sell the BMW when they're starting out.

5. *Seek grants or other aid.* There are grants, scholarships, and prizes available for people with ideas. In fact, virtually any library will carry many books detailing them. The Beverly Hills Public Library, for example, offers a handbill listing 76 books devoted to finding grants and scholarships.

6. *Try for a loan.* Loans against ideas do exist, but usually only after you already have a track record. The best will let you repay them, not via fixed monthly amounts, but by a royalty payable only after your product's on sale. A good possibility, but, again, not usually available for beginners.

All those means are straightforward, but since you don't want to sell the idea itself prematurely, your other options are fairly limited. Your best bet is to have created a war chest to carry you through the lean times of development. This doesn't have to be a fortune; even a few thousand dollars will make a huge difference.

Admittedly, economic pressure isn't much fun, but at least you can anticipate it, prepare for it, or simply gut it out.

Psychological pressure may be harder to endure—or even to recognize.

Some of it is predictable, even the clichés: the parents who want you get a "real" job; the spouse who's tired of your tinkering.

More subtle and more damaging may be the internally generated pressures: the desire for recognition or immediate riches, or the fear of being scooped. After all, somebody might get "your" idea completely independently, and if he reduces it to method first, you're probably sunk.

Dealing with Psychological Pressure You may be one of those levelheaded people whose egos never get in the way of their success, or you may be so caught up in your work that other forms of recognition just don't matter to you. But if you do feel psychological pressure, what can you do?

Support Groups You may need to confide in one or two trusted friends, people who'll tell you your work's interesting and important even before you're willing or able to go public with it. Or you may favor a larger support group. Some of these groups offer not only moral support but services such as regular speakers who share expertise, and no-cost consulting services from members with well-established careers. Here's an example:

The Writers Guild of America, West (basically, the union for stablished screenwriters) provides, along with other aids, a well-used electronic mail network. At any hour members can put out a query like, "What's the best way for a hero to stop a tank with his bare hands?" and hear back immediately from other writers possible solutions to the problem. They can also swap jokes, nasty cracks about producers, and nearly anything else.

The WGAW is for established pros, but nearly every major city has support groups for aspiring artists and inventors. To find one in the arts, just ask at local bookstores, galleries, or college campuses. The best of these groups don't necessarily critique one another's work—they give one another moral and emotional support. That can be much more valuable.

There are now about fifty inventors' groups nationwide; the largest, in Chicago, has nearly 6,000 members. For the address of the group closest to you, or advice on starting a group of your own, contact the United Inventors Associations of the USA, in St. Louis: 1-314-721-3842.

Counseling Pressures can get bad enough for you to need professional help in dealing with your problems. There are therapists who claim to specialize in treating creative people. In light of the expense of therapy, you will want to check carefully the success rate and general credentials of anyone offering these services. But if simpler methods of handling stress don't work for you, by all means consider getting professional help.

Summing Up Pressure, after all, is not necessarily bad. Some people thrive on it, and it often serves to force us to do things we know we should be doing in any case. But if the pressure ever gets so bad that it's interfering with your work or with your life in general, then you need to take steps.

Above all, take responsibility for your own feelings. Be aware of them—and respect them. Don't just let a nagging feeling of you-don't-know-what persuade you to drop a project. If you're feeling discouraged or confused, admit it—and take steps to find the solution.

14

Being Where the Action Is

MOST IDEA PEOPLE wind up asking themselves this question sooner or later: "Do I need to be where the action is in order to break in?"

Of course, the place "where the action is" will vary according to the nature of your idea, but it's certainly true that most activities are associated with a few particular places: Hollywood for film, New York for books, Silicon Valley or Route 128 for computers, and so on. Wherever the center of your chosen field, the question remains: Do you need to be there?

Why Centers Matter Centers do matter, but less and less these days. They matter for several reasons:

1. Concentration of secondary skills. "Secondary" isn't a derogatory term; it simply means production skills. Thus, in Hollywood you have not only the big studios and the offices of many production companies and directors, but also the hundreds of craftspeople, from casting directors to location caterers, who make a project go. In New York, for publishing, you have free-lance editors, indexers, designers, and so on.

2. The "social milieu." A top screenwriter we know claims that in twenty-four hours he could make any script—even one that hasn't been written yet—the hottest thing in Hollywood. All he'd have to do would be to hire a dozen people to spread out and hit half a dozen key Hollywood parties and ask other people whether they've seen the XYZ script yet. Before the evening's out, everyone will be talking about the XYZ script; by the next morning every agent in town will be getting calls from every producer in town, all desperate to get a look at the XYZ script before anyone else can make a deal.

Social impetus may or may not be a factor, depending upon your interests. If your idea is a mechanical device, being in a center probably doesn't matter. But success in some of the arts is tremendously dependent upon social contacts.

3. Credibility. Yes, you have more credibility coming from a big center. A screenwriter living in Beverly Hills may not have half the talent of one living in Butte, Montana, but the Beverly Hills writer is going to have an easier time.

4. Entry-level jobs. The chances of landing a job that gets you at least partway into the game are much better in a major center. So far, at least, no major film studio has hired script readers in Idaho.

5. Classes, contests, and advice. The educational advantages of a major center can be considerable. In Los Angeles, for example, you'll have at least potential access to two of the country's three top film schools, the American Film Institute's classes and seminars, uncountable private seminars, entertainment lawyers donating time to California Lawyers for the Arts, even such luxuries as the only computer store in the country devoted exclusively to the needs of screenwriters.

The Downside of Centers Centers *do* have their downside. The most obvious negative is that you may have to move to reach one—and that can be a tremendous burden. But also consider:

Competitive Pressure New York, for publishing, is probably as much of a true center as still exists anywhere in the United States. According to a *New York Times* estimate in June 1991, there were about 15,000 working writers living in New York City. That certainly means you'll have people to talk with—but it can also mean a pressure-cooker environment, where people eat, sleep, drink "the business," and make themselves miserable comparing themselves to competitors who are making better deals.

If you like the pressure, go for it. If not, you may be happier working where you are.

Costs Unfortunately, most of these centers are expensive places to live. For people in the arts the expenses are personal: food and housing, for instance. For manufacturers, though, the costs multiply; taxes, wages, rents, and the like can wreck you before you get started.

Summing Up There's no absolute answer, but, based upon our spot survey, the need to be in a center to make your mark is rapidly declining.

Modern technology (faxes, video conferencing, and the like) are making "centers" obsolete. Yes, most publishing is still done in New York, but successful writers, at every level, now live where they choose.

Among the few remaining exceptions is Hollywood, for films. The film community remains relatively small and closed, and to break in you need to be there, or at least to have representation (i.e., an agent) there.

In any case, don't go without an agenda. If you don't have a list of people you want to meet, courses you want to take, jobs you want to try for, you're not ready to go. Stay home and work your ideas up to a reasonable level: Write five screenplays, build your prototype, make some demo tapes, or whatever. You'll almost certainly save a lot of money and preserve your peace of mind. When you've gotten as far as you can where you are, and when you know fairly clearly what you want from the big center, then you can make your move.

15

Phonies

YOUR IDEA IS TAKING SHAPE. You're putting in the hours, sticking to your schedule, producing results. Meanwhile, the pressure's probably building for you to begin making the contacts that will let you profit from your ideas.

How do you find the right people to represent you, and the right people with whom to cut deals?

Let's be clear: there are lots of extremely honorable people out there who'll go far beyond their legal obligations to play fair with you. "Handshake" deals are scrupulously honored every day.

But until you know the players, you need to be cautious.

Outright crooks who steal your idea and run away with it aren't common. But people who'll charge you for useless services (like fake "invention marketers," who cost American inventors tens of millions annually) exist in great numbers, as do "wannabe" agents, producers, and the like, who'll tie up your material and never do anything with it.

How do you decide whether or not someone's legitimate?

1. Check references. Obvious enough. Especially with less famous organizations, a few inquiries may tell you a lot. Don't be afraid to ask for credentials and to check them. You want to know not only the deals they've done, but the way they've treated the people around them.

2. Don't be dazzled by a big name. Except in very rare cases, big firms that take you on will be handing you over to their trainees. These firms aren't phonies, of course, but they can have nearly as bad an effect, simply by letting your interests drop to the bottom of their pile. A small but reputable organization is nearly always better for you at the start of your career.

3. Make sure you share in any revenues generated. Never sign a deal (fairly common in Hollywood, fairly rare elsewhere) that says anybody else gets paid development money, but you get paid only when the product goes on sale.

4. Don't pay advance fees. Except for reasonable expenses, such as photocopying, your agent(s) should work on a percentage basis—that is, they get paid when they deliver. Never pay anybody for promised introductions.

5. Don't sign any long-term deals. (Musicians, watch this *especially.*) Personal managers and the like deserve some protection in return for their early efforts, but their best protection should be in doing a good job for you day after day. A one-year contract (ideally, with escape clauses if no results have been achieved in any 90- or 120-day period) is the longest commitment you should make.

6. See whether they'll make an investment of their own. If their services are on a fee rather than a commission basis, do they believe in your project enough to take their pay out of future profits? With high-powered people, that willingness is the best indication that they believe in your idea. With professionals, like attorneys, the best you can expect is for them to defer their own hourly fees, but for you to pay their expenses. Thus, if a patent attorney flies to Washington, D.C., for you, you'll pay the travel costs up front, but the $250-an-hour legal fees might be against future earnings. It never hurts to ask.

Watching out for phonies isn't that hard. But now you've begun making contacts with legitimate people. They start inviting you in for meetings.

What happens then?

16

Meetings

BY ONE MEANS OR ANOTHER, you've made contacts. Maybe you've mailed out your manuscripts; maybe somebody from a design company has set up a meeting for you with a venture capitalist; maybe a friend has gotten her agent to hear your demo. Somebody says they're interested.

Does your throat suddenly close up? Do you start sweating when you have to pick up the phone to arrange the meeting?

We're being melodramatic, of course, but it's remarkable how many of us are simply too shy to face these kinds of situations. In fact, one major study reported in the *New York Times* said 40 percent of all Americans considered themselves handicapped by shyness in social situations.

The fear of rejection can paralyze people. We still know writers whose hands tremble when they collect their mail, for fear of getting a letter that starts, "Thank you for letting us see the enclosed." That may be natural—but if such fear keeps you from acting, that's a tragedy.

Yes, some successful people, such as novelist J. D. Salinger, manage notable careers without ever presenting themselves in public. Still, if you shrink from public contact, you're severely handicapping yourself at the outset.

So what can you do?

The *real* secret is to take charge of your progress. Pursue as many avenues as possible. Phone calls scare you? Start calling for everything you can. Call the library for information. Call the grocery and order a loaf of bread. Don't like having to "pitch" yourself or your ideas? Practice in front of a friend.

Get out there and try. Nothing will burn you out faster than sitting home, thinking about how you wish you could get up the nerve.

You want a good formula for meetings? Try this. Put 80 percent of your effort into what you're going to say, 10 percent into how you're going to look, and 10 percent into staying calm and enthusiastic, and you're about right.

Don't let fear ruin your shot. With a little practice you'll find meetings a pleasure at best, a minor bore at worst—and certainly nothing to fear.

Most of the people you meet at these "pitch" meetings will be perfectly nice. Initial meetings aren't negotiating sessions; the buyers aren't going to be trying to beat down your price. (That will come later—if you're lucky!)

The worst thing they have a right to tell you is "no." That won't kill you, and most often they'll modify it—as in "no, but we'd like to see the next thing you do."

Once in a while, yes, you'll meet real jerks, who'll make a point of displaying their power. If that happens, just thank them for their time and leave—but leave fast. You haven't lost anything; you've kept the moral high ground, and at least you've gained some experience.

Don't Sweat Your "Image"! Huge industries in this country (from clothing to personal grooming) have spent fortunes to convince us we're not worth anything unless we look a certain way. As a practical matter, that's largely baloney.

Image is not going to make or break you. Indeed, there seems to be a growing reaction against the "dress for success" materialism of the 1980s. For everybody who lines up to throw money at you because you look like "a winner" (whatever that is), there are likely to be several who'll be turned off by your extravagance. There's much to recommend a middle course. Don't worry if you haven't got an Armani suit or a hundred-dollar haircut.

Even more to the point, remember that you're an idea person—you're not a corporate lawyer or a bond trader. On that basis, most people will grant you considerable slack.

You could probably write a long and funny essay on the different theories about image. One successful TV writer of our acquaintance, a self-described "Nebraska farm boy who made good," attends network meetings in straight "good old boy" garb, except for Gucci loafers. His theory is that the shoes show he's affluent—the football jersey shows he's different. It works for him. Lowell Ganz, the tremendously successful co-writer of comedy films like *Splash* and *City Slickers,* once told a film school class that (we paraphrase), "producers expect most writers to dress like bums—except for comedy writers, who should dress like nuts."

That's pushing it, of course, and for other kinds of ideas, like inventions, you probably want to go for good, solid, standard business clothes. The basic point remains: Relax, and remember you're there to sell the idea.

You don't have to agonize over "image." What *do* you have to think about when someone offers you a meeting?

Reach the Area Early Allow yourself plenty of time to arrive. If you're early, you can always wander around the neighborhood or review your notes. The panic of running late is the kind of stress that's easiest to eliminate.

Try to Get Everyone on Your Side This isn't an adversarial meeting; you're trying to establish common interests, even friendships. Often a deal will result two years from now, from the contacts you make today.

Don't Frighten Yourself Don't build people up into all-powerful forces that can make or break you. Nobody owns an industry. If you do hit one of those rare, unpleasant meetings, realize you're always going to get another shot. You could write a very long book about projects which were rejected by one company, then made a fortune for another. (To take one example: Columbia Pictures bounced *E.T.* as hopeless. It made a *billion* dollars for Universal.)

Above all, remember, these people didn't invite you in to yell at you; they invited you because they're interested in your work.

Humanize the Proceedings If you're nervous, say so—nobody will be put off. If anything, you may engage their sympathy. Tell them why you care about the idea—and why they should. Ask if they have questions; if they don't, explain how you'd like them to get involved.

Address Everyone in the Room You don't know who has the real power—and it's not always the character sitting behind the big desk. Divide your attention; treat them all with courtesy. It's the right way to treat people, after all—and it's also sound business.

Don't Drag Things Out Talk as long as they want, and, when it's over, say thank you and leave. Normally, if they're interested, they'll either start to set up the deal then and there or tell you when they'll be getting back to you. If they don't do either, you can certainly ask when you may expect to hear from them.

Don't Be Put Off If They Turn You Down Sometimes you'll go to a meeting, make your best pitch, and get turned down. Just be polite, try to learn what they didn't like, and see if there's an invitation for future contacts. When you get home, write up your notes: the people you talked with, what part of your pitch worked and what didn't, what objections they raised. That way you gain even if you don't make a sale. And no matter how it goes, send a thank-you note. It gives you one last chance to make a positive impression, and it helps you achieve a psychological ending to the event.

Even getting the first meeting is a big achievement. Regardless of the outcome, feel proud of yourself—and learn from it.

17

Negotiating

THE GREAT DAY when someone first says, "We'd like to invest in your idea," will probably bring you a real surge of excitement. But it also brings new challenges.

How do you handle them?

Even if you intend to let lawyers, agents, or others do your negotiating for you, you need to understand at least the basic principles of negotiating. Why? Because quite often what you expect to be a casual, informational, or informal meeting will turn into a negotiating session.

Before Negotiations Start

Decide your negotiating style. Most experts say there are two basic types of deal makers: cooperative and confrontational. (There's also rolling over and doing whatever the other side wants, but that's no style at all.)

Both cooperative and confrontational people can succeed, although statistics suggest that cooperatives do better. The main point is to have a style you can live with.

Be sensitive to the other side's MBO. "MBO" is "main business objective." If the other side needs a TV movie rewritten in seventy-two hours, your tack can be something like, "Yes, I can work straight through, but I need a private suite in a beachfront hotel, a secretary on call around the clock, and . . ." whatever else will be helpful.

Your negotiation isn't going to work unless everyone gets at least most of what they need. Smart negotiators keep both their own and the other side's objectives clearly in mind.

Know the marketplace. Whether or not professionals (agents, lawyers, managers) are representing you, try to learn about the marketplace—from books, magazines, or people already in the business. Know the players, and, at least generally, the value of your property. Remember: with or without professionals—agents or lawyers—you make the final decision on the deal.

Know what the other side is up to. Any big company, especially in a patent matter, is going to get a report on your financial condition: a Dun & Bradstreet if you're operating as a business, a TRW or comparable report if you're an individual, or both.

The other side wants to know how eager you are to deal. If your credit is shaky and you're badly in debt, they're going to assume you'll yield quickly.

They're also likely to check you out with anyone who's done business with you before, to decide how tough you're likely to be and whether you have any weak spots. Can you be intimidated? Do you fall for a pitch to your sense of pity?

There's no reason you cannot gather information of your own. If you have a hot action-adventure script and the studio you're negotiating with has not had an action-adventure hit in three years, you've got leverage. You may as well use it, right? If nothing else, knowing about the other side will give you a very useful sense of confidence. So find out what you can.

When You Negotiate

Negotiate from strength. It's easy to feel swamped as the lone individual up against a big company. Clearly, you can't match them person for person or dollar for dollar. You don't have to; you just need resources enough so that you can walk away from a bad deal. So—

Live a life that costs less than your income. With money in the bank, you can always reject an exploitative deal. In Hollywood there's even a name for this cash cushion, crude but to the point. It's called "F___k you" money. Don't leave home without it!

Communicate this strength not only to the other side but to your own team. If your agent thinks you've got a stack of unpaid bills, he or she is going to convey that (consciously or not) to the other side—and will also pressure you to take the first deal that's offered.

Be enthusiastic. Again, "enthusiastic" does not mean desperate. You want to communicate enthusiasm for your idea, even while you're making it clear you aren't desperate for the money.

Too many people try acting blasé about the proceedings, simply so they won't look desperate for money. That's a mistake; you have to be a source of excitement, for several reasons. People who are thinking about buying your product are almost always, to some degree, investing in you as a person, too. They're going to have to return to you for revisions, to do promotional work, perhaps to persuade other people to join the project. If they think you're bored with the project today, how confident can they be that you'll still be pushing it six months or two or three years from now?

Also this isn't your last project. You want a reputation as someone who's exciting to deal with, not as a blob.

Remember the phrase, "Let me think about it." No matter how well you've prepared, the other side can always hit you with a proposal you've never considered. Don't panic. Never let people put you under so much pressure to decide that you can't make a reasoned decision. If they won't give you time to consider, you're almost always better off passing. A day or so is usually all you'll need.

Watch out for last-minute changes. In every field you'll find some people who'll treat their word as their bond—and others who'll promise you the moon, until it comes time to sign contracts. In the film and music industries, above all, many people see the contract-signing meeting as the time when the real negotiating begins. If that happens to you, stay calm. Your advisers, if they're any good, should have clued you in to the situation (you're paying them, in part, to know the other side's strategies).

If you do get surprised by one of these last-minute shifts, resist your temptation to stomp out of the room. Instead, listen to the proposals, but don't answer. Unless the changes are very small and you're sure you understand them, go home and consider them. If you then decide to take the revised deal, do so grudgingly and make it clear that these are your last concessions. Otherwise, all you'll get for your trouble is another set of demands.

Lastly. Even if for some reason you don't want to use agents or lawyers to help cut your deal, you must at least get an attorney or agent to review any contract before you sign it. Whatever deal you may strike in conversation, make it clear that your acceptance depends upon (1) satisfactory reduction to writing, and (2) your attorney's approval.

Summing Up We'll just leave you with one line on negotiating. We got it from Bob Bookman, a famed agent with Hollywood's powerful Creative Artist's Agency. Each year he teaches a UCLA course on the film business. Each year the course changes, but each year he ends with the same line. Actually an old Russian saying, it nicely summarizes life in Hollywood—or indeed any creative person's relationship with the business world.

The saying?

"Make friends with the wolf—but keep your hand on your ax."

Clever folk, those Russians.

18

Collaborations

WHILE YOU WANT TO KEEP your idea in your own hands as long as possible, once you do make a sale, you generally have to compromise and collaborate to see it reach its final market.

Most creative people hate that idea. In fact, Richard Walter, the distinguished screenwriting professor, tells a story that in many ways embodies the universality of the frustration.

In all his years as writer and teacher, Professor Walter says, he never met a screenwriter who wouldn't moan and groan about the terrible things the studio had done to his or her script.

Finally, at a party, he saw Julius Epstein, the author of, among other things, *Casablanca*. Surely among the most beloved and admired scripts of all time, *Casablanca* is, of course, particularly known for its ending, with Humphrey Bogart putting Ingrid Bergman aboard that airplane at the fogbound airport, then heading off to join the Free French garrison.

Walter immediately went over to Epstein and said with perfect sincerity, "Mr. Epstein, I just want you to know I think *Casablanca* is one of the greatest movies of all time!"

"Ah," said Mr. Epstein with a sigh, "you should have seen the ending I *wanted* them to use."

Carrying through a film idea means cooperating with others—even if it kills you. But films (at $20 million-plus each and involving hundreds of creative and technical people) are clearly special.

What about other kinds of ideas?

Even the creative endeavors most associated with solitary genius (whatever that is) are very often when closely examined largely collaborative. The romantic poets? Sure, they wrote some of the world's greatest tributes to solitary genius. They also worked in groups (Wordsworth/ Coleridge, and Shelley/Keats, to name two). T. S. Eliot may have brilliantly explored individual isolation in the twentieth century, but he also let Ezra Pound whip *The Waste Land* into shape. (In fact, for a quick course in how much a critical eye can help your work, just check out the New York Public Library's facsimile edition of that famed poem. You'll get an education in collaboration.)

Inventing? Historians are increasingly showing that even legendary "solitary" inventors really worked in groups. Thomas Edison, for example, is now recognized as the inventor of the modern research lab— he realized early on that teams could create more and better inventions than could lone geniuses. It can even be argued that the main reason inventors fail is that they're too stubborn to get the help they need from industrial designers, business advisers, and patent attorneys.

You may enjoy and benefit from collaboration, or you may fight it every step of the way. In either case, you're going to have to learn to deal with it.

The key is not to react emotionally. The first time someone wants to change some idea of yours, you're probably going to have a fit. Don't!

Instead, try the following:

1. Don't say an automatic "no." Just nod eagerly (especially if you're a beginner), take copious notes, and then:

2. Go home and think about it. Try to see every possible bit of good in the suggestion, from at least three points of view:

a. Does it work? You don't have a monopoly on wisdom; is the suggestion, no matter what you think of the person who proposed it, an improvement?

b. Does it suggest something better? Often people who make even the worst suggestions have found a real weakness in your work. They may say, "Your hero is too working-class. We want him to be something more prestigious, like a painter," but they've forgotten that on page one you established that he was blind. You can go back and tell them, "Your basic idea was terrific, but what if we make him a stockbroker? That way we pick up the prestige, but we also keep the handicap, which makes him more heroic." They'll probably buy it.

 c. Is it harmless? The proposed change may be simply neutral. You want blue push-buttons, and they want green? Giving in can buy you a lot of goodwill, for free.

 If you still don't like the suggestion, then—

 3. Work out your response. Most people will listen to a counterargument, if they see you've taken their ideas seriously and if your counterargument is well reasoned and well presented.

 You've already tried using the suggestion. Save your notes and bring them to the follow-up meeting. You'll be able to show them you took their ideas seriously—and why your approach is better, or why theirs won't work. Especially if the suggestion was prompted solely by the suggesters' need to feel important, that will be all you'll need to do.

 Know the Limits of Your Expertise If you can't come up with a clear reason for your objections, it's possible that you're simply having a fear reaction to an idea outside your expertise. In that case, remember, people who know their business will generally respect your expertise; give them the same courtesy:

 • A young screenwriter named J. D. Lawton optioned a script called "$3,000" to Disney. The Disney people liked everything but the ending and the title. They decided the hero and the heroine should live happily ever after and that the movie should be called "Pretty Woman." J. D. Lawton agreed, and they made the movie.

 Pretty Woman did $180 million in domestic theatrical release alone— and J. D. Lawton made enough money to buy his own ministudio.

 • Bill Cosby wanted to do a TV show about a chauffeur and his wife. Two free-lance producers named Tom Warner and Marcy Carsey, brought in by Mr. Cosby's agent, thought a show about a doctor married to a lawyer would go over better. Mr. Cosby agreed, and at last count "The Cosby Show" had earned $800 million in syndication sales alone.

 So those folks who want to fiddle with your idea are sometimes worth listening to.

 If You Can't Compromise In some cases, you just can't find answers that satisfy both sides; either there's a genuine conflict of vision or your boss is being an unreasonable jerk. When this happens, only a few possible results remain: a) you quit, b) you get fired, c) you do it their way and never work for them again.

None of those three things is necessarily bad, provided that you handle the experience in a professional, adult fashion. That means:

1. Don't leave people in the lurch. Honor your contract(s), and even beyond that, make sure the transition is smooth, even if it means staying on a project until a replacement is found and brought up to speed.

2. Don't descend to attacking personalities, either while you're separating from a project or afterward.

3. Keep the door open for future collaboration. You'll often find, after you've cooled down, that the absolute right was not 100 percent on your side. When that painful revelation hits, why have it redoubled by the knowledge that you were ill-mannered and brattish?

Cooperation Action List

1. Expect that when you sell something, the people who own it will likely want to alter it, either to meet their own tastes, to prepare it for a larger market, or simply to assert their own power. Don't be shocked that the people who were beside themselves with joy before you signed on the dotted line now want a total reworking.

2. Behave like a professional. Since cooperation is a part of most crafts, make the most of it. Be open-minded and willing to work hard.

3. Prepare your arguments and keep them on your grounds if possible. Don't try to tell a music publisher or a movie producer what's going to sell—it's their job to know such things.

4. If compromise proves impossible, make sure you separate in a way that keeps your reputation intact. Most creative/business communities are quite small; if you get a reputation for being difficult, you'll find yourself frozen out pretty quickly. Above all, don't get in the habit of bad-mouthing people behind their backs. That sort of thing always gets around, and it only hurts your reputation, both long-term and short.

5. But by far the best approach in all collaborations is to become a leader. Don't be reactive, be active! Solicit opinions of other people who are part of your project, and, whether you use their ideas or not, make them feel appreciated. They'll work twice as hard for you, and very often their ideas will be extremely helpful.

19

Push After You've Got the Deal

YOU'VE GOT A DEAL! A producer, a venture capitalist, or a publisher has sent you a contract, with check to follow.

Are you home free?

No! If you're a creative person, your job doesn't end when you've made a sale to some intermediary, whether publisher, producer, manufacturer, or retailer. It would be nice if it did, if creative people could simply find the right folks to promote their creations and then get back to what they do best—creating.

Yes, some writers, directors, and inventors are lucky enough to find people (agents, partners, spouses) to assume the job of pushing the business side, so that they can concentrate on the creative one. If that happens to you, congratulations!

Those who don't, too often end up like a friend of ours, an extraordinarily bright fellow, who was hired by a major publisher to translate a French classic into English. He did the job; the firm was delighted and paid up promptly. Then there was a management shift, and the book was never released. That meant he got no royalties, no publicity, and—most important for a scholar—no publication to put on his résumé.

When something like that happens, what can you do about it?

If you're thinking of legal action, forget it; basically, the law says whoever buys your creation has the right to decide what to do with it. As long as he or she meets the terms of the contract, you won't have much chance of forcing further action. The law assumes the buyer has a rational interest in profiting from your work, just as you do, and if he or she chooses not to spend money on promotion, that's a fair business decision. End of story.

Can someone buy up your project just to clear the way for a competing project? Yes! And if you've sold the rights, you're basically stuck. That's yet another reason you want to make yourself a student of the market from the start of your career.

Unless you have enough clout to write into the contract that the project will be promoted or developed in certain ways, you're going have to keep negotiating with your new partners for more promotional money, more promotional efforts. Do it! You want them to send you on a promotional tour? Ask. You want them to spend money on ads or to take a booth at a trade fair? *Push!* (Push politely—but *push.*) Even after you get a deal, you're still in competition for your publisher's/studio's/retailer's time and attention. So keep asking for more. They can always tell you no.

In the majority of deals you'll get (especially in the arts), there's a huge difference between someone's representing or buying your product and actually pushing it. If you want to get all the way to your "dot," you have to be willing to do at least some of the pushing. Otherwise, you'll be another one of those screenwriters whose scripts get optioned but never made, or those writers whose books get published but never promoted, or even those inventors with a raft of great-looking patents and no products on the market.

Action List: Promoting Your Product

1. Keep in mind that generally the law recognizes no affirmative duty on the part of anyone who buys your creations to do anything to promote them. If you expect anyone to promote your work, you have two choices: Get a firm and specific commitment in writing in your initial contract, or else be prepared to do a lot of the pushing yourself.

2. From the earliest days try to accumulate market information; you should always know who's going to buy your product (not just the investor/producer, but the end buyer). Learn all you can about your prospective buyers, what they like, what they need. Often you'll be able to feed this information to your agent/publisher/retailer. Even better, you can hit them with concrete ideas for promoting your works more successfully.

3. Don't be afraid to *push*. Your uncle's girlfriend runs a morning talk show on a local station? Write her a letter, polite but enthusiastic, about how much you'd like to be on the show and what you'd be able to contribute. Ask the local library if they'd like you to give a guest lecture. Try anything; it beats *hell out* of sitting home and complaining about how your publisher doesn't answer your letters.

20

Thinking Big

HERE'S ANOTHER PART OF pushing your idea after a deal.

First, remember that increasingly there are valuable and often unforeseeable spin-offs of every sort of idea.

Take Carmen San Diego. Created by Broderbund, a privately held, fifty-million-dollar-a-year software company, Carmen San Diego was the key character in an educational/entertainment computer game. Players would attempt to pursue the (mildly) archcriminal Carmen all over the world—and in the process would learn world geography.

By 1991, though, Carmen was hot—and appearing not only in a whole series of further computer adventures ("Where in Time Is Carmen San Diego?" "Where in the American West Is Carmen San Diego?"), but also in books, puzzles, and a TV quiz show. (*New York Times,* July 9, 1991)

Carmen was one of a long line of neat but not dazzling ideas that caught the public fancy and were rapidly expanded into mini-industries. The cartoon characters Waldo and the Ninja Turtles are, of course, two other examples which succeeded even more spectacularly, expanding into TV cartoons and movies.

Interestingly, Broderbund turned down an offer of a Carmen San Diego TV cartoon show. They reasoned, probably correctly, that their target market of ten- to twelve-year-olds would be turned off by a show aimed at younger children. Broderbund was more interested in protecting the underlying value of its intellectual property than in turning a quick licensing buck.

It's a World Market

The second thing to remember is that these days you have to think globally. Ideas can make you money not only in unforeseen ways but in unforeseen places.

Take Betty Mahmoodi.

Mrs. Mahmoodi was an American woman married to an Iranian. After the start of the Iranian revolution, Mr. Mahmoodi decided to abduct their daughter and keep her in Iran to be raised as a Muslim. Mrs. Mahmoodi went to Iran to rescue her daughter and bring her back to Michigan.

It's an interesting story, with elements of bravery and pathos, but not necessarily a blockbuster. In fact, Mrs. Mahmoodi's book, *Not Without My Daughter,* co-written with William Hoffer, was only modestly successful when it was published here in 1987. It even inspired a film— which, in the polite language of the *New York Times* (July 10, 1991) "flopped."

End of the idea?

Well, guess what's the best-selling nonfiction book in the history of modern Germany? Guess what book has sold more than 2.5 million copies in France, and sits in an estimated one-of-every-two Swedish homes?

You've got it: *Not Without My Daughter,* the American so-so title.

Why? Nobody knows. Europe has large immigrant populations from North Africa and the Middle East, and Mrs. Mahmoodi speculates that international kidnapping of children from bicultural families is a bigger problem there.

For our purposes, that doesn't really matter. The point is that these days your chances for success will be greatly enhanced if you a) think globally, b) never give up on an idea as long as you still believe in it, even if the initial response in the marketplace is cool, and c) hold onto as many rights, worldwide, as you possibly can.

The Bottom Line? Be Stubborn, Be Imaginative, Keep the Faith

The end result of this is that today all the clichés about never quitting on an idea you still believe in have a new, suddenly crucial importance, simply because there are vast markets out there that few people foresaw even ten years ago.

Your book's been published and went out of circulation quickly? What about the foreign market? What about making it a computer game— or a piece of self-help software?

The "dot," it seems, is a moving target. Keep raising your sights!

21

Media Appearances

TEN OR FIFTEEN YEARS AGO it would have been sheer pomposity to consider media appearances concerning your idea. Today, though, it's more like a necessity. Whatever your idea, sooner or later, to make it succeed, you're at least going to have to try to draw media attention to it.

The great appeal of this sort of coverage, of course, is that normally it's free. And it can be extremely powerful.

As a small example, when the American Women's Economic Development Corporation opened its West Coast office in 1991, they got a few polite notices in local papers, but nothing special. AWED, a nonprofit group that trains women entrepreneurs, was well known in New York, where it began, but new to the West.

For several months they progressed slowly, with some of their classes having as few as fifteen participants.

Then the *Los Angeles Times* ran a piece praising them.

Within a week the word had spread. They were profiled on two national network programs, almost half a dozen local programs, and CNN. And by the end of that week, before the full miniblitz had hit, they had received 450 inquiries about their classes, many including checks for enrollment.

AWED has a terrific program; they would have gotten established on the West Coast in time, with or without the publicity. But you can still see how dramatically helpful even a small media blitz can be.

Unfortunately, far too many people are made nervous by media opportunities and immediately start worrying about their "images."

Media Presentations

Obviously, image matters more in some areas than in others; it would be tough to imagine, say, Madonna or Michael Jackson without their elaborate images. But what about the rest of us—writers, painters, directors, inventors, businesspeople? Do we have to worry about "image"—and can we improve ours?

The Basic Rules

If you reach the point where appearances are a regular part of your life, you may want to seek the advice of a professional media consultant. But in the meantime:

Physical Appearance Unless you have a particular image, just go for neat and simple business clothes, especially materials that travel well (you'll probably be appearing on a circuit of shows). Women are probably better off skipping anything frilly or overdecorated unless that's their chosen image. Frills are visually confusing and still tend in the eyes of some viewers to trivialize or demean you.

TV cameras emphasize the "busyness" of clothes. Avoid complicated patterns and—if you want to be extra-careful—shiny fabrics and white shirts.

Body Language More important than your physical attire is your body language, which simply means the way your body communicates your mood. You want to come across as enthusiastic, honest, and, so far as possible, calm.

You'll make your best impression of you:

1. Limber up. Emotional tension expresses itself as physical tightness. If you're nervous, deep breaths may help a little, but some physical stretching will probably help more.

2. Psych up. Remind yourself that you're the expert, that most of the people in the audience are going to be pulling for you, and that you were invited on the show because you're good. This is a treat. Enjoy it!

3. Stay cool. When you're on the air, don't agonize about your physical posture—again, the tension will show. Give your attention to the interviewer or to the audience. Talking to them as people will help make the presence of cameras and hot lights drop out of your mind, and keep your voice level, posture, and expression just fine.

4. Keep eye contact. Again, concentrating on the interviewer and the audience will automatically solve one of the most common problems: too frequently shifting eye contact.

The one major variant on this is the remote interview, where you're invited into the facilities of an affiliate station to be interviewed by someone far away. Then, unfortunately, you have to look straight at the camera.

The real key is getting across what you have to say—or, to be more frank, what you have to sell. To do this:

Expect surprises. Don't be put off if the interviewer hasn't read your book, seen your invention, heard your music, or whatever. This can be your opportunity to make exactly the points you want.

Larry King, one of the best of interviewers, told the *New York Times* he makes a point of not knowing about his guests beforehand; that way, he can ask questions most likely to interest his audience, which is also likely to be new to the topic. His approach also lets his guests talk about what interests them. An uninformed host can be your best friend.

Take control. If the questions aren't focused where you want them, turn them around—politely. If somebody asks a question you can't answer, just say something like, "Well, that's very interesting, but I think the real issue is . . ." and tell them what you want them to hear.

Enthusiasm counts. Larry King also told the *New York Times* that he liked interviewees with chips on their shoulders. The people interviewing you are in the entertainment business, and they want you to be entertaining. That doesn't mean you have to open with a couple of jokes, then zip around the stage on a unicycle, but it does mean you should keep your energy level high. Being exciting on some talk show at six o'clock in the morning may not be easy, but if you've reached the point where your idea bores you, think of the satisfaction of cashing a big royalty check. That wakes nearly everyone up!

Practice helps. You don't need a canned talk, but you probably should practice answers to the most likely questions. If you can't get a friend to listen, practice into a tape recorder.

All this, along with ordinary courtesy, explains why you should never turn down an interview. You can develop skills even with the local high school newspaper if you put your mind to it.

Focus your answers. Probably the best piece of literary advice ever written came from a famous Victorian writer: "Have something to say, and say it as simply as you can."

On TV conciseness is all. Assume you have less than one minute to answer even the most complicated question. A fifteen-second answer is better still. Don't hesitate to ask beforehand how long you're going to have on any particular show.

Basic journalism courses used to teach the "inverted pyramid" style of writing: Put your most important points first, then work down to the small points. That way, when an editor in a hurry arbitrarily lopped off the bottom half of your story, the important points survived.

You can talk that way.

Make up the questions you're most likely to be asked about your creation: Why did you create what you created? What is the most useful or important, or inspiring thing about what you've created? What is the best piece of advice you'd give anyone about it?

Now try every answer you can think of, throwing out those that draw no response from your friendly audience. Rank those that remain, then practice answering the questions with the most important answers first. When you actually get on the show, launch into your answers in the prepared sequence and keep your eyes on the interviewer, who will signal you when you've gone on too long.

Drop what doesn't fit. Sometimes you've got a great story but just can't fit it into the "sound-bite" culture, which rarely devotes more than a minute to the most complex subjects. If you can't compress it while keeping the essence clear, drop it. Someday you'll put it in your memoirs.

Summing Up Image does count, but over the long term the quality of your work is going to count for a lot more. Pay a little attention to your image, but don't let it get in the way of doing your work.

22

Your Track Record

IF YOU'RE A CREATIVE PERSON, you're going to have a lot of projects during your life. But don't think of them as separate projects; think of them as steppingstones, one project leading to another, larger, more rewarding one.

And think of each achievement as proof of further abilities.

Consider Steven Jobs, cofounder of Apple Computer. In less than a decade, he helped build Apple into a world-class firm. Eventually, realizing he lacked the skills to run a Fortune 500 company, he brought in a top Pepsi executive named John Scully—

Who promptly fired Steven Jobs.

That left Mr. Jobs, one of the industry's best idea people, out of the game just as the computer market was maturing. Mature markets are supposed to belong to big, established companies. The day of the start-up was supposedly over.

So what did Mr. Jobs do? Take the good-sized fortune he'd earned from Apple and go off to raise sheep?

No! He announced he was starting another company, Next Computers, to build "insanely great" computers of an entirely new sort. He didn't have the computer yet; even some of the basic technology was unavailable.

The result?

As soon as Mr. Jobs announced his new company, astute investors, from H. Ross Perot to Japan's Canon, lined up, waving checkbooks. Steven Jobs raised $100 million at a stage where most entrepreneurs would have been hearing, "Don't call us; we'll call you."

The first Next Computers were viewed by many critics as fancy toys, too slow and without a clear market. Early sales were feeble.

But none of Next's backers backed out; they trusted the man in charge to fix things. And within two years Next Computers were sufficiently improved that they were being ranked as some of the best machines on the market. Sales were up, and other companies were beginning to license its technology.

Mr. Jobs's happy story was made possible not only by hard work and talent but by a track record that inspired confidence.

Creating a Fortune 500 company from scratch gives a person credentials. But what does that have to do with *you?*

Even a Short Track Record Can Make the Difference

Not long ago we fielded a call from the attorney representing a major independent film company. A hot young screenwriter had offered to sell them a script for way below his going rate, provided they'd let him direct. They wanted to know what we could tell them about the young writer's directing abilities.

We could tell them only two things: He had directed a promising short student film at UCLA, which was finally tied up in legal disputes and never finished, and he had competed twice in the American Film Institute's annual directors' contest.

A brilliant record? Certainly not, but it was something. You have to know a lot just to be able to make a graduate film at UCLA or to compete in an AFI contest. Combined with the proposed director's native intelligence and screenwriting success, it was enough. The film company set out to cut a deal.

Any record helps. Still, you need to watch:

The Arc of Your Career This is just another way of saying, "Keep your eye on the 'dot.' "

People with the power will be paying attention to the course of your career. If five years ago you were writing children's books for $5,000 advances, and today you're doing the same, they'll assume you've peaked. If you've moved on to write adult books and maybe optioned a screenplay or two—even if the money's not a lot better—they'll assume you've still got the capacity for growth.

That's why sometimes after early success you'll need to walk away from an offer to do the same sort of project all over again.

Sometimes, too, you'll need to take a calculated detour. An inventor who gets an M.B.A., for example, is setting his arc toward running a company, and that can definitely be a smart move, even if it means no more patents for two years.

Sure, you want to get your rewards today, but don't lose sight of the long-range situation.

23

Playing the Fringes

IF YOU'RE LUCKY, you'll get your first deal early in the process. Even if it doesn't make you rich, it will give you a track record and enough encouragement to continue working until you do make your first big score.

But what if that first deal doesn't come? What if time goes by and your money begins running out? Well, consider this story:

In 1849 the discovery of gold at a place called Sutter's Mill sparked the greatest gold rush in American history. Prospectors from as far away as Europe and even China dashed to California to cash in on the prospect of endless wealth. There were engineers and laborers, gunfighters and adventurers, men of limitless tenacity, energy, and—sometimes—ruthlessness.

So who made the most money?

If you take the long perspective, it was probably an immigrant peddler who realized that these fellows with pockets full of gold nuggets needed pants with seams that wouldn't tear out from the pressure of all their mineral wealth. He tacked rivets onto the corners of a pair of ordinary blue jeans, guaranteed that they wouldn't rip, and after sales took off named his company after himself. Today, close to a hundred years after most of the 49ers moved on to that great gold strike in the sky, his company, Levi Strauss, Inc., is a Fortune 500 firm with a trademark that's one of the half dozen best known in the world.

Often, when a field is generating a lot of heat, *you* can generate a lot of money, without a lot of risk, by selling something on the periphery.

Today plants for making top-line semiconductors cost hundreds of millions of dollars; by the end of the century such a plant will probably cost nearly a billion dollars and only a handful of the world's largest corporations will be able to build them. Not a market where a small player would seem to have a chance.

But tiny Athens Corporation of Oceanside, California, found a way into the business. Part of the manufacture of semiconductors involves washing them in extremely strong acids. These acids create two problems: They're major pollutants, and they can easily contaminate the very semiconductors they're supposed to clean.

Athens developed equipment both to recycle the acids and to purify them. After selling the purified acids for several years, Athens found a potentially huge market: Sumitomo Corporation (which bought into the company) estimated in mid-1991 that Athens could sell about five hundred million dollars' worth of its purification *machinery* in Japan alone. (*San Diego Union,* May 25, 1991)

It's the hi-tech equivalent of selling blue jeans to the prospectors.

Let's take an even more modest example:

At a time when major drug companies were pouring hundreds of millions of dollars into AIDS research, twenty-nine-year-old Anne-Marie Corner co-founded a company to make legitimate anti-AIDS products on a shoestring. Within nine months of starting, she'd raised $250,000, hired top people to help her with everything from research to marketing, and been profiled in the *Wall Street Journal*.

How?

She licensed the rights to some safe, simple compounds that killed the AIDS virus outside the human body—and is going to sell them as products for sterilizing, among other things, medical and dental instruments. Again, a fringe of the main market, but a very good business in its own right. (*Wall Street Journal*, January 30, 1991)

Does the same approach work for the arts?

In some ways, it works even better.

It's a commonplace that actors are often discovered while working in minor jobs around film studios: from John Wayne (prop boy) to Harrison Ford (set carpenter). But you can also add people like Joel Schumacher, who went from assistant art director to major film director. Or Michael O'Hara, who went from press agent to successful TV writer/producer. Or Amy Tan, who worked as a technical writer until she sold *The Joy Luck Club* for more than $1 million.

Settling In Sometimes people do so well in the business side of their art that they settle in very successfully.

Robert McKee is an actor who wanted to be a screenwriter. He certainly knew a lot about the craft; he had the right background and an analytical mind. The only thing he could not do, despite a number of film deals, was get a movie on the big screen.

So Robert McKee became a screenwriting teacher. Concentrating on what he'd learned in the business, and exploiting his dramatic skills, he put together a course. Today, after a decade or more in the business, he packs students by the hundreds into his classes and charges $2,000 for private consultations on scripts.

Working on the business side of your art does three useful things: 1) it pays you a living while you're developing your ideas, 2) it helps you make contacts, and 3) if you're practical enough, it helps you learn the market. (That's part of what press agent-turned writer/producer Michael O'Hara told the *New York Times:* Spending years promoting other people's TV shows taught him very well what audiences liked and disliked.)

Above all, even if you never get your big break with your great idea, there's a way to be a part of any art or industry that interests you if you have imagination and persistence. If you can't strike gold, sell jeans. And sometimes you sell jeans *until* you strike gold.

24

Dealing with Prejudice

Read this paragraph! When you read this chapter's title, did you automatically translate "prejudice" to mean racial, ethnic, or gender prejudice? If you did, welcome to the largest club on the planet. You're a prejudiced person.

"Prejudice" in its strict sense means simply "pre-judgment": reaching a conclusion in advance of all the facts. And prejudice (as this faintly sneaky opening was meant to show), affects all of us in one way or another.

What kinds of prejudice are you likely to encounter in your idea career? Along with the obvious forms of racial, religious, and gender bias, here are a few examples:

Prejudice against new ideas   Prejudice against old ideas
Prejudice against career changers   Prejudice against expense
Education prejudice

And on and on. Prejudice of any kind can be extraordinarily confusing and frustrating, but you can learn to deal with it if you approach it as just another practical problem and don't internalize it as something aimed specifically against you.

Here are a few tips for dealing with prejudice:

Recognize It Prejudice can be very explicit, loud, and obvious, or it can be extremely subtle.

Understand It Does it come from ignorance, malice, or from adherence to a body of facts which no longer holds?

In lots of fields prejudice is simply based on outdated information.

Take one example. For decades documentary film making was viewed in Hollywood as an utter backwater. There were a few exceptions (usually in wartime), but mostly documentaries were considered economic nonstarters.

Then a film maker named Ken Burns produced a six-hour masterpiece on the Civil War. It was among the most talked-about programs of the year and led to everything from soundtrack albums to coffee-table books.

Even more to the point, it overturned a long-standing prejudice. How? By earning $26 million in videotape retail sales alone in its first fifteen months of release. All this from a Public Television program done on a shoestring.

Suddenly many people in Hollywood were interested in hearing about documentaries—and about historical subjects. (The same thing happened a few years earlier with animation. Animation was a dead subject until *Roger Rabbit* and a few other hits—then suddenly everybody wanted animators. The studios started paying big money to hire young animators still in film school.

Prejudices exist in business partly because they save time. In many fields—most notably film—there are far more talented people than there are opportunities. The people who buy ideas are desperate for ways to simplify the selection process. They want reasons to rule you out, not to count you in.

How do you deal with this sort of impersonal prejudice?

Prove You're the Exception Sometimes you have an exception to the rule, and all you have to do is to make it clear, on very strong grounds, why that's so. Nobody in Hollywood was interested in a three-hour-long Western (especially one told from the Indian point of view) until they heard red-hot Kevin Costner was willing to star in it for a fraction of his regular fee.

Design Work-arounds: Be Creative Ken Burns worked around the Hollywood bias against documentaries by going to Public Television. If there's an alternative pathway to your "dot," try it.

Gabe Green has a genius IQ; he was admitted to UCLA at thirteen as a chemistry whiz kid. But as much as he liked chemistry, he loved music, both performing American standards of the twenties and thirties, and writing songs of his own.

Now, the music industry isn't exactly tripping all over itself to sign up middle-class eggheads working on chemistry Ph.D.s. So Gabe Green wrote rap songs to perform in chemistry classes. A number with lyrics like, "Thus t-butyl (no surprise)/In methanol will solvolyze" may never replace "Moon River," but it did get Gabe Green noticed by Joe Piscopo, who put him on an HBO special, which led to a feature spot on "Entertainment Tonight," and so on. (*Los Angeles Times,* May 19, 1991)

Will this lead Gabe Green to a great career in music? Too soon to tell. The point is that, with imagination, you can nearly always find a way to overcome bias and get your ideas noticed.

Never give up the search for practical alternatives. Prejudice tends to be static and clumsy—more often than you'd think, you can just go right around it.

Those are approaches to prejudice against ideas. What about prejudice against groups?

The toughest problem is probably proving that an ethnic or racial or gender prejudice is the root cause of your being rejected—especially since investing in ideas is always subjective.

Essentially, you have two choices. Either you have to show that people were interested in your work until they found out you were a member of some group—or else you have to develop a statistical case, showing a pattern of discrimination.

Document It Some cases have been effectively prepared. In the late 1980s, for example, the Writers Guild documented the extraordinarily low levels of work granted to Hollywood writers who were female, members of minorities, or over forty. The industry began responding, albeit slowly, with various programs to encourage these previously excluded groups.

As a practical matter, though, probably nothing had as much impact as Hollywood's discovery that films by and about women and minorities could make money. After Spike Lee and a few other young black directors had successful movies, for example, suddenly everybody in Hollywood wanted to hire young black directors. That's yet another reason why sticking to your work can be the most powerful tactic available.

If you feel you've been discriminated against, you can try to take action alone, but you might prefer to document your experience as best you can and then take it to whatever organization (civil rights, artists', or other group) is most likely to press your case. The best advice though, might be this:

Keep devoting the largest part of your time to the project itself. As long as you can keep that moving forward, the checks of prejudice will never completely discourage you—and, more to the point, the best way to answer people who say you can't do something, is to *do it*.

Here's one last, cheery story—again from Hollywood, home of more weird prejudices than you can imagine:

The story comes from television producer David Neuman, who joined NBC in the mid-1980s, after a stint as a White House Fellow. When he joined NBC, one of the network's grand old men, meaning to be helpful, took him aside and told him there were only three absolute rules about television:

No comedy in a bar,

No old people,

No multiple stories.

Within three years of that conversation, NBC had three megahits: "Cheers," which was set in a bar , "Golden Girls," about old people, and "Hill Street Blues," which told four or more stories at a time.

So if you hit some sort of prejudice, don't worry—just keep slugging. These things always change.

Postscript: One of the Worst Prejudices of All One of the most insidious forms of prejudice is an internal prejudice, where people count themselves out of the game. Don't ever tell yourself your ideas won't go because you're too old . . . or too young . . . or the wrong color . . . or didn't go to the right school. Matt Rich was a nineteen-year-old ghetto kid when he made *Out of Brooklyn;* Ray Kroc was a nearly-sixty-year-old malted-milk salesman when he built his first McDonald's restaurant.

Are there rules about who can do what? To heck with the rules! If you want to do it, then do it!

25

Developing Your Craft

Our Last General Advice

IDEAS ARE PURE, wonderful, abstract things. But we've learned that the people who succeed with them have an almost obsessive interest in the nuts and bolts of their professions.

Yes, we're going to mention secretaries who got $250,000 for an almost illiterate film script—and yes, people who have become millionaires from vague ideas made workable by honest and honorable industrial designers. None of those odd examples, though, overturn the basic rule: Over the long haul the people who do best are the ones who learn their craft.

George Lucas (*Star Wars,* the Indiana Jones films) is certainly a man of many ideas. But what do people who went to film school with him remember most about him? That he was an inveterate tinkerer, who wanted to know the film-making process from top to bottom, and who'd stay in USC's film labs till way past midnight. When it came time to make *Star Wars,* the technical people didn't tell him what was possible; he told them.

Keep at it nonstop. We met Nicholas Meyer on the set for one of the *Star Trek* films; as its director, he was certainly an established player. But in the midst of explaining to us how sound stages work, he suddenly overheard a sound engineer playing a score for another film. So he broke off our session to go to take notes on the composer of that score. It had a strong flavor of Americana, and he thought he might need such music for some future film. So he got the information and filed it away.

You can never know too much about your craft.

That obviously doesn't mean you have to stop and study a couple of decades before you can have good ideas. Good ideas can hit you at any stage of your career. If you get one at the outset, bravo! Take it as far as you can.

Just remember that "the best never rest"—the men and women who get the most from their ideas always want to understand more and more about everything—and especially about the mechanics of their own crafts.

Part Two

THE ART OF
IDEAS

———

BOOKS, MOVIES, SONGS, AND THE VISUAL ARTS

26

Your Basic Protection: Copyright Law

IF YOU'RE AN ARTIST—musician, writer, painter, film maker, or whatever—you're lucky. Your work falls under the protection of copyright law, and copyrights are, for the most part, automatic, simple, and powerful.*

Copyright: The General Legal Protection

Thanks to the U.S. Copyright Act of 1976, whatever you create is protected at the moment of fixation (that is, whenever you commit it to paper, film, or other "tangible form"), and that protection will last for your lifetime plus fifty years, with no renewal needed or allowed. (Before 1976, copyrights were for twenty-eight years, with a twenty-eight-year renewal).

A copyright lets you keep anyone else from either reproducing your work or making a derivative work (say, a movie from a short story) without your permission.

That automatic copyright exists whether or not you have a copyright symbol on the work. On the other hand:

Use the Word "Copyright" Using this word or the "©" symbol, while it does put people on notice that you own and mean to defend the

---

*Copyrights also cover computer programs, but we'll discuss those elsewhere.

rights to your creation, does not gain the level of extra protection many people think it does. To step up your protection, you must also:

Register Your Copyright To register your copyright, you need to send the U.S. Copyright Office (see Recommended Reading for the address):

1. A copy of your work (or photographs, if it's bulky visual art); two copies if the work has been published;
2. An application form (see Recommended Reading); and
3. The registration fee (presently $20).

A registered copyright gives you more firepower if you ever have to sue anyone for infringement;* specifically, you can collect hefty statutory damages, as well as your attorneys' fees (which will often amount to much more than the damages). To gain those advantages, you need to register your work within three months after publication.

It's been estimated that only about 20 or 25 percent of all eligible works are actually registered. Clearly, you don't want to register every little scribble (the fees do add up), but if you have anything you think may be valuable, registration is certainly worthwhile.

A big note: Be very clear on this: Your copyright protects your particular expression of your idea, not your idea. You wrote a short story about an archaeology professor who has wild adventures, and two years later Paramount made *Raiders of the Lost Ark?* Tough! Unless you can prove a) they read your story, and b) the movie that followed was substantially the same in plot, characters, etc., you don't have a claim.

Copyrights Are Property Like other property, they can be bequeathed in a will, mortgaged (if somebody's willing to loan you money on them), sold, rented, given away—and divided up in a divorce settlement.

Most artists treat their copyrights far too carelessly, and so create problems. Don't wait until your copyrights are valuable before you start treating them seriously. Always keep track of what you've created, how you've protected it, and especially what rights you're keeping, selling, and giving away.

The Limits of Copyright The protection given by a copyright is not

---

*Technically, marking your works with the notice of copyright (the "©" symbol and year of creation) may help eliminate any "innocent infringement" defense by anyone stealing your work—but that's a small legal detail. More importantly, in some arenas (especially, Hollywood) marking your writing with a copyright notification will mark you as an amateur. In sum, you can mark works if you want to, but you risk little if you don't.

absolute. You—or anybody else—can use protected materials without permission in at least two ways:

Parody. Anyone is permitted to "quote" from a copyrighted work (whether written, musical, or visual) for the purposes of parody, but the quotation can be no larger than is needed for the average audience to recognize what's being parodied.

Scholarship, reviews, and the like. Again, the law allows for "fair use" of copyrighted materials for scholarly books, reviews, and the like. "Fair use" is a vague term, but, for example, if you're quoting from somebody else's book, anything under, say, 200 words would probably be considered fair.* On the other hand, the wholesale copying of books, articles, or whatever, even for classroom use, has definitely been ruled illegal. Obviously, of course, even "fair use" borrowers must give full credit to the original creator.

Aside from those uses, you basically own absolutely what you've created—until you give or deal it away.

Moral Rights Traditionally, America has lagged far behind other Western countries in protecting an artist's *droit moral,* or "moral right" to a work. Once somebody bought your work, he could distort it as he chose; in one rather notorious Hollywood case, for example, a dark tale of child abuse was turned, without the author's consent, into a slapstick science-fiction film which literally ended with the stars singing, dancing and imitating Jimmy Durante for a cast of aliens.

Today the legal pendulum is swinging the other way. In 1989 the United States signed the Berne Convention, the international protocol on copyrights, which grants far stronger moral rights to artists. Still, simply because *droit moral* is not traditionally guaranteed, try to keep yours specifically in any contract you sign.

So far we've been discussing works of your imagination. But what if you've created nonfiction: a map, a database, a mailing list?

Can You Copyright Information?

The quick answer is "no." Simply collecting and organizing information is not considered original enough to earn legal protection, especially when weighed against the public good of having that information freely available to the community.

---

*With poetry and song lyrics, though, the safe course is to get written permission before quoting. The copyright laws are very strict in these two areas.

Of course, you can copyright a nonfiction book, but what you're protecting is the form of your information, the way you said it—you're not protecting the facts. That's why so many new companies now publish "yellow pages" that include the same data you find in the phone companies' books.

This doesn't mean you can automatically help yourself to other people's information, without credit or pay. It means you can go out and collect and apply the same information as long as you use your own efforts.

Of course, this is mostly an issue for businesspeople—which is why we talk more about it in Part Four. But it does lead us into something increasingly important for creative people:

When Creative People Work from Facts

If your big idea was to sell weather data or demographic maps, you wouldn't be reading this section. But suppose, for example, your goal is to create an imaginative work, such as a play, painting, or novel, based on real people or events. What can you legitimately use?

The simple answer is that you can generally feel comfortable using any published facts—again, because facts are not copyrightable.

There are just two points that need concern you:

1. The right to publicity. The courts believe that famous people have a right to profit from their names. If you create a "work of art" which seems to cut into that right, (for example, you want to create a piece of "performance art" which consists of your doing Michael Jackson's act), they're going to stop you.

2. Technical transformations. From digital sampling to the hi-tech manufacture of sculptures, artists are increasingly using technology to let them "capture" and swiftly transform other people's ideas. Increasingly, though, the courts are sticking up for the people whose materials are borrowed. Thus, in 1992, the courts for the first time upheld a music infringement suit against a rapper who incorporated a digital sampling of someone else's work into his own album. The album was pulled off store shelves worldwide, and a large money judgment was likely.

And cases are becoming more frequent. In 1991 Wall Street trader-turned-artist Jeff Koons was sued by postcard maker Art Rogers, after Koons sent a copy of a Rogers photograph (of Rogers, his wife, and eight German Shepherd puppies) to Koons's studio in Italy, with instructions to his workmen to create a sculpture "just like the photo." Koons then sold three copies of the sculpture for a total of more than $350,000. Rogers felt his work had been ripped off and wanted some of the profits; Mr. Koons felt he'd made legitimate use of something that inspired him.

Who was right? In April 1992 the Federal Appeals Court in Manhattan ruled that the sculpture was an unlawful copying and that Rogers was entitled to monetary compensation, perhaps even treble damages.

Before you borrow from anyone else's work, make sure that the core of what you're creating is really your own. If you feel in your heart you're playing fair, odds are you'll be okay. If you have any doubts, then either alter your project or seek written permission for the borrowing.

Those are the basic rules of copyright. The truth is, most artists work their whole careers without ever landing in a dispute. So take the basic steps to protect yourself, then spend most of your time focusing on developing and selling your ideas.

27

Books

PROTECTING YOUR RIGHTS to a book isn't hard: Once it's finished, you can register it with the copyright office. Moreover, most publishers have very high ethical standards, and the most common practice is that, if they buy your book and you haven't yet registered it, they'll do it for you, in your name. If money's tight and you're worried about someone's ripping you off, you can always use the tactic described in Part One: Simply mail yourself a copy via registered mail and store it unopened when it arrives.

But that still leaves the business side of writing books, so let's start with—

The Cold Facts about Money

The sad truth is that if you're expecting to get rich writing novels, the odds are against you. In 1990, according to the *New York Times*, only 54 novels published in the United States sold over 100,000 hardcover copies. At a rough $20 a copy, and royalties usually at 15 percent, a sale of 100,000 copies would mean roughly $300,000 in royalties to an author. Of course, paperback rights and film deals can multiply that considerably, but still, we're not exactly talking Steven Spielberg's income here. Add in the fact that most of those best-sellers came from long-established authors, and you see that writing fiction, while one of the world's most emotionally rewarding pursuits, is scarcely the quickest road to wealth.

That being said, how can you do the best for yourself?

Building a Name If you want to get rich writing fiction, your best bet is to try to make yourself into a brand name: a Stephen King or Danielle Steele. It's going to take a while before you can do that—and you may not like the accompanying pressure to write the same sort of book time after time. Still, you need to start out as soon as you can to build a track record.

How do you begin?

Agents and Houses Compared with, say, the music industry, publishing is fairly simple for the idea person: You'll normally deal with only one agent and one publisher at a time.

In fact, matters are getting simpler all the time, although in a rather sad way. Increasingly, major publishers are refusing to read "over the transom" manuscripts, those not represented by agents.

You can't really blame the publishers: reading unsolicited scripts is expensive, and the payoff has always been small. In twenty-seven years of reading unsolicited scripts (probably far more than 50,000 of them) the Viking Press found exactly one that met its standards. True, the book (*Ordinary People,* by Judith Guest) did very well for them, but probably not well enough to justify nearly three decades' work. Today Viking (now Viking Penguin) reads only books submitted by agents.* Yes, many publishers still say they read query letters, but our spot check of aspiring writers suggests most publishers take months to respond, and that very few of their responses are positive.

As a practical matter, then, your best move is probably going to be finding an agent. First, though, let's talk about few other options:

Vanity Press Should you pay someone to publish you? As a general rule, you shouldn't. We haven't been able to discover any recent writers

---

* Actually, a few big names (such as Arthur M. Schlesinger, Jr.) do represent themselves; and, of course, any publisher would be happy to read their unsolicited works. Our comments here apply strictly to beginning writers.

successfully published by the large vanity presses, unless you count the mere satisfaction of appearing in print as "success." In any case, it stands to reason that you should try the mainline publishers first.

Self-Publishing This is another prospect altogether. There have been some really remarkable successes with self-publishing, and, under certain circumstances, self-publishing is certainly worth considering.

In the spring of 1992, two of the top-ten books on the *New York Times* best-seller list were self-published: a short volume of sexual advice, and a book on the Kennedy assassination. Their success was unusual, to be sure, but by no means unprecedented. The career guide *What Color Is Your Parachute?* was self-published by a minister named Richard Nelson Bolle in 1976. Since then, it has sold some 2.5 million copies. Now owned by the Ten Speed Press, it's still going strong, with new editions every year. (*New York Times,* April 20, 1992)

At the other end of the scale, even a very modest project can pay off if self-published.

Donna McKenna was a schoolteacher in rural Maine. When her husband lost his job in 1990, she not only took on a second job of her own, but worked out menus to feed her family of six on $30 a week.* Friends urged her to publish her ideas, but she waited nearly two years before borrowing the school's word processor and writing a 60-page pamphlet. The pamphlet was publicized by another self-published venture, *The Tightwad Gazette.* In short order, Mrs. McKenna had sold 6,000 copies by mail order at $5 a copy, been featured on CNN, and had book agents coaching her on how to write a full-length book.

The evidence suggests nonfiction is probably your best bet for self-publishing. If you have information and a potential audience, you have a reasonable shot at succeeding on your own, even if the major publishers have turned you down.†

Academic Presses In recent years growing numbers of academic presses have ventured into limited publishing of fiction. Often, they pick either highly "literary" subjects, or books which have been published, then dropped, by the mainline houses. Probably the best-known recent example was *The Education of Little Tree,* which fared poorly when published by Delacorte, but topped the *New York Times* best-seller list

---

* At a time when U.S. food stamp regulations allowed a family of six $100 per week.

† Self-published fiction success, while rare, *does* sometimes happen: Roddy Doyle took out a "car loan" to self-publish *The Commitments,* his novel about an Irish rock band. It ultimately became a feature film directed by Alan Parker.

when reissued by University of New Mexico Press nearly a decade later.

Academic publishers (and small independent publishers) have two primary disadvantages: They are usually painfully slow to respond (you can wait over a year to hear from an academic press), and they spend little or nothing on promotion. Still, they can sometimes work to your advantage.

Specialized Houses If your book is well-enough focused, you might consider trying one or two highly specialized houses.

Mega-selling author Tom Clancy sold his first blockbuster, *The Hunt for Red October* "over the transom" to the Naval Institute Press. The Naval Institute, though founded to promote a strong U.S. Navy, has only informal military connections. Mostly it publishes naval nonfiction; given its orientation, though, it was an inspired choice for a place to send a Cold War naval thriller.

All these are reasonable places if, for some reason, you want to be your own agent.

Overall, though, your plan, if you want to make money, is going to be simple: Find a respectable agent to represent you to the major publishers.*

How do you start? One of the country's top literary agents gave us these tips:

1. Learn the business: Read *Publishers Weekly* and the *New York Times* or *Los Angeles Times* for news about the field. Learn why publishers buy, and how they buy. Hang out at your local bookstore to see what's selling and why: Get a sense of everything from shelf-life of books to what motivates a typical reader to buy.

2. When you write query letters or proposals (see below), work as hard on them as you would on the book. Above all, the structure of your proposal should show thought and planning. Good agents can tell at a glance if you wrote a proposal off the top of your head—and they won't want it. If there are competing books, show you're aware of them, and explain how yours will be different.

3. Style and content carry roughly equal weight in the first viewing

---

* If you *do* want to be your own agent and to send manuscripts to major publishers on your own, at least find the name of an appropriate editor. The *Literary Market Place* annually indexes virtually everyone in American publishing. Even better, simply call the publisher of some similar book that you admire, and ask the editor's name. Then address and focus your letter accordingly.

of a project (of course, extraordinarily "hot" topics might make content more important).

4. Queries and proposals shouldn't sell the book; don't estimate sales, praise yourself, or anything of that sort. You should show how your book differs from existing competitors, but otherwise, the *agent* is the business professional—and mostly wants to see a) how well you write, and b) how well you know the topic. Sales pitches are amateurish and a major turn-off.

5. The big money provided in some first deals has to do, most obviously, with the quality of the project. But the next biggest factor is timing, which can mean either a topic that's suddenly hot or a company that needs a project of that type. If a publisher feels it needs, say, a blockbuster foreign intrigue novel on its schedule and hasn't been able to land one for several years, it may well spend big bucks to plug a gap in its lineup. An agent is in the best position to understand those facts, but you can improve your own understanding if, again, you learn the market.

6. It's easier to break in if you aim at an established genre. Many houses have formal or informal quotas for these—say, three mysteries or sci-fi's a month—so the demand is steady. You do need to worry about being typecast, but you can always branch out within the genre, or if necessary, write other types of books under pseudonyms.

7. First books are proverbially easier to place than second ones; they haven't got a track record for publishers to use against them. So don't worry if you're just starting!

Finding an Agent

Good agents, as you've probably gathered, are invaluable—and certainly earn their money. They help shape a proposal and will send it to the right people—editors with whom they already have strong relationships. They'll negotiate your deal (with your input) and later handle the sale of such subsidiary rights as first serializations, film and foreign sales. (Your publisher will handle most other rights, including paperbacks and book clubs.)

And here's another big benefit: An agent will get a publisher's response within days or weeks, whereas an unsolicited manuscript may languish at a publisher's for months before you get a reply. A quick rejection is far better than a slow one: No long weeks of holding a deathwatch at your mailbox.

Okay, agents are worth the money. But how much money are we talking about?

What Agents Cost The standard fee for literary agents used to be 10 percent, rising somewhat (but never to more than 15 percent) for certain subsidiary rights. Nowadays agents often expect higher fees, with some expecting 15 percent of basic book sales, and 20 percent of certain subsidiary rights, such as foreign sales. Unfortunately, the less well established you are, the more likely it is you'll be obliged to pay the higher fees, partly because an agent will have to do more work to place a lesser-known author.

Many agents will ask you to sign a contract at the outset, although some of the best of them work on an old-fashioned "handshake basis," and will simply attach a rider to any publisher's contract they ultimately secure for you.

The larger agencies often pay all duplicating and similar costs related to selling your book; some of the smaller agencies may bill you for their photocopying and mailing expenses, simply because they have less financial wherewithal. Paying these costs is fair enough, especially if you're an unknown, but get it clear, in writing, exactly what expenses will be charged to you. These fees should total no more than, say, $200 for a fairly long campaign.

Other Agents' Services Increasingly, smaller literary agencies are trying to build revenues (and manage their workloads) by charging additional flat fees for other services.

Many smaller agencies, for example, will provide "readings" of submitted scripts for fees of, say, $100 to $250. That can be fine—if you understand what you're getting. Most of these will be relatively brief one- to three-page summaries of the book's strengths and weaknesses, usually written by an agency assistant or trainee. Only if the assistant's response is strongly positive will an agent be likely to read the manuscript. Such an agent may then choose to represent the book as is, suggest specific changes that may make it marketable in the future, or simply pass outright.

Caution: While many of these services are legitimate (if expensive), many others are simply ripoffs, intended to separate overeager would-be writers from their money. Always check a firm's reputation or references. In addition, do not pay for any services that should be a part of the normal work of agenting, such as a "marketing fee." That's what commissions are for.

A good agent is a virtual necessity. How do you get one? And how do you know if you're approaching a good one?

Reputable agents generally belong to a trade or professional association, such as the Society of Authors Representatives (SAR), which has established a code of ethical behavior; the listings of agents in *Literary Market Place, Writer's Market,* or *Literary Agents of North America* will tell you which agents or agencies are members. The biggest agencies, international in scope, are nearly all headquartered in New York (often with second offices in Los Angeles), but some very effective agents work away from the media centers. Amy Tan's agent, for example, has her office in Del Mar, California.

The big agencies may have more prestige and a wider range of contacts, but unless you're lucky, you can easily get lost in the shuffle. For first-time writers a smaller "boutique" operation may serve better.

Above all, you want a good personal match between you and the agent. If you have an agent you trust and who's willing to work hard for you, that's far and away the main thing.

Right now, of course, you're probably trying to get any agent. How do you start?

Approaching Agents

A letter of introduction can do wonders. If someone—a published writer friend, writing teacher, or published expert in your field (for nonfiction)—offers to contact an agent for you, by all means accept.

But don't contact an agent, either on your own or via friends, unless you have done at least this much:

1. Written a detailed outline or synopsis of your proposed book. The synopsis should probably not exceed eight or ten pages for nonfiction, and twenty for fiction. But it should be clear, complete, and exciting— one draft won't do it.

2. Written the book's first two chapters (plus the Introduction, for a nonfiction project) and then at least one other chapter you think is especially strong.

With at least those under your belt, you can write your query letter. This is simply a brief letter asking whether an agent or editor would care to see part of what you've written. You send the letter first by itself, without the proposal package.

As an author, you're dealing with people who care about writing; if you send them something flat, wordy, or ungrammatical, they're going to treat it as a fundamental flaw.

Beyond that you want to avoid egotistical statements, any discussion of the money you expect to make (or any other demands), and too-obvious sales pitches.

You do want to mention:

• What the topic is, and why you're excited about it.

• Your intended market.

• Your relevant credentials (if they're modest, be modest about them, but mention them).

• Any particular reason you have for approaching or admiring the particular agent to whom you're writing, but only if it's sincere.

One page or less is the right length.

If you start writing your query letter, but can't say clearly why the project matters or what angle you'll take, or if, after several drafts, you still don't feel comfortable about what you've written, you're probably not ready to write the book. Don't push things. If a project interests you even a lot, but you aren't ready to carry it forward, just go on to something else and return to it in a few weeks or months.

The Responses You May Get   Agents normally respond to queries quickly, usually within two or three weeks. You're likely to get a great many rejections before your first offer to read your proposal. That's why most agents understand you'll be querying many of them at the same time.

When you do get a positive response, your proposal should be ready to go; you just want to give it the once-over and mail it. Lots of writers use private overnight services, because they're quicker, they look more impressive, and they let you phone in to confirm delivery—you don't have to wonder if the packet arrived.

Unless you're dealing with a super-hot topic, you don't want to fax your proposal; presentation matters, and few faxes are letter quality.

If your project is returned quickly, with a form letter attached, it was probably read and rejected by the agent's assistant. Getting a couple of those doesn't mean much, but if four or five arrive, try redoing your proposal, maybe after getting a friend's criticisms. Obviously, if you receive a personalized rejection from an agent which raises specific objections, make sure you answer those objections when you send out your next letters.

It's standard advice at this or any later waiting stage to start working on another project while you're waiting. Nothing's worse than passivity—you should always have a backup project going.

Landing an Agent Sooner or later an agent will respond positively to your proposal. Maybe he or she will want changes, but you make them quickly.

It's a big step, and you're on your way, but your agent still has to sell the project to a publisher.

If you've landed an agent with a strong track record, your odds are now good enough for you to start pushing to complete the project, on the assumption that sooner or later it will sell. But you may still have to wait several months or even longer before you know one way or another whether the book will sell. Most agents will try at least half a dozen editors before losing interest in a project. If early responses are positive, the agent will often try dozens if necessary.

Normally, your agent will get a response to a proposal within, say, two weeks, and will relay the news to you: by letter if it's a rejection, or by phone if it's an acceptance or a request for more.

If your agent got merely a simple no from a publisher, he or she will probably send you a copy of the rejection, with a quick cover note telling you where the manuscript or proposal is going next.

As your writing improves, though, publishers' replies will probably become more detailed. Rejections of writers who are getting close to being publishable often change significantly. You may hear, "Great writing, but we're publishing a book on this topic next month," or you may start getting more detailed criticisms. Sometimes your agent may even have an inside line on why the publisher passed, and will call you with an explanation.

When this happens, cheer up and work even harder. They won't say you're getting close to publication unless you are.

When Editors Ask to See a Revision Before They'll Buy Sometimes the editor will say something like, "This is close. Give me one more draft, and I might buy."

What do you do then?

It's a tough call, but basically "spec" (that is, unpaid) rewrites are probably worthwhile if you're still at the outline-and-sample-chapter stage, but not if you've got a whole book. For a whole book you're probably better off saying "thanks" and moving on. Those revisions take too long and pay off too rarely. (If your agent thinks a rewrite's worth the risk, though, trust your agent.)

Two Final Notes:

1. We've said it before, but it bears repeating. You'll get more money for a completed project than for a proposal, but you risk more in finishing at your own expense. The choice is yours, but do think it through.

2. This is pretty obvious, but the amount of your advance is going to vary hugely according to your track record and (if possible) public name.

Solid previous sales will be worth money, but so, to a lesser degree, will your reputation in the industry. If your last book didn't earn scads of money but you were pleasant to work with, made your deadlines, and delivered quality work, you'll probably get a kind reading for your next idea; but if you were difficult, and commercially unsuccessful, they'll probably pass.

Someone offers you a contract. What do you look for?

28

Book Contracts

JUST BEEN OFFERED your first book contract? This is definitely a time to celebrate!

But after you've celebrated—and before you sign and return the contract—sit down and read the thing. Even better, especially if you have questions, have a lawyer read it. (An hour with a volunteer lawyer for the arts usually runs about $35.) And feel free to ask your agent questions—that's why he or she's there.

Basically, publishing contracts are short (usually five or six pages, compared with, say, thirty to sixty pages for a retail property lease) and understandable.

But they still contain some potential zingers.

Basic Rights Before we discuss the zingers, let's talk about the good and easy stuff:

Copyright law assumes the creator owns all the rights—that anything not specifically bargained away in the contract remains yours.

Out of this bundle of rights, you, as a first-time writer, will be giving up relatively little; hardback publication is the main thing. Then there will be a set of minor revenues (like data retrieval systems). Normally, you'll split the revenues from these fifty-fifty with the publisher. Lastly, the publisher will normally have the right to try to sell paperback rights for another advance (to be shared with you), or else to publish its own paperback and to pay you a royalty on sales (but without another advance).

Obviously, you want to improve the ratios in any royalty splits if you can, but your agent will probably have already tried that before you get your contract.

Typical Royalties Basic royalties are simple enough: on hardbacks, you usually get 10 percent on the first 5,000 copies sold; 12½ percent on the next, 5,000, and 15 percent thereafter. For paperbacks, the peak royalty is usually 10 percent.

The more money you get, the more rights you'll be giving up. In fact, in some megadeals, the author will be giving up all rights. Thus, one of the biggest deals of the early 1990s was Jeffrey Archer's three-book deal for a reported $20 million. That was a ton of money, but Mr. Archer gave up, among other things, film and serialization rights, and even the rights to use the characters in future projects.

Most other clauses, like the number of author's free copies, are too minor to talk about. But here are two you want to note:

Changes in Proofs You get various chances to correct your manuscript for free, but after the proofs (that is, sample sheets printed from the actual typeset) are made, you have to pay for any changes exceeding, usually, 10 percent of the first typesetting costs.

This is less of a problem with today's computerized typesetting, but you still want to limit your changes on the proofs; otherwise, you can find yourself billed for the work.

Author's Warranties You warranty that you haven't plagiarized anything or slandered anybody (especially nonpublic figures, who have the best standing to sue). If you thought it was funny to name the serial killer after your noisy next-door neighbor, this is the time to change the name. And if you have any doubts about *anything* you've written, show it to the publisher's lawyers.

Increasingly, publishers are naming authors as co-insureds on their

Media Special Perils Insurance policies. If they're doing it for you, it should appear in your contract. If they're not, ask about it.

Audits Your contract will probably give you the right to audit your publisher. Fine, except that, unless the audit shows you were short-changed by more than 5 percent of the amount paid to you, you pay for the audit. Unless you're receiving substantial royalties, this isn't very helpful.

At least two parts of authors' contracts should concern you, even though, as a beginning writer, you may not be able to do much about them: (1) demands for return of advance, and, (2) publishing industry accounting.

Demands for Return of Advance Traditionally, the system of advances and royalties worked pretty smoothly in this country: An author got an advance to write a certain sort of book, wrote the book, and the book was published.

But with the escalation of advances in the 1980s, some authors saw an unpleasant trend beginning: Publishers offered big advances for books that sounded good (especially on hot topics), but when the books actually delivered, if the topic was no longer hot, the publishers allegedly began crying, "This isn't what we ordered. Give us back our money."

The publishers, meanwhile, have claimed that more books are being refused because more authors are doing a sloppy job.

Who's right? We're not sure. But from your point of view, the key points are:

1. Make certain that the book described in your contract is the one you want to write, and the description in the contract is as clear as possible. If you have doubts, ask your lawyer.

2. Work with your agent and publisher, so that if important changes come up, they're informed as you're making them, not when you plop the book down on their desk(s).

Payment Schedule The publishing business is often portrayed as old-fashioned. In some ways that's wonderful: The ethical standards are, in most cases, very high.

In other ways publishing is a mess. Few publishers have invested in modern data processing equipment, and their accounts are, by many reports, nearly chaotic.

Most publishers pay writers twice a year, but when you get, say, your June statement, you may well find it covers not the sales for the preceding six months but for the six months before that. The publisher, in short, will be holding onto some of your money for almost a year before handing it over.

And it gets worse, because of—

Reserves for Returns Publishers have historically taken back unsold copies from bookstores virtually forever; a store could keep a book on its shelves or in its back room for five years, then return it to the publisher for a refund. Indeed, the rule-of-thumb is that about 50 percent of all books ordered by bookstores will eventually be returned to the publisher for credit.

Unfortunately, publishers ask you to bear part of their risk on returns. They do it by holding on to a percentage of the royalties due on books bought by bookstores as a "reserve for returns," usually for eighteen months after publication. That's not a very appealing system, we know, and it's a subject of frequent tussles between authors and authors' groups and the publishing industry. Better computers and tighter inventory controls throughout the business should improve the situation somewhat, but you can add your voice to those (politely!) urging further reforms.

Before you get too hot under the collar waiting for your royalties, though, remember: The surest solution would be for publishers to clamp down on returns. But how many bookstores would take a chance on unknown writers if they knew they were going to be stuck with every copy they ordered?

The return system, in short, has both its good and bad sides for beginning writers.

Overall, book contracts are straightforward, but you have to read them, understand them, and try to improve them when you can.

29

Screenplays

Is your idea for a screenplay? Congratulations—and welcome to a very large club! Screenwriting is probably to the 1990s what novel-writing was to the 1930s: the first choice of everyone with a story to tell.

Since you won't lack for competition, how can you get to the front of the line?

The first step is to learn something about the business.

Here are the facts. Despite everybody's advice to the contrary, amateurs persist in mailing unsolicited ideas and scripts to the major studios and independent producers. Because these are mailed by the tens of thousands every year, sooner or later nearly every possible idea is suggested. Then, when some studio makes the movie, some person who mailed in the idea inevitably decides he or she has been ripped off and tries to sue the studio. Indeed, almost every successful Hollywood film produces at least one major plagiarism suit.

Virtually all those suits are dropped or thrown out of court. Still, nobody likes being sued, not even Hollywood studios. To minimize the number of stupid lawsuits, the studios and most production companies have a simple policy: If you send them a script or some ideas, they'll return your material either with a note saying they don't read anything unsolicited or else with a waiver form.

The waiver form will, basically, require you to give up any and all legal right forever to sue them over what you send them.

Lots of experienced people in the business will tell you to go ahead and sign the waiver, that you can still sue anybody, no matter what you sign, and that otherwise you'll never get read.

Maybe so, but you're still giving up a lot, and you're much wiser to put all possible effort into getting an agent, both because agented scripts are read without waivers and because:

• Increasingly, producers and studios are opting out of the unsolicited manuscript business altogether: Spielberg's Amblin' Entertainment Co., for example, quit reading them about 1988.

• Even if you do get your scripts read by a studio, that's probably the last thing you want at this stage.

Studios keep staffs of readers who "cover" submitted scripts; that is, for each script, they write a one-or-two-page report, which they then forward either to the head of the reading department or to some particular executive.

Unfortunately, a script sent by an unknown, with no "elements" attached, will almost certainly get a negative reading. You get a rejection letter and the coverage goes in the file. If anyone in subsequent years tries to re-place the script at that studio—even if the script's much better and has a major actor attached—that bad coverage will almost certainly kill the deal. Since there are only a handful of major studios, you can burn up your chances pretty fast.

Those, frankly, are just a few of the reasons an agent is probably essential if you want to break into Hollywood.

What Makes a Good Agent? The basics are the same as for book agents: You want a film agent with contacts, integrity, and a passion for your work.

But there are a few differences, mostly because your "dot," whether you want to be a pure screenwriter or a writer/director, is not just to sell a script, but to make a movie. That means bringing together a lot of separate talents—and that makes a lot of people think they need a "packaging agency."

Packaging One of the longest-running disputes in Hollywood is about the morality or even the existence of packaging.

In television, packaging has long been a recognized and respected practice. The big talent agencies would bring together all the key elements for a new program—writers, director, stars—along with the idea itself, and then sell the whole package to a network. Since there were for many years only three networks, the method was said to help balance the networks' overwhelming power. The agency then collected, along with its fees for representing individual talent, a "packaging" fee of, say, 10 percent off the top.

In film, the practice is controversial, because in theory the big agencies, by controlling the few true "box-office" stars, would be able to dictate terms to the studios. Not only would they be able to get huge salaries for the stars, but they'd be able to insist the studios use the agencies' highest-priced writers and directors, thereby blocking out younger talents. The agencies have long denied such tactics exist.

Call it what you will, the big three agencies (CAA, ICM, and William Morris) certainly do work to bring together the elements of a successful film. But they definitely also do work with screenwriters represented by smaller agencies if those writers have the right script.

In short, don't worry about big agency or little agency; at this stage of your career a small agency is probably your best, perhaps, your only choice.

So whether you want a big "packaging" agency or not, you want an agent. How do you proceed?

Preparing Your Script: Learn the Form!

You probably noticed that, in talking about selling a book, we said almost nothing about the form of the book itself. That's because books have few formal demands beyond the obvious, such as good grammar and clean typefaces.

Hollywood's different. Here, format does matter—a lot.

Some years ago a major independent film producer told a UCLA film class he had just paid $250,000 to "two secretaries from the Valley" for a screenplay. The screenplay was (to put this nicely) poorly done; in fact, it bordered on the illiterate. But because they had worked around the film business and knew screenplay formatting, they made the first cut—and then he bought the script for its idea. (Yes, he did have to hire someone else to write the real script, but the film got made and did fairly well.)

In general, Hollywood cares a lot about formatting. In fact, format is a standard "cutout"—improper format is the first excuse for bouncing a script without reading it.

How can you avoid getting cut?

Watch the length. Screenplays, correctly formatted, generally run between 100 and 130 pages. Comedies and action stories can be shorter—as short as 90 pages—simply because a line or two of description ("the Marines shoot their way up the hill") can translate to several minutes of screen time.

Don't number your scenes, and don't give camera angles or other technical details. You're writing a "selling script," not a "shooting script." A shooting script is what the director will use to make the movie; he or she will decide the camera angles, number the scenes, and so on.

Write your script in "master scenes": that is, describe each scene once, briefly, at the start, then just give us the dialogue with a minimum of additional narrative.

You want something that resembles a shooting script without interfering with the story—its drama, humor, pace, and excitement. Stuff like—

G-26 INT / EXT-POV THE SUBMARINE-SUNSET (F/X, MOS, "Binoc" Matte, Undercranked)

High camera angle. As water crashes over the conning tower, Rhett clings desperately to the deck gun.

SLOW FADE TO:

—won't make you sound like an insider; will make you sound like an amateur.

Water crashing over the conning tower and Rhett clinging desperately are fine—but F/X and MOS ("special effects" and "without sound"), and "high camera angle" only break up the reader's experience. Just write in "master scenes," separated (if at all) by simple "CUT TO"s:

EXT-SUBMARINE-DAY

As water crashes over the conning tower, Rhett clings desperately to the deck gun.

CUT TO:

INT-WARDROOM-NIGHT
Gunny and Mac nurse cups of coffee at the wardroom table.

MAC
I'll miss old Rhett.

GUNNY
Yeah. He owed *me* money, too.

—and so on.

Keep descriptions brief. Avoid long physical descriptions. If you're describing a room, for example, you may need only a few words—or none at all:

INT-JOE'S KITCHEN-DAY
High-tech and yuppie.

We've got the picture—now give us the action and the dialogue.

You should, of course, mention important props, which impact the action of the scene, but otherwise you're not a set designer—right?

Don't tell the actors how to give their lines. Avoid parentheticals describing how lines should be delivered. Every actor in the world immediately on receiving a script goes through it to line out the parentheticals, and since producers and directors know this, you'll only mark yourself as a rookie if you include them.

The only exceptions to this are a) where the line is delivered to someone in particular, and b) where there's a chance of ambiguity:

> JOHN
> (to Fred)
> Wait here.
> (to Charlie)
> Come with me.

—or where the reading is other than what would first be expected:

> JOHN
> (affectionately)
> You fat idiot.

Otherwise, forget the parentheticals. If the line delivery isn't clear from the context, rewrite the line.

Don't cast the movie. Never describe your characters in terms of actors: "JOHN, a Mel Gibson figure of a man." In fact, try not to narrow the type at all. Why say your hero's six-foot-four and blond? How many six-foot-four, blond leading men are there today? Just say, "JOHN, a dashing man of action."

The Last Details Don't agonize: The rules we've given actually make your job easier. You only have to write the story, not direct it, too.

The point is to be clear and readable. Just remember that the way to look like an insider is simply to tell a good story and leave all the "film" stunts for later. Our Recommended Reading list cites some good books that can teach you much more about screenwriting.

Once your story's in shape, only a few details remain:

Polish your script. Get yourself a good, clean, carefully proofread copy, one following the rules above and free of typos, missing words, and grammatical errors. If you're working on a computer, spell-check the script, and then read it again for all those places where you've used the wrong word but spelled it properly.

If you can, laser-print your script. You want the clearest, most readable copy you can get. When you make the photocopies, have them shot onto three-hole paper and then check each copy to make sure there are no missing pages.

Keep covers simple. Oddly enough, for such a visually conscious industry, film has an aesthetic of simplicity for binding manuscripts:

1. Use simple card stock, front and back. No plastic, no fancy graphics on the cover.

2. Scripts are always done on three-hole paper, held together with

three brads (you'll normally want to use one-and-a-half-inch brads). The reason is simple: Brads allow readers to hold the script open to a page with one hand, but also to disassemble it quickly and easily for copying and such. (Don't ask us why the convention in publishing, where manuscripts are always submitted loose-leaf, is different. In cases like these, rules are rules.)

Does Format Really Matter?

TV writer/producer Lew Hunter tells a story about his early days as head of the script department for Disney. He had received a story he loved, but he couldn't get anyone higher up to pay the slightest attention to the coverage. Finally, in desperation, he recalled the coverage and reread it. It was a rave; he couldn't understand why the people with authority wouldn't ask for the story.

Finally he noticed the coverage was single-spaced. Hoping against hope, he had the coverage retyped, double-spaced, and resubmitted it to his bosses.

Almost immediately he got a call. "Where has this great script been hiding? Why didn't you tell us sooner?"

Disney did the deal and made the movie. It was called *True Grit,* and it won John Wayne his only Oscar.

So put the time into being clear and readable.

Finding an Agent Finding a screenwriter's agent works the same way as finding a book agent (some, in fact, do double duty). Always start with a query letter and build from there.

The main difference, though, is that there's no shortcut comparable to the "outline and sample chapter" method. To make a serious try at getting representation, you probably need at least:

• One really strong script—a "kick butt" script, as it's sometimes known.

• One or two backups, in case they want to see more. Ideally, these should be in other genres (if your main script's big-budget sci-fi, your backup might be a small, personal film). These should be as highly polished as your "calling card" script, though they may not have quite so brilliant an idea.

• At least half-a-dozen well-worked-out ideas, to ready you for that Hollywood oddity, the Pitch Session.

Once you have all or most of the above, you're ready to look for an agent. There are a number of handbooks out—try your local library or write:

> Writers Guild of America, West
> 8955 Beverly Boulevard
> West Hollywood, CA 90048
> Attn: Agency Department

For a small fee (presently $1), they'll mail you a copy of their Agency Directory, listing all the screenwriters' agents who are signatories to the Guild's Artist/Manager Agreement, which provides important protection for writers.

Take the list and start writing query letters (even shorter than novel letters, if you can) to the agents listed. As always, a letter of recommendation would help; otherwise, stress your enthusiasm and (if any) credentials.

Agent Contracts Your agent absolutely must be signatory to the Guild's Artist/Manager agreement. You'll see that immediately when you're offered a contract, but most nonsignatories have contracts that are downright predatory. You want a contract that either a) incorporates all the Guild's contract provisions, or b) (as is more commonly the case) includes the Guild's contract rider (sometimes called "Rider W").

The Guild provisions give you crucial protection. (For example, they let you out of any agency contract if the agency hasn't found you a legitimate offer of work in 90 days.) Good agents have no objections to these clauses. If your proposed agent isn't a Guild signatory, keep looking.

Once You Land an Agent He or she will begin sending out your scripts—mostly to independent production companies. If you're lucky, you should pretty quickly get either an offer to option (or, if you're really lucky) to buy your script outright. Or you may get invited to a:

Pitch Session Often, if your writing's good but the company doesn't want the particular story, you'll be invited in for a "meeting" or "pitch session."

Pitch sessions are often ridiculed; there's an idea that you have to sell your movie in one sentence—the so-called high concept.

There are famous stories of great pitch sessions. One writer allegedly walked into a meeting, spread his hands, and said, *"American Graffiti with beds!"*—and got a deal for a film called *Dorm*. The movie *Outland* (with Sean Connery playing an interstellar sheriff cleaning up a distant asteroid) was supposedly sold as *"High Noon* in space," and the alleged winner for the all-time shortest successful pitch is usually said to be the meeting where the studio bought the idea of a comedy film based on the TV show "Dragnet" when the movie's proposed star walked into the meeting, whistled the show's famous theme—and stopped.

Yes, pitch meetings can be totally wacko, but far more often they're exploratory meetings like those in any other business.

Some low-level development people in Hollywood take meetings to make themselves appear useful, but most are really hustling and looking for a project. Very few people you'll meet at this level will have the power to spend any money, but if they like your idea and they're hard workers, they can do a lot to push it up to the next level.

Part of the meeting will be "get-acquainted," but the meat of it will be to see whether you have a great idea for a movie—either a written script or simply something that interests you.

They'll probably ask you offhandedly, "Working on anything else interesting?" Make no mistake—this is your chance to pitch. Start throwing ideas at them; if they say one's not right for them, pitch them another one and just keep going! They'll expect you to have at least half-a-dozen ideas that excite you, and they may have the patience to listen to a dozen.

There *is* something to the "pitch meeting" folklore. Hollywood does place great emphasis on short, punchy communication—in scripts and in conferences. You may not need a one-line plot summary, but you'd better be ready to summarize any idea you want to pitch in 60 seconds or less. Then you can elaborate if they're interested.

Sometimes they'll ask you if a certain idea of theirs interests you. Run with it if you can. Probably more real writing assignments come out of these questions than out of pitched ideas.

If you strike out on all counts, try to wind up the meeting quickly and cheerfully. Ask if they'd mind hearing from you again with more ideas. Shake hands all around and leave.

Then, when you get home, write a letter to them and to your agent, if you have one, itemizing the ideas pitched. It's a good habit, both because it gives you a chance to sharpen the impression you made and because, if there's ever a dispute, you've created a record of what you discussed.

You may take in a lot of meetings without results, but if you keep getting invited, keep going. Oral presentation will be part of your career as long as you're at it. Besides, pitch meetings are where you meet the people who'll be running the studios ten or fifteen years from now. And most important of all, eventually somebody's going to offer you a deal.

When You're Offered a Deal   Don't mess around. If someone offers you a film deal, you need both an agent and an entertainment attorney. If you lack either, get them on your team before you sign anything. Yes, they're expensive, but you need pros. These contracts are just too tricky.

Take just one example:

Your contract offers you 5 percent of all the royalties the studio earns from video sales. That sounds good; the video is going to sell for $89.95 in the stores, which means somewhere around $54 at wholesale. Assume it sells a million copies, and that's $54 million in gross sales. You get 5 percent of that, which is a cool $2.7 million.

Fine. But here's what happens:

The studio, call it 19th Century Wolf, creates a company called 19th Century Wolf Video Industries. Then 19th Century Wolf sells its video rights to 19th Century Wolf Video. Just to be fair and square, it gets a 5 percent royalty from its subsidiary.

A million copies are sold, but 19th Century Wolf books only *its* 5 percent royalty ($2.7 million), and pays you 5 percent of that. Your $2.7 million just became $135,000.

And that's why you need an entertainment lawyer in Hollywood.

How Much Money Will You Make?   Yes, you can make a lot of money as a screenwriter. You can even—weird as it sounds—make a couple of hundred thousand a year without ever getting a movie made— simply because of "development deals": A studio or production company "buys" your script, takes it a certain distance toward actually making it, then drops the project. Some people have sold half-a-dozen projects— have even sold the same project to more than one buyer through "turn-around" deals—with never a project on the screen.

On the other hand, remember that those big-number deals you read about, especially for first-time screenwriters, are often wildly inaccurate, simply because so many projects get dropped. A "$250,000" deal may really pay the writer only $100,000 (before agent's and lawyer's fees) at the outset, with more paid out in bits for, say, each draft and "polish," and then a final lump of perhaps $100,000 payable only if the film is actually made. (Technically, the last payment is usually due at "commencement of principal photography.")

That's still good money, but perhaps only one in forty projects put into development actually makes it to a finished film.

Your "dot," then, should be more than just selling a script; it should be getting your movie made.

How can you improve those 40-to-1 odds, or even improve the odds of getting a deal in the first place?

Attaching Elements One of the ways you'll know your script is hot, and one of the ways your agent or producer will earn his or her money, is by the attachment of elements. "Elements" is defined as the director and the stars. The commitment of a major star will virtually guarantee a film's being made; a major director, while not quite so influential, will still help a great deal.

Hang around Hollywood even a short time, and you'll hear dozens of people tell you that this or that star is "considering" or "interested in" their script. Usually that means they've put a copy in the mail for the poor star, but sometimes people do get their scripts to the right person and a film deal results.

Can You Reach the Big Players? Oddly enough, this does some-times work, especially if you have a script with a particular slant and know of a director or star who might share that slant. You probably have a better chance of reaching a director than an actor.

The method is easy. Write or call the Directors Guild of America or the Screen Actors Guild and get the address of the agent of the person who interests you. Then write a letter in care of the agent, with a cover letter to the agent, explaining your idea and why you think the particular actor or director would be interested.*

If you write a graceful letter and your reasons for asking the particular actor or director to consider the script make sense you may well get a positive response. The odds are too poor to base your campaign on, but on a one-shot basis, it can't hurt, and people do get lucky.

But play fair. If you don't have a strong reason for thinking a director will care about what you're doing, don't make the approach; you won't get anything for your trouble, and you'll make it harder for others. Why mess up a system that can get a break for unknowns?

Getting Hot One thing that Hollywood offers that probably no other place on earth does is the phenomenon of becoming suddenly, blazingly in demand.

In mid-1991 a friend of ours had been in Hollywood for six years.

---

*Be realistic. Steven Spielberg reportedly gets 100 *job résumés* a day, and his company (Amblin) stopped reading unsolicited scripts several years ago.

He'd been a Rhodes Scholar, graduated from Harvard, and was finishing up a Master's at UCLA film school. He'd had a few modest option deals and had written a couple of short pieces for "reality-based" television, but not much more. Certainly he was getting read, but he was scarcely making a living.

Then our friend and one of his writing partners (call him "Joe Smith") wrote an adventure script. They spent nine months writing it. Previously they'd both done long runs of the pitch-meeting-after-pitch-meeting routine, and, while they had come close a number of times, they were both getting pretty discouraged by the time the new script was ready to make the rounds.

Warner's received the script on a Monday afternoon. The studio gave it to star Steven Seagal, who decided that evening he wanted to star in the film. By late the next day Warner's had agreed to buy the script for a cool $500,000.

Even more than that, the script—and its authors—were suddenly hot. The top agents of the big three agencies, even the president of the top one, were offering meetings.

How weird did it get? When Joe Smith stopped by one of the big-three agencies to visit a friend in the mail room, word spread that "Joe Smith is in the building." The next thing Joe knew, Clint Eastwood's agent was dragging Joe into his office for a meeting. And there, on the agent's desk, was an almost unreadable, seventh-generation "sneaked" photocopy of the suddenly hot script.

Twenty-four hours before the script sold, none of these people would have returned a phone call. Now every one of them was desperate to get into business with our friends. And that's how the game is played.

It's been called a "feeding frenzy"; more popularly, it's known as becoming the "flavor of the month"—because, unfortunately, that's about how long it usually lasts. Still, it's that element of fantasy success, the way it comes on in a huge wave, that sustains the enthusiasm of would-be screenwriters. People who've been through the process offer three tips:

1. Remember that this probably won't last.
2. Enjoy the hell out of it while it does.
3. Don't let it go to your head, because the descent may be as rapid as the rise.

Above all, remember that selling the script doesn't get you all the way to your "dot." You still have to survive several further steps.

Development. Development means that the project has been moved onto a studio lot and the studio has committed a certain amount of money (generally, under one million dollars) to refining it to where it can be scheduled to be made as a film. That is, the script is reworked, the stars and director are signed (in addition to any who may have been added earlier) and a shooting budget is prepared.

If all goes well, at the end of the process, the producer (perhaps with the director, a star, and/or the studio person who's backed the project) will present the developed project to the studio heads, who will *"green light"* it—that is, okay it for production.

If your project is the lucky one in forty (one in seventy-five, at some studios), and actually gets green-lighted, then triple congratulations!— you're really on your way. If not, the project is either kaput, or, if you're lucky, put into "turnaround."

Turnaround means one of two things. Sometimes it's just a polite way of saying the studio has dropped the project. More formally, it can mean a project has been dropped by one studio, but picked up by another. That's quite common in Hollywood. It happened, most famously, to *E.T.*—but lots of successful films have struggled.

48 Hours, for example, kicked around Hollywood for more than a decade; it was set, at various times, in the Wild West, and even in outer space. When it finally appeared, of course, it was a huge hit and made a star of Eddie Murphy.

Credit. When your story finally becomes a film, you may have one last issue to confront.

Because a project can go through years of development and script after script, it often becomes hard to determine the actual writer. Since screen credits largely determine what you'll get paid for future projects, you have to fight for your fair share. Your lawyer and agent should try to keep unwarranted names (like the star and/or the producer) from being listed as writers.

Ultimately disputes over credits are settled by the Writers Guild, which appoints arbitrators to settle credit. The all-time greatest number of credited writers is said to be seven, for *Tootsie.*

You now know the basics of the script business in Hollywood. A few tips on breaking in:

Film Schools For any film discipline—writing, directing, producing—film schools are definitely worth considering. The "Big Three,"

UCLA, USC, and NYU, share three big advantages: top faculty, alumni networks to help you make contacts, and access to top media people who will often advise or lecture on campus. Still, many schools have good, basic film programs.

Don't let your present career or lack of background stop you. A large percentage of students at the top film schools are "second career": lawyers, doctors, teachers. It most cases, schools decide whether or not to admit you on the basis of your submission: a sample of writing, film making, or even animation.

Contests. Most film schools offer prizes of various sorts, and there are other contests (like the FOCUS awards) that are national but open only to full-time film students. The one major screenwriting contest open to everyone (worldwide) is the Nicholl Fellowship Contest, administered by the Academy of Motion Picture Arts and Sciences. It gives five $20,000 fellowships each year, and the prestige is considerable, but more than 3,500 people enter annually. For information and an application form, contact:

> Academy Foundation
> Nicholl Fellowships in Screenwriting
> 8949 Wilshire Boulevard
> P.O. Box 5511
> Beverly Hills, CA 90209

Presently the entry fee is $25, and submissions have to be postmarked by May 1, but inquire early, because the rules change often.

If you really want feedback and industry attention, and care less about the prize money, consider the Writers Workshop. The workshop accepts scripts from all over the country. For $65 you get a reading by two industry readers. If they turn down your script, you get one or two pages of their comments and suggestions. If they accept your script, within nine months it will be presented as readers' theater by the Actors Repertory, in front of an industry audience. The reading will also have a Guest Moderator, often a high-powered writer like Ray Bradbury or Larry Gelbart. You get feedback from the audience and probably some useful contacts.

Even better, while about eighteen scripts a year get that very nice treatment, two are chosen for Special Event readings at major studios, with a still more select industry audience and even more opportunity for contacts and prestige.

The Writers Workshop is certainly legitimate, but in comparison with some of the better-known contests, it demands a lot in return for what it offers. To enter, you not only have to pay a $65 reading fee and perhaps a few hundred dollars in later fees, if your script is chosen for performance, but have to sign a three-page contract, committing you to various steps which might delay your marketing of the script. You also agree to help the Workshop profit from any script deal you may cut. Get the contract, then decide for yourself if the Workshop is right for you. Write:

> Mr. Willard Rogers, Director
> American Film Institute Alumni Association
> Writers Workshop
> P.O. Box 69799
> Los Angeles, CA 90069

With any big prize comes a brief rush of interest. Win any respectable contest and you'll hear from agents, studios, and production companies. With luck and persistence, you can parlay that into a deal, or at least representation.*

One Last Tip about Screenwriting In "Recommended Reading" we've listed some books generally considered first-rate. You know there are university courses, even complete degrees, in screenwriting. You can also sign up for some very expensive seminars.

But the primary text at the UCLA screenwriting program (ranked by many as the best in the world) is Aristotle's *Poetics*. Before you launch into expensive courses where "experts" tell you how many minutes can elapse to your first-act turning point, try sitting down with the Old Master. You'll learn a lot.

---

*With screenwriting and with most of the arts there are a lot of phony contests, where you send in, say, $50 to compete for a $5,000 "award." Most of the people running these have no industry standing at all. If you want to fiddle with these contests, okay, but watch out. Some of them make you sign away development rights as a condition of entry. Don't do it!

30

Television

OBVIOUSLY, TV and the movies have much in common, but generally, taking your ideas to TV means:

* More money for the artist,
* More intellectual freedom,
* Quicker action.

Unfortunately, it also means:

* Less prestige,
* Lower production values,
* More time pressure.

More Money The money to be made in television often dwarfs what is to be made in films. Here's how the co-creator of a hit 1970s half-hour sitcom described selling his show into syndication:

"It felt like somebody was stopping at my house every week and dumping a truckfull of money on the front lawn."

How much is a "truckfull"? At the peak of the market, the top people of a hit show that went into syndication sometimes earned $50- to $100 million each.

On a per-project basis, you'll get more working in films, especially when you're starting out, but TV will give many more chances to work, and as you move into producing your own work, which is common in TV, you'll rapidly get into the big money.

Television also provides more:

Intellectual Freedom Especially since the rise of cable, TV has become far more open than film to new ideas. That's partly because it needs so much more material, and partly because it risks so much less money per project (at a rough ratio, a theatrical film costs from eight to ten times more than a made-for-television movie). It's easier to risk four million dollars than forty.

"Intellectual freedom" is a vague concept, of course, but here are two examples:

Controversial subjects. TV made its first movie about AIDS some six years before Hollywood tackled the subject, and even then the "Hollywood" film *(Longtime Companion)* was made only after it got backing from public television's *American Playhouse* series. In general, TV's record on tackling controversial subjects (from drug abuse to racism) beats Hollywood's handily.

Historical projects. Hollywood's view of historical projects is perhaps best summarized in two words: "We'll pass." Meanwhile, television in the 1990s has taken on everything from the Josephine Baker story to the Civil War's Battle of the Ironclads.

Quick Action TV has an edge in its ability to make a project quickly. If a TV movie or series is going to be made, it'll normally be on the air in less than a year, while a Hollywood film can take from four to five years or more.

Television has clear strengths for idea people. What about the negatives?

Prestige For many people TV is still synonymous with the mediocre and the repetitious: the "vast wasteland," as it was once described.

Is that fair?

Ten years ago, when the three networks had a virtual monopoly on the TV business, we would have said "yes."

But the late eighties and early nineties saw television, even the three networks, increasingly willing to solicit the ideas of major film writer/ directors from Jonathan Sayles to George Lucas. Even David Lynch, best known for "out there" films like *Eraserhead* and *Blue Velvet,* scored a series hit with the equally "out there" "Twin Peaks."

Our guess is that TV will eventually catch up with Hollywood's prestige, especially as HDTV brings film's visual quality into the home. Still, today, Hollywood is probably the prestige medium, and for many people that matters.

Production Values Television can offer big-name writer/directors creative freedom and a fast transition from the idea stage to the finished product. What it can't offer them (or you) are elaborate production values: casts of thousands, two-million-dollar handcrafted pirate ships, or the like.* Clearly, though, if you want to tell a "small" story, that's not a factor.

---

* One of the most interesting TV developments of 1992 was George Lucas's announcement of an Indiana Jones TV show. Mr. Lucas said he was sure that with good management, on

Time Pressure TV is an assembly-line business. Programs have to go on the air, every day, exactly on schedule. That translates to major time pressure on everyone in the business.

Those are points to consider before deciding whether TV's right for you. If TV *does* interest you, read—

Our Sixty-Second Course in Television Economics

Most television shows are commissioned by either the major broadcast networks or one of the cable networks, but most shows are actually made either by divisions of the major film studios or by large independent production companies (like Cannell Productions).

The networks, then, simply pay (currently about $250,000 for a half-hour episode) for the right to air a show. Their money usually buys them a first showing, plus one or two repeats; after that the show reverts to the control of the production company. Since nowadays the network fee rarely covers the full cost of making an episode, a production company whose series airs but then flops after a year or two will lose a lot of money.

But TV production is a gamble—the winning ticket comes when a company's show stays on the air for at least 100 episodes. Then, especially if it's been a big hit, it's eligible for *syndication*. That simply means that a group, or syndicate, of independent television stations agrees to buy the airing rights. This is a straight deal between the production company and the independent stations, with no studio middleman. The revenues can be gigantic—hundreds of millions of dollars—and it's almost pure profit for the producers, because most or all of the production costs have already been paid for by the networks or cable channels.

Increasingly, syndicates are sponsoring shows from the outset. Many are low-budget, but a few, like "Star Trek: The Next Generation," are top grade.

The syndicates, composed mainly of independent stations or those trying to fill time before network programming begins at 8:00 P.M., are mostly interested in buying half-hour sitcoms. Projects like miniseries and TV movies find very few secondary markets, though a few succeed

---

a TV budget, he could make an episode look like a feature film. The show debuted to uneven ratings but universal agreement that it looked great.

on videotape. The biggest money, then, is in creating a long-lived sitcom.

Getting a TV agent is just like getting one for film. In fact, if you have a film agent, he or she will likely be putting you up for TV jobs, unless you've specifically said you don't want any.

If you sign with an agent specializing in TV, he or she will probably focus your work in one of two ways: either full-length dramatic pieces or sitcoms.

Selling Your Ideas:
A MOTW or Miniseries

Selling a MOTW ("Movie of the Week") or miniseries idea works almost exactly like selling a regular film. You need an agent to go at it large-scale, but you can sometimes get read by particular production companies on your own if you write a convincing query letter.

Network-Approved Writers Ten years ago, when the three networks were all there was of television, the biggest single bugaboo for people trying to break in was the idea of the "network approved writer." Particularly for the prestige projects (movies and miniseries), this was an almost classic Catch-22: You couldn't do a project until you were network approved, and you couldn't be network approved without a project under your belt.

Nowadays, of course, the networks matter less. But the network-approved writer list still exists. There are at least four ways to get on the list.

1. Get an approved writer to guarantee your work. (The writer agrees to rewrite your work for free if the network rejects it. It takes a writer of rare generosity to undertake this commitment, but some do it, for beginning writers they believe in.)

2. Establish your credentials in another medium.

3. Get a recognized producer to back you for a specific project. If they have the weight to get you on the list for this one project, you're in—and once you're in, you stay in.

4. Get the rights to a work or story the network wants, and swap them for the chance to write.

If the networks turn you down, though, it's not the end of the world; nowadays there are options from the "premium channels" (like HBO) to the "mini-networks" like TNT and Fox.

How TV Deals Are Structured

Here comes the paradox: Even though we've said that, overall, TV offers more money than films, the pay per project is much lower, especially at the entry levels.

Basically, TV deals are controlled by the WGA-MBA, the Minimum Basic Agreement worked out between the Writers Guild of America, West, and the signatory producers of filmed entertainment. If you're serious about TV, you'd be well advised to get a copy of the MBA and read it. It costs $15.00, direct from the WGAW; please see Recommended Reading.

The Basic Deal TV movies differ from theatrical films in that you get most of your money up front. The fee for writing a two-hour network film normally runs between $45,000 and $80,000, with a modest bonus (generally under $20,000) if the film is actually made. There are also small additional payments if, for example, the program is shown multiple times or broadcast overseas.

If those prices discourage you, remember: (1) they're not bad for openers, (2) a far higher percentage of TV movies actually get made, and (3) once you break into TV movies, you'll get far more work than you would as a writer of theatrical films. Finally, remember that in TV, far more than in feature films, writers can move up to be the producers of their own shows, and that's where the money becomes huge.

"Quotes" The actual price you get will depend partly on your leverage (e.g., do you own the source material?), but largely on your history as a working writer. For that, they'll ask you or your agent for your "quotes," key terms of your previous deals. If you don't have any previous deals, just be honest; they'll certainly check.

"Letter Riders" Later in your career this may become more complicated, because Hollywood often uses "letter" riders to contracts. These are terms between you and the producer which are favorable to you, but which never go into your contract, so the producer won't have to admit how much you're getting paid. (That way, other talents can't use your deal as leverage in *their* dealings with the producer.) You're honor-bound never to refer to these riders unless you and the producer get into a legal dispute. That's okay, but then you can't use it for your "quotes." Hollywood's a very tricky place!

Your MBA contract will probably require you to give the producers a story, a first draft of the script, two sets of revisions, and a polish. (A "polish" is loosely defined as minor revisions; often this will come about when somebody decides a certain scene won't play.)

As a beginner, you want to be as cooperative as possible. If the producers want minor changes not called for by the contract (and they've been honorable up to this point), help them out: It's worth it for the sake of goodwill.

Beware of "Cut-Offs" Probably more of a concern from your point of view is the possibility of a "cut-off" deal. These can take various forms, but the worst is the one that lets the producers drop you from a project after you've done only the story. If that happens, you may receive only about a third of the money you would have gotten for going all the way through to the polish stage.

Special Deals and Extra Pay Can you up the pay for a MOTW? As with anything else, it depends on your clout. If you're well-established, or have the rights to a hot story, you (or your agent) can probably wrangle a producer's credit of some sort—the fee for this averages somewhere around $25,000.* And, of course, by owning the story outright, you can also collect a fee for the (TV) movie rights. These can be worth another $50,000 or (rarely) much more.

Other Rights As a rule, you're going to have to surrender the majority of other rights; the one you can most often keep is the right to adapt your story as a book. The MBA has minimum fees you're entitled to collect for such things as foreign and videotape revenues, but these are all quite small sums. You can do somewhat better if you have leverage, but the money will never approach theatrical film levels.

Perks As a first-time writer, you aren't going to get many perks. The studio or network will certainly pay your reasonable secretarial, photo-copying and faxing expenses. In addition, you can probably get a reasonable allowance for research if it's a legitimate part of the project. (For that matter, paying a young writer, say, between $1,500 and $3,000 for "research" when no research is really needed is a fairly common way producers sweeten deals without technically paying over Guild minimum for a first project.)

Beyond that, the good perks—the offices and secretaries and choice

---

* This habit of doling out producer's credits (with names like "co-producer, co-executive producer, associate producer, and so on) has perhaps cheapened the value of the title. Probably the one term still containing a measure of significance is "line producer"—the poor slob actually on the set every day to handle the myriad details of film making, and keep the project from collapsing.

parking spots on the lot—will have to wait. For now, forget about the prestige and concentrate on doing the writing.

Another Way into the Business: Pressure Rewrites In fact, it's likely that your first TV movie deal won't be a writing job, but a *re*writing job, one that arises when a network under time pressure can't find an established writer who is both free, and willing to work under that much stress. Many MOTW writers got their first break when their agent called to say, "NBC [or CBS or ABC] has a script with a lousy first act, and they're starting shooting on Monday morning. Can you rewrite it?"

If you're up to working 72 hours straight through, you're in! But you'll get these offers only after people have seen your work and, even if they haven't bought it, have been impressed by your talent.

Beginners don't get rich doing TV rewrites (perhaps under $10,000 for a quick polish, although top people get more than $100,000 for two weeks' work on big projects) but just remember, it's your union card.

Now, what about the real El Dorado—writing for a series?

Selling Your Own Ideas: A Series

Just as with films and MOTWs, the people who make series television shows may well invite you in for a meeting, but it will be a meeting with a difference.

As a practical matter, selling your own series ideas to television, if you're a beginner, is almost impossible. Set aside the idea of pitching an entirely new television idea; you have to work up to the point where people are willing to trust you with the money to make a show of your own.

Instead, expect this:

You walk into the meeting. The producers or their reps say they loved your sample script. You say you love their show. Then they'll tell you how—just off the top of their heads—they've been thinking about an episode where, say, the hero inherits a llama farm in Peru—and ask whether you think you could do anything with it.

What do you answer?

Let's not be stupid! Of course, you tell them it's the greatest idea since "Leave It to Beaver," and you'd walk on hot coals for a chance to write it. Probably then they'll give you videotapes of half a dozen of their favorite episodes of their show and tell you to come back with a first draft of your script in, say, two weeks.

And that's it. They may solicit your ideas for new plots (not series), just to get a sense of your creativity. But nine times out of ten the offer (if it arises) will be to write up one of their ideas.

The deal part of this will be handled by your agent. Again, the governing minimum agreement will determine almost exactly what you make on a first deal, and again you're mostly interested because it's your entry into the business.

Becoming a Staff Writer Clearly, your goal is to deliver a good enough script to be offered a position as a staff writer. Not only is the pay great, but you can then advance up the chain: head writer, producer, and finally creator and owner of your own series.

By far the best-paying staff jobs are in series comedy. While staff comedy writing burns out many people, it also provides astoundingly good training in the art of comedy writing. Just consider the names of four guys who wrote together for NBC's "Your Show of Shows" in the 1950s:

Neil Simon—Mel Brooks—Larry Gelbart—Woody Allen.*

Do bear in mind, though, that TV comedy is the most collaborative art form: you'll get rewritten and rewritten (even while taping/shooting's going on). If that bothers you, forget TV comedy.

Summing Up The old barriers between TV and movies are falling: in the future, very likely creative people will move freely between the two media, in order to take advantage of the particular strengths of each.

31

Directing: Making a Movie

FOR MANY PEOPLE the ultimate project in the arts is directing a major motion picture. At least in theory, you have a budget in the millions, absolute control over hundreds of people, and a chance to play

---

*That in turn leads us to our single silliest fact: According to Mr. Simon, the reason he got to run that crew of geniuses was that he was the only one who could type! We'd make that into a piece of advice if we knew how.

a part in what we're sometimes told is *the* art form of the twentieth century.

Actually, directing is often a lot less glamorous than that, and a lot more rigorous than anything you can probably imagine, but that doesn't stop a lot of people from wanting to make their own movies.

That being so, how do you begin?

As we've shown in the example of Matty Rich, you can film just a fragment of a feature-length movie, then use that to raise the money for the rest of the film. You can also write a surefire screenplay and then agree to sell it only if you're allowed to direct.

A third strategy, though, is to make a "student" or "calling card" film, which lets people see how well you can tell a complete story on a small budget.

Money: "Calling Card" Movies How small a budget are we talking about?

In 1990, the average American film cost somewhere between $15- and 20-million—before advertising. But with an all-volunteer cast, and paying only very nominal fees for technical help, you can probably make a "student-length" film (generally, somewhere from twenty to forty minutes long) for about $20,000. Of course, that's still a considerable amount of money, but probably not beyond reach of most of us.*

How good are these films? Some have absolutely astonishing technical "values"; others, frankly, are quite crude. Steven Spielberg's was a sweet boy-meets-girl miniroad film, entirely devoid of special effects.

Industry people watching student films will discount anything they know was done at great expense. What they say, over and over, is that they're looking for the ability to tell a good story, with good characters, on film.

Casting and Crews While movies are complicated, and some types are fantastically expensive, as a beginning director, you have one huge advantage: There are a lot of people out there as crazy as you are about the movies.

---

*Increasingly, too, a considerable amount of high-technology film making is within the grasp of beginners. For example, the stunning special effects of the "liquid metal" terminator in *Terminator 2* took a year's work by 35 experts, working on $3.5 million in high-tech equipment. About two months after *T2* premiered, though, Silicon Graphics announced a new machine capable of the same effects—for $8,000. That doesn't mean you could make your own *T2* for that price, of course, but it does mean that ever-fancier effects are becoming ever more affordable.

That means that, if you have a good script, the kind that catches people's imagination, you'll probably have relatively little trouble recruiting people to work on your project.

The usual rule is that you provide food and (nonalcoholic!) drink, plus travel and housing, for anyone who travels a long distance to help you. Remember, though, that all this is negotiable; some very desperate first directors avoid providing even food, while others (like Richard Linklater, whose $23,000 film *Slacker,* about Texas drifters, got critical raves and made a considerable profit) have actually gone back and paid salaries to their volunteer casts and crews.

Actors, in particular, love (and need) to work. If you post a "casting call" announcement in any college drama or film department, you'll probably get a generous turnout; all you need is a single 8½ × 11″ sheet describing the project in a few words. Most beginning directors also add a few (often incomprehensible) photostats of snapshots.

Student actors are fine, but don't forget how many other sorts of people love the limelight. Lawyers are probably as good an example as any. In 1991 a dramatized educational video on insider trading on Wall Street called *Think Twice!* was shot by a Manhattan financial printing company for about $75,000. They used the standard tricks for keeping down costs (like using their own offices as "Wall Street" sets) and recruiting unknown actors, but they also got some big names: Many of the hotshot attorneys who appeared in the actual Wall Street trials of the late eighties played roles for free, just so they could be in "the movies." (*New York Times,* July 20, 1991)

In short, never underestimate the panache and appeal of film making—and never hesitate to play it for all it's worth.

Producers and set designers (or artistic directors) have to be great scroungers; if you try to deal exclusively with film supply houses, you're going to break your budget your first day out. (Try $300 a day to rent, say, one eighteenth-century costume). You don't create a schoolroom set; you borrow one.

When you find out how expensive props and costumes are, you'll probably find yourself rewriting scenes to accommodate what you can borrow. Nothing wrong with that!

One tip. The largest variable unscroungeable cost for making a first movie is probably film processing. In New York or Los Angeles a lab will probably charge you about $6,000 for what becomes a thirty-minute film. If you have time to send it to another city, you can get the same quality work for roughly half the price—a $3,000 savings you can invest elsewhere.

Getting shown. If you're in any of the big film-making centers, your work-in-progress may well get its own bit of local "buzz" (that is, become a topic of conversation among people in the business). Or you may meet people at social gatherings and so get festival organizers to ask to look at your film. Otherwise, you need to consider submitting it to festivals on your own initiative. It's quite possible you'll be offered a deal to distribute your film simply by reason of its having been shown at a reputable festival.

The main thing is to be persistent and innovative. Never overlook a venue, no matter how small.

Consider *Slacker,* that $23,000 film made by Richard Linklater. It took roughly two years of hard promotion before the film caught fire. According to the *New York Times,* Mr. Linklater was rejected by any number of film festivals before he booked the film into a small theater in Austin, Texas, where it ran for a record eleven weeks. On the strength of that, it was accepted by the Seattle Film Festival, where suddenly everyone loved it. On the strength of the reviews there, Orion Classics offered a distribution deal, blew the 16mm negative up to a more commercial 35mm print, reworked the soundtrack, and got the film into circulation. In its first month in national release, it earned almost $220,000—not exactly *E.T.* territory, but nearly ten times what it cost to make. Once that happened, of course, the offers to direct feature films arrived from several Hollywood studios.

Minor tip. Don't assume you need to start with the key media cities to launch a movie. The record suggests you might do much better picking some of the smaller cities (Austin, Seattle, Minneapolis) that have a reputation for supporting original films. *Slacker* was no fluke in that regard.

Selling an Independent Production We don't want to build false hopes, but, surprisingly, it's quite possible these days to sell a feature film with far-less-than-studio-quality production values. The success in past years of films, from Spike Lee's *She's Gotta Have It* to Michael Moore's *Roger and Me* to *Straight Out of Brooklyn,* has raised studio interest in independent projects.

The studios can't afford to make films like these (their huge fixed expenses require much larger-dollar projects), but they can afford to distribute them, and today most of the majors have small divisions designed (like Orion's Orion Classic) to do just that. You can contact these divisions yourself, or you can try to interest an *independent* producer's representative, who will act as the film's agent.

Straight to Video Most books about the film business will tell you about major studios and about the lucky free spirits who make art films. They sometimes even mention the "major independents," like Roger Corman *(Little Shop of Horrors)*, who hire young writers and directors to turn out a steady stream of low-end theatrical films, usually on budgets of between one and three million dollars.*

But there's another way into professional film making almost nobody knows about. If you're interested in action films, and have a bold and risk-taking nature, you might want to try it.

The films are called "straight to videos," because they almost never see theatrical release. They're usually made on budgets of under $500,000, and the people behind them are masters of getting a professional-grade product on the cheap, both because they're splendid freeloaders, and because they know how to exploit the many talented people desperate to break into film.

Consider this description of the shooting of a scene for one of these films, from a friend of ours who went along as observer.

(While you read it, remember that "guys dangling from helicopter" scenes are usually shot this way: The camera is placed low and relatively far away, with a telephoto lens to flatten depth perception. Then the copter actually flies a few feet over the roof of a building, but the audience imagines it as a wild flight over a city.)

"In downtown L.A. there's a forty-story office building owned by Hong Kong investors waiting to move here after the mainland takes over the island. They've rented out the ground floor, so the place won't look abandoned, but they're keeping the rest empty for themselves.

"Anyway, the film company arranges to use the top floor and roof of this building for free to shoot some scenes. We're up on the roof, waiting for the stuntman to grab onto the runners of the copter, so it can fly low over the building and we can fake the shot.

"Suddenly the stuntman yells, 'Screw it! I want this for my reel!'†

---

*Mr. Corman surely rates a special tip of the cap for having given early breaks to, among many others, Ron Howard, Martin Scorsese, Jonathan Demme, Francis Ford Coppola, and Jack Nicholson.

†That is, for the reel of clips he shows producers as his "calling card."

He signals to the chopper pilot, grabs onto the runners, and the next thing we know, this guy is dangling from a copter, flying hell-bent-for-leather all over downtown L.A. We got a *great* shot, and all it cost was a two-hour rental on the chopper."

Most of these companies operate by raiding crews from small TV and film production outfits in places like Provo, Utah. They suffer inordinate losses from location injuries (even deaths), and they don't win any Academy Awards. But they make movies—and, more often than you'd think, they make money.

If that sort of excitement appeals to you, by all means consider starting with a straight-to-video company. Here's how:

At your local video store, comb the action-adventure, horror, and/or science fiction sections for films you never saw in the theaters, put out by companies other than the big studios. Check out a handful of titles with recent copyright dates, take them home, and watch them.

For any videos you like, note the names of the production companies (not the distributors), and call Information for the 310 or 213 (Beverly Hills / West L.A. or Hollywood) area codes for their phone numbers. Alternatively, you can use the *Pacific Coast Studio Directory* or the Hollywood Reporter's annual *BluBook* [sic] to find addresses and contact names for many of these companies. Phone the companies, pitch your abilities, and ask if you can send them a tape of your work or come in for a job interview.

You can probably talk your way into a job with these companies faster than with any big Hollywood studio. Just don't let them talk you into taking any helicopter rides.

There are a lot of tricks to the direct-to-video trade. The real way to learn them is to come to L.A. and hook up with people already in the business. They'll give you a chance to learn, provided you in turn are willing to—guess what?—work cheap!

Whatever level of film making you want to try, you probably need to think about at least the following technical details:

Insurance. You're taking a big risk making any sort of film without insurance. Especially on location, you're dealing with ambitious people in strange locations doing unfamiliar things under intense time-and-money pressure. That's a prescription for accidents.

Bonding. Film bonding is a separate matter: The bond is put up to ensure completion of a film by a certain date. Bear in mind that, technically, a bonding company can either close down or take over a film's production if it falls behind certain markers in its completion schedule. Films that are taken over by the bonding company—even if they're finally finished with a company-chosen director—are almost never released. Unless you have investors putting up substantial amounts of money to make your film, you won't have to deal with bonding companies.

Union crews. The Hollywood unions aren't really a consideration for people trying to make films on their own. Nobody in these unions expects a student or beginner to hire a union crew. With overtime and Sunday work, a union director of photography can cost you more in a week than most students have for their whole budget.

A warning. If you're a beginner and don't have the properly trained people, forget using guns or explosives. Even the pros have had disasters; the promising young actor John-Erik Hexsum blew his brains out while playing with a gun at a studio commissary. He was under the impression that "blanks" are harmless. In fact, of course, blanks are simply shells with thin wax plugs, instead of a lead slug, to hold the gunpowder in place. The explosive force of the gunpowder, in a confined space, is more than enough to kill someone.

You would not believe the sorts of accidents firearms and explosives can create around a set. In Los Angeles a student actor was shot because, while somebody had checked the clip of an automatic pistol being used in a scene, nobody realized there could still be a bullet in the gun's chamber.

Technical assistance for firearms and explosions is very expensive; you'll likely be out at least $2,000 for even a modest bang. If you need it, okay, but don't try doing it yourself.

A Film Miniglossary

These are the main people involved in making a motion picture. If nothing else, now you'll know who are all those people credited at the end of films.

PRODUCER: As discussed, the producer is the financial organizer/ director of the film. Recent years have brought a profusion of titles, such as "associate co-producer" and the like. Many of these lack any definition and are simply complimentary terms for people who have some sort of leverage (e.g., they helped attach a major star to the project, or they knew the producer's best friend's hairdresser).

D.P.: Director of Photography. If you're making a first feature (however modest), a competent D.P. can save your tailfeathers, especially when you consider how expensive film is. Alfred Hitchcock supposedly never looked through a camera in his life; he let his D.P. set up every shot.

SOUND ENGINEERS: They are responsible for the basic "live" sound. Ask your sound engineers if they know what "room tone" is; if they don't fire them. (Every acoustic space has its own background sound. Engineers record some of it for use in the final "mix" of the sound track.)

ADR: "Additional Dialogue Recording." Just as you'd guess, the people who record and edit the dialogue, including redubbing ("looping") of muffed scenes. Traditionally, American films have tended to use as much live recording as possible, European ones much less.

FOLEY EDITOR(S): Basically, the sound-effects specialist(s), named after an early great practitioner of the craft. Foley rooms are great fun, full of sandboxes, bells, buzzers, and other gadgetry, both high and low-tech.

EDITORS: Almost no major motion pictures have ever been shot in chronological sequence.* For obvious financial reasons, all the scenes in one location are shot at one time. Editors then not only help the director choose among different takes and camera angles, but assemble the story into its proper chronology, with proper rhythms. Probably the most famous editing job of all time is *High Noon,* where the "metronomic" re-editing, with some additional shots of the clock as it edged toward the showdown time, turned a relatively dull Western into a classic.

GRIPS: Traditionally, the set carpenters; nowadays, the term refers more generally to the people who do all the basic construction work.

BEST BOY: An archaic term that used to mean assistant to the head grip.

GAFFERS: Electricians on the set.

WRANGLERS: They handle any animals used in the production.

STAND-INS: Not often credited, they simply stand in for the actors

---

*The great director John Ford tried to shoot in nearly a one-to-one ratio, so that the studio executives couldn't re-edit his films. A more normal ratio for feature films is probably closer to ten-to-one (ten feet shot for every one finally used). That means much of the art of making a film comes in choosing which foot out of every ten to use.

while scenes are being set up. Ideally, they should match the actors' size and coloring, since they are used mainly to help the crews test out camera angles and lighting. In contrast—

DOUBLES: Appear on-screen for actors. "Body doubles" are often used in the nude shots, as well as in scenes where the actors' faces would be hidden or indistinct, like long-shots of people riding in cars. "Stunt Doubles" are those used for the physically demanding or dangerous scenes.

Schools and Contests A more traditional way into a directing job is to attend a good school and direct a student film. Just remember that the cost of the schooling is in addition to the cost of making your film.

Of the big three schools (USC, UCLA, and NYU), only USC traditionally provides cash financing for student films. The others provide some support, including use of sound stages and gear.

Presently USC funds the production of five student scripts a year; the student directors each get a budget of $35,000. That's a good bit of cash—but remember, USC owns the resulting film. Also remember that after the school picks the script, it also picks the director—who may or may not be the person who wrote the script.

Many film programs provide smaller grants and prizes for students, and each of the big three runs an annual festival of student films, generally with a good number of industry people in the audience. Any good student film can lead to work in the business; a few, like *THX* by the young George Lucas, will lead to a chance to *re*make the story as a full-scale theatrical film.

If you're not ready for three years of film school, consider these alternatives:

AFI and the Sundance Institute. There are several industry-supported film institutes that provide film training. Probably the most impressive is the American Film Institute, which, among many other functions, maintains a Los Angeles campus for training people in all aspects of the film industry, but especially in directing. Created by a 1965 Act of Congress, AFI has a national membership and program of activities.

AFI also runs an array of contests, fellowships, and programs, from a Sony-sponsored competition for VHS-based productions, to special Directors Workshops for women and minorities.

For information on AFI, call their toll-free number: 1-800-999-4AFI. They can send you lots of useful information, including listings of film and television grants, scholarships, and college and university programs available throughout the United States and, indeed, the world.

The Sundance Institute is probably better-known to the general public because of its annual film festival in Utah, but it offers less for absolute beginners. The "Sundance Projects" are films of "near-major-theatrical," or better, quality. They clearly favor projects outside the mainstream, and the competition is fierce. Each year they consider about a thousand proposals for roughly between ten and fifteen slots in their Screenwriter and Director labs. The up side is that it costs only $15 to be considered, and that to start the process you need to have only a two-page synopsis of your story, whether you want to write or direct.

You can contact the Sundance Los Angeles office at: 1-310-204-2091, or write them in care of Sony Studios, 10202 W. Washington, Culver City, CA, 90232.

Well, that's a basic introduction. Yes, film making is the most expensive of the arts. Just remember this: Spike Lee made *She's Gotta Have It* for $18,000—and less than a decade later, he was able to go $5 million over budget on a $25 million film. Is this a great business, or what?

32

Music

> It doesn't take long to find out that *if you're not care-ful,* the music business is nothing but one big, gigantic rip-off. —*American Federation of Musicians*

Welcome to the Music Business As that little quote suggests, music is one tough racket.

Warning stories? They're endless.

Back in 1957, an Arkansas country boy named Billy Riley had a modest hit called "Flying Saucer Rock-and-Roll" for Sun Studios, the label that launched Elvis Presley.

In the fall of 1957 Sun released Mr. Riley's next single, "Red Hot." Legendary deejay Alan Freed declared it a smash hit—and Mr. Riley walked into the office of Sam Philips, Sun's owner, to find three telegrams from distributors, each ordering 10,000 copies of "Red Hot." The band (hastily renamed "The Little Green Men") seemed bound for glory—

Until Mr. Philips arrived a moment later, saw the telegrams, and immediately called the distributors. He told them Sun wasn't shipping "Red Hot." Instead, it was shipping a record by the band's piano player. The piano player was named Jerry Lee Lewis, and the record was "Great Balls of Fire."

Mr. Riley responded by going out to get "really plastered"—and returning to rip up the Sun offices.

Mr. Philips intercepted Mr. Riley as he was overturning the file cabinets, and convinced him that Sun had promoted "Great Balls of Fire" only because it needed "to get Jerry Lee's record out of the way." From then on, Sun was going to push Mr. Riley. Mr. Riley calmed down and went home.

Of course, the only place Sun ever pushed Mr. Riley was out the door; he left the label a year or so later and spent most of the next thirty years recording under various pseudonyms for small labels. Jerry Lee Lewis went on to stardom. (*New York Times,* July 20, 1991)

That's the music business—then and now.

Certainly you can win at the music game. Never forget, though, that the pop music business has long preyed upon the financially and legally unsophisticated people, often from disadvantaged communities, who produce so much of our popular music. To protect yourself in this racket, you need to rely on a fairly elaborate team.

Anybody who hopes to make a living from musical ideas will need one or more of the following: personal manager, business manager, attorney, and/or agent.*

A *personal manager* is much like the general manager of a business, where your career is the business. At least in theory, he or she will make all your key contacts and career decisions. In exchange for this full-service relationship, a personal manager takes between 15 percent and 20 percent of, essentially, your total pretax net earnings.

Personal managers generally expect long-term contracts, up to five years or even longer. You've heard their logic before: They're investing

---

*Since in recent years the music industry has focused mainly on songwriter/performers, this chapter is aimed at that category. Even if you are interested only in songwriting, however, it still is to your advantage to learn something of the big picture. Remember, too, that the industry's ideal of a performer continues to change. Thus the rise of MTV has created a demand for musician/performers who are photogenic as well as talented. (For the best and most sympathetic treatment of management teams, see Donald Passman's *All You Need to Know About the Music Business.*)

in you today and don't want to be dumped a year or two from now, when their hard work begins paying off. There's some sense to that argument, but five years is still too long. Unless you're being signed by somebody with an absolutely golden reputation, try for two years.

Also watch the provisions for "post-term" earnings. Those are earnings on contracts negotiated by your old personal manager, but paid after you've left him. While not necessarily expecting full commission on another manager's deal, your new manager will be working with you while you fulfill prior contracts, and will expect some compensation. Try for a "phase-out" clause, where your old P.M. agrees to accept half his normal percentage on post-term earnings. That leaves you able to offer the same half-normal percentage during the phase-in of your new P.M.

Attorneys. You need a music lawyer to help structure your deals. At the least, a lawyer with legitimate music industry credentials should review any contract before you sign it, especially as the dollars involved rise.

Lawyers are commonly paid by the hour—the last thing you need is another partner. Make sure you know their billing rate, and get solid estimates of what each negotiation will cost you.

In New York and Los Angeles plenty of attorneys claim they handle music clients, when all they've done is, say, settled a star's parking tickets. Again, check those credentials.

Music (or "booking") agents differ from film or prose agents in the narrowness of their activities. Music agents handle only live performances and so should not participate in profits from records or songwriting.

Agents are effectively licensed (the industry term is franchised) by the various musicians' unions. Because each union has its own rules, any agreement you sign with a legitimate agent will really be a bundle of agreements or riders.

As with the WGAW agreement, union-approved agreements allow you to drop your agent if he or she hasn't brought you legitimate work in 90 days. The maximum an agent is allowed under any union agreement is 10 percent. If you sign under union terms, the union will help you negotiate any problems. If not, you're on your own.

If your personal manager, attorney, and agent do their jobs, you're going to be making money. Handling that money is your *business manager's* job.

Appallingly, in some states a person needs no credentials to be a business manager. That means you need to be doubly careful. Get references and check them. Ask what degrees the person has and from what schools. Find out if he's or she's a CPA and/or a CFP (certified financial planner). Finally, trust your gut reaction—even if everything checks out, pass if you don't trust someone.

Never trust your business manager unquestioningly with the investing of your money. Veto out-of-hand any "private" placements of your money. These will almost always mean she's cutting a deal with her friends, who are a) wacko, b) crooked or c) both. Until you get very sophisticated about money matters, make sure your money is being placed in well-known financial instruments like CDs, treasury bills, major stocks, or mutual funds. And for heaven's sake, never let a personal friend be your business manager. Friendship and money rarely mix.

Discuss periodic audits. Even though you're probably not going to spend the money (more than $10,000) to run an audit, a potential manager's response can tell you a lot. If he or she blanches at an audit clause, keep looking.

Finally, whomever you sign with, keep your right to fire your business manager at any time.

However, if you're still at the starting stage and wondering how you get your first deal, consider these tactics for:

Breaking In The classic discovery scenario is that an industry professional hears a live band, then jumps onstage waving a pen in one hand and a record contract in the other.

It's a great image, but these days the pros more often want to listen to a demonstration tape of your music in their office.

Having a professional demo made. The professional way to make a demo tape is to engage a recording studio to record you and to mix the result down to a cassette (not DAT) tape.

How sophisticated should that recording be?

Music industry people will give you two answers. In theory, they'll listen to anything with a vocal track. In practice, the technical standards are so high these days that to get a serious hearing you'd better also have at least a rhythm track and a piano or guitar accompaniment. (Of course, everything but the vocals can be simulated electronically.)

We asked Michael Shiflett, a Hollywood arranger/producer who teaches courses on how to avoid getting ripped off by studios, for some basic tips. Here's what he offered:

• Those low-priced "studio packages" promising to cut you a demo for, say, $80 can be legitimate as long as you walk in ready to record, need the bare minimum of technical support, and make no mistakes. Few people manage that, because:

• Costs jump as you add live musicians, of course, but also because beginners rarely do their homework. Astonishing numbers of people walk into music studios intending to record, but when somebody asks for their "charts" (that is, the written-down music), they say, "Oh, the song's in my head." They end up paying full studio time (plus any talent fees, for backup musicians or engineers) while they hum the tunes, and other people try to work out the chord changes and the like. Hours go by, and nobody's even thought about recording.

• Plan ahead. If you have a friend who plays an instrument, ask him or her to get at least the melody and basic chord changes down on paper. If you have to pay someone to do it, okay. Just get it done before you go to the studio.

• A good studio can get you competent backup musicians, but give them time to do the job right: at least a week. They can also provide professional "demo singers," who, by singing on pitch the first time out, will save you money. Of course, if you're a performer/writer, you'll have to sing the song yourself, even though few amateurs can sing on pitch without several run-throughs.

Figure the average demo tape takes from eight to fifteen hours of studio time. Multiply that by the studio's hourly rate (with engineer), and you have an idea of the cost. If you allow fifteen hours at $25 an hour (a typical figure for a modest big-city studio), you're looking at up to $400 per demo.

Doing your own demo. If you're constantly writing new material and updating your tapes, that money adds up fast, and you may well want to make your tapes at home. Today that's quite possible if you're willing to buy and to learn to use the gear.

The lowest figure we've been given for equipment adequate to making a demo tape is $500, but most people say you need to spend about $1,000. A serious professional, on the other hand, will spend from $30,000 to $40,000 for good-quality home studio with 8-track capability. As with all electronics, the cost of MIDI and recording gear is dropping rapidly.

Once you have your tapes, you're ready to approach publishers (if you're strictly a songwriter), record companies, or both. Or:

Can You Make and Sell Your Own Records? Modern technology has made it steadily easier (at least in theory) for musicians to make and sell their own records. In general, you have to think about this as a very small business; selling 1,000 copies is going to be a lot of work. The problem isn't the technical quality of the music; it's with distribution, which is tightly controlled by the big- and mid-sized companies.

Most people do their own albums either because they want complete artistic freedom or because nobody else will offer them a contract. Still, a few people do make significant money; some albums have grossed nearly $150,000. Manufacturing a CD will cost you about $2.80 a copy (in runs of 1,000), and bring you about $5.50 a copy (for every copy you sell to a store). If the idea interests you, we'd recommend two sources: *How to Make and Sell Your Own Record* by Diane Rapaport, and a *Wall Street Journal* article (November 13, 1991) called, "More Musicians Start Their Own Labels," which makes the whole thing sound like fun.

Also consider: A homemade CD, especially one that covers its costs, makes a great demo even while it gives you the start of a public name. And since you own it, there will be no problem with re-releasing it after your name gets known.

Pitching Your Songs Basically, this will depend upon whether you are a pure songwriter (in which case, you pitch your songs to the music publishers, who will then try to pitch them to various performers and producers), or a songwriter/performer, in which case, you pitch directly to the record companies.

In either case, the approach is simple. If you have any contacts, you use them; if you don't, get the names of people at various companies interested in new talent, and write them a query letter, telling them briefly about your music and asking for an appointment to come in and play your demo tapes. The American Federation of Musicians suggests that you state in your letter that you'll be calling in a week to set up the appointment. When you call, ask for a meeting to demo three or four songs. You may simply hear, "Just mail us your tapes." If all else fails, do mail them in, but your goal should be a personal meeting.*

How do you decide the best places to try?

Picking a Record Label The major labels are those with full-scale

---

*Lately some performers have begun offering to include video footage of their work. In the age of MTV, that's not a bad idea. We're talking about simple video footage, not the professionally made videos you see on TV. Your record company will pay for those when you reach that stage.

distribution capability—that is, the ability to get records in stores everywhere. Then there are the "mini-majors," an oxymoron meaning, basically, labels with big names (like Motown) but with no distribution. They distribute through the majors (Motown, for example, distributed through MCA, before their deal collapsed in litigation).

Finally, there are many "independent" labels, generally small companies devoted to one or two specialized sorts of music.*

Is bigger better? Unquestionably, the big labels have the clout to underwrite major advertising campaigns. On the other hand, small companies can still do a great job for you. One of the hottest bands in the country going into 1992 was Nirvana, whose second album, "Nevermind," shot past even Michael Jackson's $10 million spectacular "Dangerous," to top the charts. "Nevermind" was put out by DGC, a label owned by legendary producer David Geffen, but Nirvana actually made its mark on a small Pacific Northwest label called Sub Pop. While Sub Pop couldn't back the group with the huge publicity a major company could have managed, they did a great job promoting Nirvana through the so-called underground channels, especially the alternative, or college, radio stations, which have launched so many groups in the last five or so years.

Demo or record deal? The ideal is a record deal with one of the majors. Failing that, you'd probably like a deal with the largest company you can find. And below that comes the "demo deal," where the company puts up enough money for you to do a short, professional-quality tape, so they can see whether production values can make you into a salable act. A demo deal isn't much, but if that's all that offers, grab it.

Where the Money Comes From

The Incredible Shrinking Royalties, Pt. I If you thought what we said about *movie* profits was scary, wait till we tell you about record royalties.

Royalties are set as a percentage of the suggested retail list price (SRLP), the music company's idea of what the retailer should charge. Technically, royalties for tapes, CDs, and the like are negotiated, and

---

*Because so many of these specialized independents have been bringing in smash hit records in recent years, many of the majors are now underwriting what we might call "pseudo independents"—owned companies with large measures of independence.

superstars can get as much as 20 percent of SRLP. As a beginner, though, you'll normally settle for the basic deal, which is about 10 percent.

That sounds pretty good. If a cassette retails at $10.98, you should get 10 percent of $10.98, or roughly $1.10. Sell 100,000 copies and you pocket $110,000.

But first you have to deduct "packaging" (a mythic figure, much like "studio overhead"). For cassettes, the deduction is 20 percent.

So: $10.98 - ($10.98 \times 20$ percent) = $8.78. That $8.78 is your true royalty base. You get 10 percent of it, or 87.8¢ per cassette sold; 100,000 copies makes you $87,800. That's still not bad, although the "packaging" on a CD jumps to 25 percent.

Unfortunately, you still aren't down to the money you actually get to keep.

The Incredible Shrinking Royalties, Pt. II: Production Costs If musicians have cause to envy prose writers, it's in the matter of production costs. An author sits at a computer, writes his book, and mails a copy to the publisher, and that's the end of his production costs.

Taking musical ideas to where they can be duplicated and sent into the marketplace, on the other hand, takes a lot of money—and you pay the bill.

How much money are we talking about?

Someone like Luther Vandross may require $800,000 or more to produce an album. Michael Jackson reportedly spent $10 million on "Dangerous" (including, of course, some very expensive video work, and the recording of some fifty songs, of which only about fifteen were used).

Obviously, no one's going to spend that much on your first album; you aren't even going to be in the Luther Vandross league for a long time. Still, a budget of a couple of hundred thousand for a first album on a major label isn't unreasonable, and even an independent label may spend $50,000 or more.

Nobody expects you to write a check for that; the record company's going to advance the money, to be repaid out of—you got it!—your royalties. That's fine, so long as you remember that whole amount has to be repaid out of the royalties you earn, if not on this record, then on your next.

The Incredible Shrinking Royalties: Pt. III: The Producer A record producer supposedly "creates" a record: finds the songs, chooses the studio and backup musicians, oversees budgets, files union reports. Some producers (Quincy Jones is perhaps the best known) actually make artistic contributions to albums.

Unfortunately, producers have two negatives: a) they're expensive, and b) you pay for them.

In theory, a record producer gets paid out of the artist's royalties. Usually, the percentage is between 3 and 4 percent of the SRLP. Since, however, most first albums never earn enough to pay back the artist's advance against royalties (let alone pay a producer), the record company pays the up-front producer's fee, then charges it against the artist's royalties.

Not only will the producer's fee chop down your advance; it will also whittle your basic royalty. If you're getting 10 percent and paying the producer 4 percent, your net royalty is now just 6 percent of the SRLP. Not only that, but you don't see royalties until you've earned enough to pay back not only your advance but the money the record company handed the producer.

In short, a first album can often sell 200,000 copies without any royalties reaching the artist's pocket.

The Last of the Bad News The truth is that you make your first album or your first two or three not to make money but to make a reputation, so that then you can start making the big money, both touring and recording.

Still, here's one more point to remember:

Just as with books, unsold records can be returned to the record company for credit (the credit system isn't as generous as that for books, but it does exist). To prevent having to pay you royalties on records that are ultimately returned, it's customary to hold a reserve of 35 percent against units shipped for two years. Since there can be further delays because of reporting periods, you may not see your money for as long as two and a half years.

So don't order that Rolls-Royce yet!

Now we come to the revenues that matter both to songwriter/performers and to pure songwriters.

Songwriting: mechanical royalties. Every time a song of yours is played in a commercial setting (in a jukebox, or wherever) you're entitled to royalties. These mechanical royalties (from the mechanical reproduction of sound) cover all forms of reproduction; probably the most important of these royalties come from what are called compulsory licenses.

As a song's author, you will, of course, own the copyright and so have the exclusive right to record it. However, once it has been recorded, you or your publisher must allow others to record it.

Any such licensee must in turn pay you royalties. These are capped at the rate established by the Copyright Royalty Tribunal. Presently the rate is about 6¢ per song, for songs lasting under five minutes (it then rises by about 1.2¢ per additional minute of playing time).

Actually, that statutory rate is the maximum; since people know they can automatically get rights to record your song for that, they try to negotiate down from there. Still, it gives you a ballpark figure; if somebody agrees to license your song for a 5¢ mechanical royalty and sells 100,000 copies, they owe you $5,000.

Music publishers handle the licensing of your musical copyrights, issuing licenses, collecting money , and, at least in theory, promoting you and your songs. A music publisher can be as small as a single person or as big as those owned by the major record companies. Traditionally, income on any deals cut by a publisher is split 50-50 between songwriter and publisher.

Successful performer/songwriters nearly always have their own publishing companies, which can be major profit centers. Indeed, some superstars (Paul McCartney prominent among them) use their companies to acquire ownership of other publishers' song catalogues. Thus, the ex-Beatle owns, among many other pieces, the old standby, "Happy Birthday to You."

Songwriters whose music sells only a little also commonly establish their own publishing companies run from their homes. You can affiliate with one of the performing rights societies and occasionally collect a royalty. Affiliation is also to let people who might want to hire you find you through the society.

Your publisher sells other people the right to record your songs, but how do you collect when someone performs them—or (more valuably) when someone plays one of your songs over the air?

Performing Rights: ASCAP and BMI Obviously, you or your publisher would go batty trying to pick up a tiny fee every time one of your tunes got played in somewhere in the hinterland. Instead, he or you signs with one of the performing rights societies (normally ASCAP or BMI). These societies then issue blanket licenses to all the nightclubs, TV and radio stations, and the like around the country, collect the fees, and pay you and your publisher your shares. The publisher/writer split is 50-50; the society collects off the top, of course, but it does all the work.

Technically, you as writer can affiliate with only one society. If you have some reason for affiliating with both, you can create extra publishing companies and affiliate them as you choose.

Songwriters are paid by the societies four times per year, with a holdback period of roughly one year. The biggest of the societies, ASCAP, distributes more than $100 million to publishers and artists annually.

That's our mini-major tour of music revenues. But here's a question. Since it's easy enough to pop a cassette in the mail, do you really need to move to one of the big music centers in order to succeed?

Being in a Center

Every expert we asked agreed: If you want to make it in music, you're going to have to put in your time in L.A. or New York. In theory, you can mail music to publisher or to a record company's A & R people;* in practice, you'll likely just be ignored if you try.

We've already said that publishers and record companies will often let you come in and play your tapes. Obviously, you can't pitch in person unless you're in the town. But there are other reasons for spending time in Los Angeles or New York.

Along with the contacts and the deals, centers are where you'll find the greatest wealth of courses and contests and free advisers.

• New York's annual C.M.J. Music Marathon brings together alternative rock bands and record executives, with both sides eager to re-create the magic that launched R.E.M., Talking Heads, and Nirvana. Also on the program: discount-priced (for students) courses on the nuts and bolts of the music business.

• On a far bigger scale, the New Music Seminar brings to New York musicians from all over the world and, according to a *New York Times* estimate, some 8,000 music industry people trying to spot new trends. Both the Seminar and the Marathon are buttressed by New York's unmatched array of clubs, where the music can be heard.

---

*"A & R" comes from the now-obsolete division of record companies into "business" and "Artists & Repertoire" departments. Today "A & R" simply means anyone on the creative end of the record business.

• In both New York and Los Angeles, ASCAP runs its Showcases, a growing series of weekly evenings where songwriters aspiring to the great old tradition of "standards" writers like Cole Porter and George Gershwin can perform their works for an industry audience.

• In Los Angeles, BMI underwrites the Los Angeles Songwriters' highly entertaining Songwriters Showcase every Tuesday night. You can try out for "Cassette Roulette": if they spin the wheel and pick your cassette, an industry expert and the audience will listen to 90 seconds of your song, then the expert will give you feedback. They do about fifty songs a night, then turn the floor over to producers seeking music for some particular project. For details: 1-213-467-7823.

• Los Angeles also has the National Academy of Songwriters, a nonprofit association underwritten by some of the biggest names in the business. It offers everything from master classes with working pros, to discount legal advice, to a registration service much like what the WGA provides for screenwriters. In California: 1-213-463-7178. Elsewhere: 1-800-463-7178.

When you get your music in shape, you've still got to get it to one of the two big cities—or, of course, to Nashville for Country/Western.

Now let's just touch on one last way to profit from your musical ideas:

Movie Music: What It Pays One of the best ways to make money and to extend the life of your music is to sell a tune (especially a title tune) for use in a movie.

The up-front pay varies hugely. While the license to use a key song, like "Let It Snow" in *Die Hard II,* can top $40,000, and writer/performers who do title tunes can make $250,000, plus royalties, even the best pure songwriters will rarely get over $25,000 for an original song.

But the really big money comes from soundtrack sales. In the year after the Disney film *Pretty Woman* hit the theaters, the soundtrack album, including the Ray Orbison song which gave the film its name, sold some three million copies.

And How It Works You break into writing for films the same way you break into any other part of the business, except that, if you're in L.A., you'll be able to attend open "pitch meetings," where film producers talk about their projects and describe the kind of music they want. You'll also develop a network of contacts who can turn you on to jobs and even put your name in for them.

Once you have a few credentials and people trust you, you'll often be shown the rough cut of the scene that needs the song, to which the sound engineers have attached a "sounds like"—that is, an example of the sort of song the film's director or producer wants. Usually this will be some smash pop hit. Instead of licensing it for $250,000, they want you to write a tune that sounds like it for about $5,000 or $10,000. The pay you get for this is usually called a "synchronization fee"; sometimes they'll ask you to throw in the song's copyright. Try to keep the copyright if you can; in any case you should also get royalties from sales of soundtrack albums and the like.

Speed Is Everything As with most things related to films and especially TV, speed will serve you well. Most beginners get called in when films are at the "post-production" stage (that means the footage has all been shot), and when deadlines are at hand. In our spot survey the shortest time songwriters were given to provide a finished song was three days. On rare occasions, the search for the right song can last for months—you may be asked to submit a blues number one day, then told the next day your song was fine, but they've decided they want reggae, and will you try again?

As long as they keep asking, you should keep submitting tunes. Be fast, be flexible, and be stubborn—and you can sell music to Hollywood!

Summing Up As a business, music is probably the roughest of all the arts. If you're careful, though, you can survive very well.

Yes, plenty of musicians get hammered by the system—and probably more, by drugs and alcohol. The counterpoint is creative people often succeed handsomely in music. A few get rich; a good many manage stable creative careers; and large numbers at least have the satisfaction of seeing their music recorded and hearing it performed.

Above all remember this, from Barbara Jordan, a songwriter/producer who works in both TV and films, teaches marketing courses for the N.A.S., and has an M.B.A. from UCLA business school:

If you're serious about selling your music, 50 percent of your time should go to marketing yourself. That means writing query letters and going to pitch meetings—but it also means getting out and getting known. It means going to parties and shaking hands. People who've met you will be far more willing to hear your tapes or to recommend you to others.

Especially if you want to write for movies and TV, you'd better get out and get known!

33

Art and Animation

IN THIS CHAPTER, we're going to try to cover a lot of terrain: the visual arts, including everything from animation, to crafts, to higher "art." We're going to be able to hit only the high spots, but don't worry: we'll give you some other good sources for more detailed information, and for starters we'll at least show you the basic legal pitfalls and financial opportunities.

These general issues will matter whether your art is "high" or "low."

Introduction: *Droit Moral*

For most of our history American visual artists have gotten the short end of the legal stick. While most of the world accepted the Berne Convention of 1928, which recognized the French concept of *droit moral,* or moral right, the United States did not.

Under *droit moral* an artist has the right to have his or her work kept unaltered by any buyer. Under traditional U.S. law, though, the new owner has had the right to rework the art, to delete objectionable elements. Thus, Rockefeller Center once forced the great Mexican muralist Diego Rivera to remove a picture of Lenin from a mural he'd painted, and, more recently, the copyright owners of classic American black-and-white films have "colorized" them despite the strong objections of their creators.*

Beginning about 1981, individual states began passing their own visual arts laws. The model was probably California's Art Preservation Act, which prohibits the owner of a work of art from altering, mutilating, defacing, or changing a work of "fine art" without the creator's permission.

---

*In all the debate over colorization, people tended to overlook one of the main incentives for doing it: The copyrights for those great films were all expiring, but a colorized work technically qualified for its own copyright as a new "derivative" work.

Today the pressure is growing for the United States to accept *droit moral* completely. Still, if you have an important work and want it to stay unaltered, make sure your attorney writes a *droit moral* clause into your sales contract.

Can You Make a Living from Arts and Crafts Ideas?

Many people have ideas for beautifully made objects, whether wooden boxes or decorative plates, which fall right on the line between arts and crafts. If your ideas run along those lines, can you make a living from them? And how do you start?

We spoke with Pamela Ross, founder of the very successful Following Sea stores in Hawaii, California, and Colorado. The Following Sea stores—they refer to themselves as "shops and galleries"—are decidedly up-market, located in the fanciest malls and centers, and feature a blend of top crafts and modern art. Though they now carry goods from around the world, they were originally founded, in Ms. Ross's words, to "celebrate American arts and crafts."

Best of all, in Ms. Ross's estimation, 90 percent of the artist/crafts people in her employ actually make a living from their work—a remarkably high percentage, and one that should give you considerable hope.

Like many other people who sell arts and crafts, Ms. Ross feels artists need to be more aggressive in promoting themselves. That doesn't mean being pushy; it simply means getting your work out where it can be seen. That in turn can mean taking your work to as many shows as possible, or sending out sets of slides of your work, or simply calling shops you like and asking if they'd care to see some of your work.

The Basic Deal In typical deals for shops like these, work is either taken on consignment, with proceeds of any sale split 50-50 between dealer and artist, or bought outright and paid for in 30 days. You can sometimes arrange a better deal, but normally, most of your gain will come from the higher prices your work will command as your skill and your reputation grow.

Artist's reps. If your work is more in the nature of crafts, you may well want an artist's representative to handle your work. A rep can take your work to more stores. He or she is essentially your agent.

The craftspeople with whom we've spoken have generally had more negative than positive things to say about reps. Too often they simply try to place goods anywhere, without any care for the quality of the stores, or the effect such stores will have on your reputation.

Pam Ross's Following Sea stores won't deal with any craftspeople with representation. Ms. Ross wants the feeling of a personal bond to her artists and feels a rep simply interferes.

So think carefully about representation before you sign any contracts.

Exclusive rights. Some shops and galleries will try to sign you to a contract naming them your exclusive retailers. Should you agree?

There's no way to generalize. You need to consider: (1) the shop/gallery's reputation and size, (2) the strength of its commitment to you, (3) the volume of sales it's projecting.

Most agents will say an exclusive to a small region is fine, as long as it runs for only a limited period, say, from 90 to 120 days. You can even write in a mutual termination clause in case sales fail to reach a certain level.

Dealing with Big Stores: A Warning

One time aspiring artists get burned is in going from representation by small shops to representation by major stores. If you're used to selling four pieces a summer and making, say, six thousand dollars, you can slightly lose your head when some big New York department store orders fifty thousand dollars' worth of your stuff.

But read that contract. Most major stores will want return clauses, which means that if they don't sell your material quickly (and we're talking 90 days), they have the right to give it back to you or to mark it down virtually as much as they want. You can find out very quickly that your "$50,000 sale" makes you about $5,000. It's all perfectly legal; most department stores simply assume artists know the game, and the stores don't intend any deception. So learn the game, and if you're not sure what's going on, ask a lawyer. (You can usually find volunteer lawyers who help beginning artists for very little charge.)

Fine Arts—The Basics

For fine artists, how do you get seen?

Many people will say that New York City remains a center for the visual arts, and certainly, if your goal is to become a superstar, New

York is probably where you or your works have to be. On the other hand, many artists maintain successful careers outside the "center" city.

You can start your career anywhere and send out work to galleries. As you gain confidence and reputation, you can pursue ever more prestigious venues for your work.

What You Send Out You're supposed to be a visual artist, so put some art into your presentations. If you're not a photographer, try to get a professional to do the work for you, perhaps through a swap of services deal.

If you don't know the gallery or don't have an introduction to it, phone ahead and get the name of the owner—if possible, try to speak briefly with him or her. Most gallery owners will give you a few minutes. Ask whether you may send in a slide portfolio.

Basically, you want 35mm slides, carefully packaged. Each slide should be clearly labeled, and marked "copyright," with the year of creation. (Of course, this isn't the same as actually registering your copyright in Washington, but it does make you look more professional.) You should also include a short, neatly printed résumé about yourself, including art education, previous shows, prizes won. Finally, you want a short cover letter, letting the gallery know you appreciate their time and trouble and offering to provide any other information they wish.

Political Art—Does It Kill Your Career? Many serious artists consider themselves radicals of one sort or another, or at least they have strong social or political concerns. Luckily, the arts community is notoriously open-minded, and if anything, controversy has been a selling point through most of the twentieth century. Take one example:

Deborah Small is frequently listed in articles about rising Southern California artists. In the mid-1980s, though, she created a much-praised installation piece which she had virtually no thought of selling.

Why?

Because, several years before the topic became fashionable, she looked ahead to the 500th anniversary of Columbus's voyage to America. Instead of praising the Discovery, her creation was a beautifully crafted assemblage of contemporary accounts of the torture, enslavement, and murder of Indians. It was a stunning blend of art and history, but it was also a very strong political statement.

So who bought this radical piece?

Actually, it was a subsidiary of a Fortune 500 company, and they bought it for public display and paid a healthy price for it.

The point is, do what you believe in, be it political, religious, or anything else. In the visual arts community good work will serve its moral purpose and find its audience.

What else do aspiring artists need to watch for?

Work for Hire: Who Owns What You Create? Probably the most common question lawyers get from visual artists goes something like this: "Somebody hired me to draw a logo for a new business. Now she wants to put it on a line of clothes [or of toys, or whatever]. What I thought was going to be a pretty small-potatoes piece of artistic creation is likely to become a big deal. How do I get my fair share of the revenues?"

The best answer is for you to reserve as many rights as you can in the original contract.

Meanwhile, though, realize that the basic element of copyright law most likely to come into play here is called "work for hire." It goes like this:

Ordinarily, copyright law says that the creator owns the work and all attendant rights. However, when the work is created under a paid contract, it most often becomes a "work for hire," and whoever paid for its creation gets some or all rights under the contract.

What does that mean in simple English?

If you sign a blanket contract to create art for someone else and don't specifically reserve rights or royalties for yourself, you're out of luck.

Artistic Rights: What's Standard Practice? When you go to sell your first work of art, the buyer or his or her attorney may well tell you they're offering a "standard" contract. Actually, there's no such thing. Individuals or individual companies may have their own policies, but over the whole world of the arts, nothing is standard except the idea that everybody's looking out for himself.

The Rocketeer's rights. In San Diego in 1981 a young cartoonist named Dave Stevens penned a six-page saga for the back of a comic book called *Starslayer,* published by an outfit called Pacific Comics. The story, about a test pilot who finds a rocket pack, was so well done that before long the character, known as "The Rocketeer," had his own comic book. Amazingly, the people behind *Starslayer* (who probably deserve a monument built to them by artists everywhere) made a point of returning all their copyright claims to their artists.

For Dave Stevens, that meant a tremendous windfall when, some ten years after the first Rocketeer story appeared, Walt Disney Studios made a feature film about his character. Dave not only kept all the money Disney paid for the film rights, but had the chance to help organize the project from the ground floor up (getting the film made was no easy project, but he succeeded).

The Huge Money: Licensable Ideas You can make a living with crafts; you can potentially make a lot of money in the arts. But the real fortunes in visual arts ideas, as the Rocketeer story suggests, come from characters who become popular enough, first, to support large sales of their images, and then to be bought by other manufacturers to be used on their own products—in short, to be licensed.

The money here is downright astonishing. The Teenage Mutant Ninja Turtles, for example, were licensed for use on some $2 billion in goods in 1991, according to the *New York Times*. Figuring a 5 percent royalty, that means the creators of TMNT, which began, actually, as a counter-culture comic book, are raking in about $100 million a year.

With that much money on the line, creating licensable characters is something of a national craze these days. In fact, several major corporations have actually set up research groups to try to invent marketable characters. Probably the biggest such success to date would be the Care Bears, created by Those Characters from Cleveland, a subsidiary of American Greetings.

No matter how you come up with your great licensable idea, how do you license it?

First of all, if your work gets any attention at all, people will probably come to you asking to license your work.

As an alternative, of course, you may need to take the initiative. One way is to attend a licensing show. The largest in the country is the International Licensing and Merchandising Conference and Exposition held every June in New York. Booths there are expensive, but the show always gets a lot of media attention, which can help jump-start a product.

A business tip. If your idea gets hot, you may be in the enviable position of having a lot of people competing for licenses. When that happens, your instinct will probably be to cut deals with the biggest companies, because they have the most prestige and money to promote your products.

However, historically, small entrepreneurial firms have done best with licenses. The Ninja Turtles, for example, are licensed almost exclusively to small companies, which, together, sold that huge $2 billion a year in goods.

Think about it a minute, and you'll see why. Licenses usually go to products that are small, inexpensive impulse purchases; nobody's ever likely to sell a New Kids on the Block mainframe computer. Small companies know how to sell those products and know how to move fast, while a fad's still alive. Moreover, big companies often resent paying the licensing fee, and put their best efforts into products they've invented themselves.

Whether you're dealing with big or small entities, licensing your arts ideas is not terribly difficult. Still, you almost certainly want a lawyer to represent you:

1. Negotiating deals. From a legal standpoint, arts licensing deals aren't particularly complicated, since they generally provide for a clearly restricted use of the licensed character or design.

The usual licensing fee is 5 percent of sales, but that's by no means an absolute rule. Certain long-established groups, with proven staying power, get much higher fees: Major league sports teams, for example, routinely get 10 percent for use of their logos on products. Try for 8 percent, then be ready to compromise.

You (or rather, your lawyer), should also pay close attention to at least:

2. Collecting revenues. Payouts can be annual, semiannual, or quarterly—semiannual payouts are probably best. The person getting the license is going to want a holding period, to make sure she or he actually collects the monies owed before having to pay you. Just keep it short, say, six months.

3. Policing the licenses. When your idea gets popular enough, people will start ripping you off. When that happens, you're going to need people to police your licenses—that is, to track down pirates and unauthorized users.

If you come up against this nasty problem, you need an enforcement program; for that, please see "Knockoff and Counterfeit Goods" in Part Four.

Do You Want Your Own Licensing Company? Of course, there's no practical reason you can't run your own licensing company. Many artists do that in effect, when they're just starting out: they cut their own first deals, perhaps with a lawyer's help. If demand for their hit idea grows fairly slowly and steadily, some (like Jim Davis, creator of Garfield the Cat) simply scale up their licensing to a first-class, corporate effort.

Royalties—Serious Art Another major sore point for visual artists, especially during the huge run-up in the prices of artworks during the 1980s, was the question of royalties. The argument went something like this: "I sell a painting to a gallery for $2,000 so I can pay my rent. The gallery sells it to a collector for $15,000; he sells it to another collector for $75,000; and she sells it to a museum for $300,000. Where's the justice? Why don't I get at least 5 percent of each of those transactions?"

Well, royalties on future sales have always been legal (as long as you could get a buyer to agree to it contractually), and increasingly, both the law and the social climate are making such deals more common. The key, as usual, is simple: Get a royalty on future resales *written in the contract!**

Now, let's talk about a topic a lot of artists prefer not to consider:

Organize Your Estate This may be a terrible thing to have to think about, but given the blows struck to the artistic community in recent years by drugs, AIDS, and the ordinary depredations to which the flesh is heir, you're probably being unwise if you don't sit down with a lawyer and plan for the disposition of your works. If you don't care who gets what, fine—but if you do, then you need to plan.

Part of the problem stems from the culture of the visual arts. Artists frequently trade pieces, lend them to each other, pledge them as collateral for loans, deliver them in unfinished form with promises to complete later—in short, they handle them in a charmingly carefree manner which ends up giving some poor attorney gray hairs years later.

Artist's estates. Even when they do trouble to make wills, artists are often offhanded in disposing of the rights to their creations. It's not uncommon for a probate attorney to discover that an artist has left the royalties to an artwork to one person, but control of those royalties to another—technically legal, but practically, a mess.

As an example, take Jean Michel Basquiat, who died of a drug overdose in 1988 at the age of twenty-seven and was one of the first African-American artists to become a superstar in the economic sense. While some have challenged his merit as an artist (as they have, indeed, many of the superstars of that period), in his short life he produced paintings collected by such museums as the Whitney and the Metropolitan in New York, and he worked in collaboration with artists like Andy

---

*As we went to press, the U.S. copyright office was holding hearings on the feasibility of a federal law on artists' resale royalties. Since the late 1970s California has actually had a law "guaranteeing" artists resale royalties, but it appears to be widely violated, mostly because few artists understand their rights.

Warhol. In 1990, two years after his death, his paintings were being sold at the major auction houses for prices pushing $600,000 apiece. Despite all that, here are a sampling of the legal/financial problems, as reported by the *New York Times,* created after his death:

• One dealer is suing the estate for $900,000 in damages, because Basquiat allegedly never delivered three paintings she bought in 1982 for $12,000, and on which she had deposited a total of $3,000.

• A review of warehouse receipts revealed that Mr. Basquiat had settled restaurant tabs by handing over paintings which a couple of years later were worth a fortune.

• The estate had to borrow money to pay $700,000 in back taxes, because Mr. Basquiat hadn't bothered to file his tax forms for several years before his death.

Perhaps you don't wish to involve yourself in business or legal affairs, and that's your privilege. But if you fail to find someone to manage those affairs for you, expect to be victimized.

Summing Up The basic rules for visual artists:

1. No matter how much you love your work, and no matter how noble the values it embodies, you need to promote it in a businesslike fashion and to protect it legally.

2. Never enter into contracts without legal advice. Artists can often get this advice for as little as $35 from a local chapter of a lawyers for the arts organization.

3. If your work, whether cartoon or high art, becomes valuable, step up the level of your legal protection accordingly.

34

When Someone Steals Your Arts Idea

DESPITE your best efforts, someone may steal your arts idea, that then proves valuable. What can you do about it?

The law is set up to make plagiarism hard to prove. In the first place you can't protect an idea. In the second place, artists traditionally inspire one another; until the Romantic movement of the early nineteenth century, it was expected that artists would use the same stories or images, usually from the Bible or classical mythology, over and over. Originality was not, historically, considered a virtue.

Today, of course, the arts are big business, and artistic ideas have huge cash value. So you can win a plagiarism case, although it's still darned hard.

Let's take an example from the film industry, which has always spawned the most lawsuits.

Plagiarism: What You Have to Prove

Basically, you have two problems to overcome: the industry, and the law.

The film industry is close-knit to a degree almost unimaginable to outsiders. Everybody knows everybody else, and nobody wants to get on anybody's bad side. People who serve as expert witnesses in Hollywood plagiarism cases make it clear you're going to need an extremely strong case to win their support.

Add to that the fact that your opponents are likely to be extremely well-heeled. They'll likely fight you to the bitter end, hoping you'll wear out or go broke before the case is decided.

The law, meanwhile, makes your task relatively simple. You will have to establish at least two things: *access* and *substantial similarity.* That is, that the person you claim stole your work actually saw it, and that he or she later produced a work in significant measure the same as yours.

Can these cases be won? Yes, sometimes—within limits.

One of the most successful movies of the 1980s was called *Look Who's Talking,* a comedy about a baby, told from the baby's point of view, written and directed by Amy Heckerling.

In January 1990 two women, Jeanne Meyers and Rita Stern, filed suit in Federal Court, charging that Ms. Heckerling's film had actually plagiarized a project of theirs: a comedy about a baby, told from the baby's point of view.

Virtually every successful Hollywood film gets sued by one or more people claiming they had the idea first. This case, though, was different. In 1984 Ms. Meyers had actually filmed a short version of her baby story as a student project at the American Film Institute. Moreover, she and

Ms. Stern could establish that they had rights to the original short story on which the film was based, and that they had shown the film, the story, and their own treatment for a feature-length comedy to Ms. Heckerling. Ms. Heckerling apparently took an interest in the project for some months before writing to say she was no longer interested.

How did the case come out?

In April 1991 the judge in the case turned down a motion for dismissal by Tri-Star and Ms. Heckerling. The judge reported that the facts in the case both showed "substantial similarity" and "suggest[ed] copying." He cited specific passages to support his views and said that the case should go to trial. At that point, Tri-Star and Ms. Heckerling settled the case for an undisclosed sum. *(New York Times, June 14, 1991)*

Note that the final issues of guilt or innocence were not resolved, nor are we trying to settle them. All we're talking about are the requirements for putting forward a case worthy of being tried. The two plaintiffs were able to establish 1) that they had at least three pre-existing, solid pieces of work resembling the one accused of plagiarism: a short story, a student film, and an extended treatment for a feature film, and 2) that Ms. Heckling (usually through an intermediary) had access to those materials over a period of months and had taken clear interest in the project.

In short, you can win—if you can establish substantial similarity and access.

If you have less than that, you're probably on thin ice in trying to sue someone for stealing your arts ideas. That's why your best defense is probably a) to take the steps we've outlined previously to document your work and to control and record its distribution, and b) to work, whenever possible, through legitimate, trustworthy intermediates.*

---

*You may have read about a 1991 case, Buchwald *v.* Paramount, in which humorist Art Buchwald successfully sued the film company over their movie *Coming to America,* which contained his idea about an African prince seeking a bride in America. Note that Mr. Buchwald had a contract saying Paramount would pay him if they made any films using ideas he submitted. He sued and won on that contract—he did not prove (nor did he have to) that Paramount or star Eddie Murphy stole his idea. So don't get the idea that studios are paying off to ordinary people who mail them plot ideas.

35

Case Study: Novelist/Screenwriter/ Director Nicholas Meyer

THE FIRST TIME Nicholas Meyer saw a theatrical film, he ran screaming from the theater.* Not the most propitious start for someone who would go on to become a major writer/director for both film and television.

And yet from the very outset Nick Meyer knew he wanted to be a storyteller. A writer from the age of five, a film maker from the age of thirteen (when he began a five-year project to shoot his own "feature-length" version of *Around the World in 80 Days*), he took scant interest in formal schooling. What interested him were the great adventure stories written by Jules Verne, Arthur Conan Doyle, and Alexander Dumas.

Like many creative people, Nick Meyer approached formal education with reluctance at best, hostility at worst. He graduated from high school with grades insufficient for an Ivy League college. That left him with only one likely choice: the University of Iowa, famed above all for its Writers Workshop, probably the best-known program for prose writers in the country.

From Nick's point of view, Iowa was the perfect choice. Rigorous but unpretentious, the school provided strong cultural opportunities without the snobbery of Eastern schools: It was the ideal place to feed his "ravenous cultural appetite." At Iowa, too, Nick found perhaps the only mentor of his career, Howard Stein, the writing teacher who brought "structure, form, and technique" to Nick's writing. No one can make you an artist, perhaps, but a skilled teacher can teach you the craft.

Getting Ripped Off Well before he started college, Nick was thinking about ways to bring his favorite stories to life. At seventeen, he made an interesting observation: that Shaw's play *Pygmalion* was a structural

---

*The film was the Olivier version of *The Beggar's Opera;* the terror came from the impending hanging of the hero, dashing Captain Macheath.

rip-off of Arthur Conan Doyle's Sherlock Holmes.* From that, Nick deduced that, since *Pygmalion* made a great musical *(My Fair Lady),* Sherlock Holmes ought to do the same.

It happened that Nick's parents knew a well-regarded Broadway producer, and at a party Nick and the producer were introduced. Inevitably, Nick relayed to the producer his exciting idea for a Broadway play. Now, big-time producers aren't usually known for either their hospitality to seventeen-year-olds or their patience with would-be writers, but this one was all grace and good manners. He listened to Nick for the best part of an hour, then sent him on his way with a word or two of kind but condescending encouragement.

Six weeks later the New York papers carried an interesting little theatrical note: that a certain famed Broadway producer was negotiating with the estate of Arthur Conan Doyle for the rights to make a musical based on the story of Sherlock Holmes, tentatively to be called *Baker Street.*

What was to be done?

Absolutely nothing. Nick realized he had given away his idea. There was nothing for it but to head off to college and to take a certain satisfaction a good while later when the Sherlock Holmes musical, *Baker Street,* proved a resounding flop.

Breaking In Nick's college years brought him training in writing, a wide cultural background, and a lesson in how the big boys play in the arts. But what do you do with a college degree in creative writing?

Unless you're willing to hustle, not very much.

There is a lesson in tenacity in the way Nick Meyer broke into the film business. In June 1968 he graduated from Iowa and returned to New York. Once there, he sat down with a copy of the Yellow Pages and wrote job application letters to everybody listed who had anything to do with the film industry. (In 1968, more so than today, New York was the film industry's corporate and financial center, just as Hollywood is its production center.)

From all those letters, sent out over a period of months, only one positive reply came back. Paramount Pictures told him that, while he

---

*How is *Pygmalion* a Holmes rip-off? Consider the similarities: Sherlock Holmes, bachelor with an analytical mind, shares rooms with the not-very-clever Dr. Watson, just back from Afghanistan. Henry Higgins, bachelor with an analytical mind, shares rooms with the not-very-clever Colonel Pickering, just back from India. . . . You get the idea. A fascinating theory, even if unprovable.

was probably "overqualified," they had an opening in their publicity department.

Not exactly the big leagues, but it was a step closer to film than the job he had—since very few people get tapped to make movies while selling pipes in Bloomingdale's tobacco department.

A Foot in the Door Publicity was not necessarily the worst job in the world. Nick spent most of his time "translating" press releases from "Hollywoodese" into plain English, and says the training prepared him for the art of "pitching" film ideas.

In his spare time Nick wrote screenplays, as many as he could, even though they were going nowhere.

Then he got a break, though it seemed small enough at the time.

Paramount was making a movie of a novel, written by a Harvard professor, called *Love Story*. The studio needed a unit publicist (one who writes publicity blurbs from the set), and since *Love Story* was shooting in Boston, Nick talked his way into the job.

Four things came out of that: Nick finally got to see a real movie being made; *Love Story*'s producer optioned one of his scripts; and, on the strength of the option, he got an agent. Then, (remember what we said about developing *all* the aspects of your ideas and experiences?) he sold a book about the making of *Love Story* for a $3,000 advance. At twenty-three, he was sure he was on his way.

He was on his way, all right—to the story department at Warner's. The producer, having failed to place Nick's story with a studio, let the option lapse, and six months later Nick appeared to be virtually back where he had started.

Nick's agent, meanwhile, had done nothing for him, so Nick decided to force matters. In the spring of 1971 he loaded everything he owned into the car he'd driven in college and set off for California. He had no friends there and only one contact: the West Coast office of the agency that had represented him so ineffectually.

The West Coast office (Nick called them from a phone just off the freeway, the minute he reached town) said they wanted to handle him. And for a brief moment they did seem eager to represent his work.

Then they lost interest. In fact, Nick later learned that the agent who had sounded so eager to represent him had actually turned Nick's affairs over to an office boy.

Bad Timing and the Big Break Nick probably couldn't have picked a worse time to come West. He had scarcely begun the usual young writer's struggle for a break when a particularly long and nasty Writers Guild strike froze all the work in Hollywood.

Was it a disaster?

Actually, it was a classic case of problem-become-opportunity. Nick's girlfriend, tired of his haunting used bookstores in search of arcane essays on Sherlock Holmes, and of his insisting he could write a better Holmes story than any done since Arthur Conan Doyle, finally called his bluff. Now he had time on his hands—where was the great Sherlock Holmes story?

Nick sat down and wrote it.

He called it *The Seven Percent Solution,* and when it appeared in August 1974, it headed straight for the *New York Times* best-seller list. It stayed there for forty weeks and for the entire year was outsold by only two books, one of which was Benchley's *Jaws.* Hollywood producers were lining up to buy the film rights.

Nick's agent told him he was entitled to climb atop the famous Hollywood hills sign and thumb his nose at the whole town.

Instead, Nick learned from this what he calls his great life lesson: From that day on, he never undertook any project "except for my own interest and pleasure." While he warns it's far from a universal rule, it's served him very well.

Nick advanced his career by a very common tactic, which he has dubbed "leapfrogging." He didn't sell the film rights to *The Seven Percent Solution* until they agreed he could write the screenplay. When that film was a hit and he was in demand as a screenwriter, he traded on that to be allowed to direct. He wrote and directed *Time After Time,* a film which blended his interest in Victorian England with modern events, as H. G. Wells chases Jack the Ripper to modern-day San Francisco.

Nick's track record was already considerable when a childhood friend, producer Karen Moore, introduced him to Harve Bennett, who was in charge of Paramount's *Star Trek* film project. Nick and Mr. Bennett became friends quickly, and Nick got the assignment to direct the second *Star Trek, The Wrath of Khan.* *Khan*'s success gave impetus to the series, which continued through 1991's hit, *The Undiscovered Country,* which Nick both directed and co-wrote. More than most ongoing projects in Hollywood, *Star Trek* has been the product of a consistent team, with various members taking different roles at different times (the series' two stars, William Shattner and Leonard Nimoy, each directed one of the six films), but certainly Nick has remained a key member of that team.

Mistakes It's almost impossible to have an active career without mistakes. Nick Meyer has been luckier than most in that regard, but probably the one clear failure of his career was his film *The Deceivers*. Based on a novel which in turn relied on historical events, it told the story of an early-nineteenth-century British soldier who infiltrated and helped destroy India's murderous Thugee cult.

Financed by a small, independent film company (Merchant/Ivory, best known for *Room With a View*), *The Deceivers* offered both the best and the worst of the independent experience, since there was maximum freedom and minimum money. Yet neither the strengths nor the weaknesses of the process seems to have much influenced the final film.

Looking back on the project today, Nick says he had thought he'd be crossing *The Four Feathers* (a classic adventure story, best captured in the Alexander Korda version of 1939) with *Heart of Darkness*. "The idea was to create an extraordinarily resonant *Four Feathers* kind of story. It never occurred to me that I'd get an extraordinarily flat *Heart of Darkness*."

Calculating a Career Perhaps the toughest part of a director's career is balancing creative impulses with the scary realization that, every time you get up to bat, you're risking as much as $60 million of somebody else's money—and that if you strike out more than about twice, you're out of the game.

For creative people in Hollywood that creates extraordinary tension. As Nick Meyer puts it, "The goal always is to live a life untrammeled by self-doubt." Against that, though:

"I've always paid at least lip service to reality. In my case, that means recognizing that I've got a wife, two children, and a mortgage." For many writers and directors that can frequently mean undertaking work which, if not personally fascinating, still pays a lot of bills.

For Nick, the solution has, in part, been different. He refers to it as a "franchise," by which he means an ongoing series with strong popular appeal, but which he also finds personally engaging.

Nick Meyer has been associated with two "franchises" in his career: Sherlock Holmes (for his two novels), and *Star Trek*. Of the six *Star Trek* films, he was director and/or co-writer on three.*

Franchises have their limits, of course. Nick has resisted writing a

---

*Of course, "franchises" are scarcely everyone's solution. You can create a franchise only if you do the first installment well enough so that people clamor for a second, so, by definition, franchises work only for artists who know how to reach a mass audience.

third Holmes adventure simply for fear of being too closely identified as someone who lives by working a few successful ideas to death.

A Moral Focus   But here's a more important point perhaps: Artists, those who really matter, have values they want to cast into artistic form. At worst, that means "propaganda" films—which almost always fail. At best, though, strong beliefs make entertaining films into far richer experiences, which audiences love.

As Nick Meyer puts it, "My job isn't to make what the audience wants; it's to make the audience want what I want." In large measure, that means producing stories that work on his terms, supporting values he supports. Those values would seem to range from tolerance *(The Seven Percent Solution),* to the peaceful resolution of international conflicts *(Star Trek VI).* Hardly exotic values; most decent people would share them. But Nick has been unusually successful in expressing them within a context of traditional Hollywood entertainments, usually action-adventure films liberally spiced with humor, which find large audiences.

Taking Risks   In fact, only one Nick Meyer film probably approaches straightforward moral polemic: *The Day After,* his 1983 made-for-television film about the aftermath of a massive nuclear strike on the United States.

This was the one subject where neither humor nor adventure could lighten the tone; the screenplay's unrelieved bleakness had marked the whole project as a flop in the making.

Nick was the fourth director brought onto the project. The talk about it ran something like this: "If the movie's ever shown, it'll be a disaster, but don't worry, nobody will ever show it." The temptation to walk away was considerable, until Nick's closest adviser challenged him: "This is where we'll find out what you're made of."

Nick stayed the course. So did ABC television.

The Day After was shown. It was the highest-rated made-for-television movie in history and sparked a nationwide debate on the arms race.

Sometimes the risks pay off.

Unmade Projects   There's a lovely dream in Hollywood that once you reach a certain level of success, you can make whatever films you want.

In fact, of course, the expense and risk of film making mean there is tremendous pressure on studios to make "safe" projects. Success gains you a little leverage, not perfect freedom.

In mid-1991 the *New York Times* ran a fascinating piece on famous directors' unmade projects. Nearly every major director in Hollywood was discussed. Nick Meyer was listed as having one favorite project he couldn't get filmed. In fact, at the time, he had three. One in particular had a highly praised screenplay, but was set in a region of the world and had a topic that made actual violence against the crew and cast a real possibility. Another was seen as too "literary," and the third was bounced because it was a "period" piece.

The reasons for having projects turned down will vary hugely, and they'll follow you as long you have a career. We tried to learn whether anyone in Hollywood could consistently make whatever films he or she wanted to. Steven Spielberg was listed as one possibility, but only because he has enough money to pay for the films himself, which is a risk he'd probably never be rash enough to undertake.

Realistically, then, you'd best assume that, however great your success, you'll still be dependent on the marketplace. Expect to fight for what interests you, and be prepared to take projects simply in order to stay alive and active in the business. Then the trick will be to infuse them with your vision and your ideas.

Summing Up Six points in particular struck us as interesting about Nick Meyer's experiences in New York and Hollywood:

1. People will take advantage of you if you let them, but you can't let paranoia keep you from getting into the game.

2. An agent won't make your career. Your creations make your career, with, ideally, an agent's help.

3. Go with what you love; if you can't take satisfaction in your work itself, you may get no satisfaction at all. Remember that your job is to make your audience want what you want—and "audience" in your early days will mean readers at agencies and production companies.

4. Keep pressing. Never pass up a contact, and if you don't have any contacts, get out the Yellow Pages.

5. When you start getting breaks, don't be afraid to "leapfrog" your successes. If they want your book, make them buy your screenplay; if they want your screenplay, make them give you the directing job.

6. Even after you make it, expect that you'll still have to fight for projects you love.

Part Three

THE
MACHINERY
OF *IDEAS*

———

YOU AND YOUR INVENTIONS

36

What Inventors Must Remember

> The two major reasons that an entrepreneur often
> receives little or nothing from his invention are
> inexperience and poor marketing—not lack of inven-
> tiveness. —*American Bar Association Section on
> Patents, Trademarks, and Copyright*

IF YOU WANT TO MAKE MONEY from your invention, never
forget that reaching your "dot" requires a three-step journey:

1. Idea. The simple notion of what you'd like to invent.

2. Method. An idea which has been "reduced to practice"; that is,
developed so it actually works.

3. Product. A method (usually, but not always, patented) which has
been polished for the marketplace.

Far too many inventors stop short. They set their sights on getting a
patent, but never ready their product for the marketplace. When their
patent doesn't bring them any money, they give up in frustration.

Think about it this way. If your idea was for a book, instead of an
invention, you would have sold your manuscript to a publisher. The
publisher would have provided the editors, copy editors, designers, and
salespeople who made the rough manuscript into an attractive product
that people would be willing to buy in their local bookstore.

Unfortunately, there's presently no industry set up exclusively to do
for inventions what publishers do for manuscripts: turn them into products that can win in the marketplace.

In the following chapters, we're going to show you how to overcome the problems facing inventors and take your idea all the way to success. In fact, we're going to show you a variety of pathways, so that you can find a route to success no matter how much time or money, or how many technical skills, you have in hand.*

We're also going to talk at length about a new resource: industrial design firms for inventors. These new firms are bringing together networks of manufacturers, retailers and patent attorneys. By combining those networks with their own strengths in product design, industrial designers seem to be creating what inventors have long needed, "one stop" centers that can turn ideas into successful, money-making products.

37

Evaluating Your Chances

Run to Get a Patent?

YOUR FIRST THOUGHT once you hit on a really good idea for an invention is probably to run out and file for a patent.

That may be the right thing to do—or it may not. While theft of inventions *does* occur, as an American inventor, you have considerable protection. The United States is the only industrialized country which protects inventions on a "first to invent" rather than a "first to file [for a patent]" basis. As long you take the proper steps to document your work, you can relax and approach the whole process in calm, even cheerful fashion.†

---

*Please note: Books have a linear nature, which means we have to list the steps in some fixed order. Where inventions are concerned, there is no one right order. Thus, while we talk about industrial designers first, patents second, you may find it wiser to speak with a patent attorney first, if you are particularly eager for a patent search or worried about protection. Stay flexible!

†The "first to invent" system is threatened by efforts to "harmonize" American patent law with the rest of the world's system, which uses a "first to file" system. Most independent inventors think "first to file" is stacked in favor of the big companies, which can afford to file as many patents as they want, without having to worry about cost or ultimate success.

Even if you put your product on sale (or otherwise make it public), you still have one year before you lose your right to file for a U.S. patent, so there's no need to rush into action.* Instead, take the time to evaluate your idea as a business proposition, then start thinking patent. Where do you start?

Tip Number One: Find Your Local Inventors' Association

One long-standing lament about the inventors' community in the United States has been that inventors are (forgive us!) egotistical loners, and that the ones who succeed usually adopt a "so long, chumps" attitude toward those who are still struggling. Thus, while film schools are always able to bring in famous and successful writers and directors to train beginners, inventors' groups tended to collect oddballs and losers.

That's changing. Between 1985 and 1990 the number of patents granted each year to individual Americans rose by 40 percent, and along with that came a revitalization of inventors' associations. Driven both by increased federal support and by the creation of groups like the United Inventors Associations of the USA (UIA-USA), inventors' groups are being steadily upgraded. Today they are often a valuable resource. You'd be well advised to find your local group. If you can't find it in the phone book or by referral, just call UIA-USA at: 1-314-721-3842.

A good inventors' group will provide moral support, educational materials, and tips on the best local patent attorneys and industrial designers. A few will even provide low-cost, professional evaluation of your invention's market potential or patentability.

Is Your Idea Original? Before you spend any significant time and/ or money, make sure your product, or something close to it, isn't already on or nearing the market.

Think about your likely buyer. Check stores and catalogues aimed at that buyer to see if your product's already on sale. If you can, visit trade shows aimed at those same markets, where you'll be able to see the

---

If you think the United States should keep "first to file," contact your U.S. representative. If the United States has gone to a "first to file" system by the time you read this, you will probably need to file a preliminary patent application as soon as you have a workable method for any idea you think has potential.

*However, offering your product for sale before applying for a U.S. patent will make that product ineligible for any foreign patents. If you have any feeling that you might want to seek overseas protection in the future, be sure to contact a patent attorney before you do anything else.

products that won't be hitting the stores for another three to nine months. All too often, people caught in the first rush of creative enthusiasm waste time and money trying to protect and develop a notion that's already in common use.

Not long ago, we were approached by a potential client who wanted to commercialize a clever idea: a "900" (pay-per-call) phone service to enable people to find out the "blue book" value of their cars. A good service? You bet! Unfortunately, we had to point out that *Car and Driver* magazine already offered it. The client, though, was convinced she could do a better job, if only because *Car and Driver* aims at auto buffs. We pointed out that *Consumer Reports* also offered the service. Competing against two well-funded, big-name organizations seemed risky, but the would-be client persisted. Finally we named two other firms offering the same service, and added that most people's banks would give them "blue-book" quotes for free.

The client's reaction? Look for a more cooperative attorney and keep on with the project.

People often get so caught up in the thrill of their own inventiveness that they ignore the facts and convince themselves they'll be able to work miracles. Investigate your market before you spend serious money. That's common-sense Rule # 1.

If the product doesn't appear to be offered for sale anywhere, the next questions are:

Does Your Idea Have Commercial Potential? Is It Buildable? One reason your idea isn't on the market may be that it lacks commercial potential. Another may be that it's simply too difficult to build.

How can you answer those questions?

If a big company wants to discover an idea's commercial potential, it will commission a marketability study, at a cost of anywhere from $10,000 to more than $1 million, and have a professional organization research the market, most often via focus groups—carefully selected consumers who are paid around $50 each to spend an hour or two answering questions about products they might buy.

You can do your own modest marketability study. You simply write a short questionnaire describing the purpose (not the method) of your invention. Then you ask at least two multiple-choice questions:

How interested would you be in buying such a device?

- Not at all interested
- Slightly interested

- Greatly interested
- I'd absolutely buy it

How much would you be willing to pay for such a device?

- Under $2
- $2 to $5
- $5 to $10
- $10 to $20

(Obviously, the range of prices should match the range you would be likely to charge—the point is to try to pin things down.)

The questionnaire can be more detailed, of course; you could, for example, ask what extra features would be worth a higher price. Just remember, the more questions you ask, the more information you're giving away, and the more likely you are to lose potential respondents. More people will give you sixty seconds than will give you ten or fifteen minutes.

Then visit places likely to have a concentration of your likely buyers (the beach, if your idea's for scuba-diving gear, for example), and ask people the questions. Or hire some students to do the asking.

Lots of inventors never do any market studies; they either trust their own instincts or go on small hints, like the number of friends who like their idea. That's fair enough as long as you make the choice consciously. There's just one approach you absolutely want to avoid:

Invention Marketing Scams The one thing you absolutely want to avoid is hiring an "invention marketing" organization, because the vast majority of these are either useless or downright crooked.

Invention marketing firms prey on people who have ideas for inventions; they usually promise to do a "market analysis" and then to help find someone to license your product and pay you big royalties.

The scam usually works like this:

You respond to a radio, print, or TV ad promising great things for inventors. The company says that, for a modest fee (say, $500), it will evaluate your invention. You send in a drawing or a description, and a few days later someone calls you and declares yours is the greatest invention since bread. All you need to do is to send the company more money (usually, between $5,000 and $10,000), and they'll develop a complete plan for you, sometimes including patenting your invention.

If you send them the money, a few weeks later you'll get a big stack of form printouts about the general market for, say, scuba gear, plus perhaps a second stack of form letters addressed to companies in the scuba gear business. The first stack is completely useless, the second you could have assembled by going through back issues of some scuba magazine. Worth $10,000? No way—but the *Wall Street Journal* estimates that would-be inventors lose upward of $10 million a year to these scams, so don't be fooled!

The sad truth is that there are probably some honest organizations out there, but they're being swamped by the crooked ones. If for some reason you are inclined to trust one of these outfits, check them out in every way possible: Better Business Bureau, district attorney's office, and the Federal Trade Commission, at least. And be sure to get and to check at least three references to satisfied customers.

Is Your Invention Buildable? Whether you trust your instincts or do a marketing study, you decide there's at least a potential for your product and that it's not already on the market.

But what about buildability?

Buildability, as we're using the term, means both that your product will work and that it can be built at a cost low enough to enable you to sell it for the price people said they'd be willing to pay.

The rule of thumb for cost is simple: The manufacturing cost of your gadget should be no more than 20 percent of the price people said they would pay. If people said they'd pay $25 for your gadget and you get a firm bid from a manufacturer or an estimate from a consultant of $5 or less a unit, you're all set.

For opinions on the buildability of your product and whether it will really work, there's a new and excellent option. The eighties saw the start of a rapidly growing movement on the part of American colleges and universities to provide low-cost analysis of the potential of inventions. For a fee of usually between $150 and $200 you'll get an engineering-faculty member's opinion of the strengths and weaknesses of your idea. Try your local college or university or ask your local inventors' association for the name of the nearest such academic center.

Finally, you can simply go to manufacturers with your design and ask for quotes—but frankly, this involves risk. If you haven't taken the steps to patent what you've invented, you absolutely need to have them sign a confidentiality agreement approved by your lawyer.

Summing Up You can take a measured approach to inventing: Before spending more than a few dollars, you can scout the market to see whether your idea already exists; talk with other inventors for advice about the most trustworthy players in your part of the country; get an estimate of what people will pay for your invention and what it will cost you to build.

If turning your idea into a product is already beginning to seem burdensome, though, your best next step might be a talk with an industrial designer.

38

Designing Your Inventions

LET'S SAY you're in one of these situations:

• You have a terrific idea for an invention but lack the mechanical training to turn it into a patentable device.

• You have an invention in hand, but don't know how to make it into a finished design, appealing enough to sell in the marketplace.

These two situations make a lot of would-be inventors quit. Don't! The solution is neither as complicated nor as expensive as you think.

What you're looking for is a good industrial designer.

Industrial Design—What Is It?

In its traditional, big-business context, "industrial design" has meant the art of refining working mechanical devices so their looks and manners of operation make people want to buy them. Thus, one famous early example of industrial design was putting glass windows in the first electric clothes dryers; people were much more willing to buy a product that offered entertainment along with the clothes drying.

Increasingly, though, industrial design is taking on a much broader meaning for inventors. The best young designers are helping inventors turn their ideas into products, even helping them find the right patent attorneys, manufacturers, and ultimately buyers or licensees.

Indeed, plenty of successful recent inventors have left the whole design process to the professionals. In our experience, though, your work with designers will get better results more cheaply if you take a minute to think about a) the elements of design, and b) the kinds of designs you like.

Elements of Design

Some elements of design are largely culture-specific. For years, for example, Americans liked fake wood in their car interiors, while the English used real wood, and the Germans used black, matte-finished plastics.

But much of design seems immutable. You always care about:

> safety
> efficiency of use
> efficiency of manufacture
> aesthetic appeal: harmony of colors, materials, shapes.

Helping Your Designer You want your designer to attend to those basic issues, but you should also have enough idea about designs you like to be able to spot a good designer when you see one, and then to help him or her work effectively.

How do you begin?

Take a tip from the Japanese, who, while they have a superb national design tradition, have consistently exploited world markets by making products that "borrow" design elements from far more expensive "prestige" products made by others.

Should you imitate Japanese products? There's probably no need to do so. It does make sense, though, to find out who makes the best-regarded products in the area that interests you, and to ask yourself what about those products works and why.

You've invented a new can opener? Go to the fanciest gourmet shop in town and ask to see their best. What colors are most common? What materials? Shapes? Are the products you like best lightweight or heavy? Do they respond to a very light touch, or do they have built-in resistance, which can make them seem more durable, more "industrial grade"?

Hiring a Designer

You have at least a general sense of how you'd like your idea to look and work. If you don't feel comfortable designing the product yourself, how do you find a designer?

1. Find out who has worked on your kind of product. Choose a design firm that has had experience in your sort of product. You don't want to hire toy specialists to design industrial forklifts.

2. Study portfolios. Once someone passes your preliminary check, ask to see his or her portfolio—that is, samples or photos of his or her previous work. Someone might be very well recommended and perfectly honorable without being able to do the kind of work you happen to like.

3. Get references and check *them.* Ask especially about timely completion of work. Some designers have brilliant ideas, but are such perfectionists they never deliver on schedule.

4. Discuss price. You owe it to yourself and to the designer to do this before you get too far into the process.

How Much Will It Cost? It's hard to put a price on design, both because complexity varies tremendously and because some design firms are just expensive. Thus, the folks at Image Design & Marketing, who designed Mattel's wildly successful Power Glove, told the *Los Angeles Times* that any entrepreneur should have "at least $500,000 in seed capital." Maybe that's so for players in their league, but some extremely successful design firms will do the job for you for under $10,000, including complete, approved specs and drawings and a "looks like, works like" model.

In fact, for a simple gadget, the process breaks down something like this:

Initial consultation. The designer signs a "confidentiality agreement" promising to keep your idea secret. Then the two of you discuss the idea and what might be done with it. You get an opinion about the idea's potential and what it might take to design a working prototype. Cost: usually under $100.

Design with plans. The designer moves on to give you a complete set of plans for the device, but no model and no additional help or advice. Cost: varies widely, but usually between $2,000 and $5,000.

Design, plans, and model. Probably the most useful approach in most cases, this gives you not only complete drawings, but what's called a "looks like, works like" model. This isn't a working or manufacturing prototype model. Instead, it uses mock components to let a potential buyer see how the real thing would look and feel. Thus, a "looks like, works like" model of a coffee maker probably wouldn't actually heat the water, but would let a buyer see that "the water goes in here, this knob sets the timer," and so on—enough for a skilled buyer (that is, a buyer for a major store, not an individual customer) to make a decision. Cost? Under $10,000.

Of course, prices go up if you keep throwing in changes in specifications or turn down many of their proposals, but still, that $10,000 is a very workable ballpark figure.*

As with any technical service, reputable designers will tell you up front about all the costs you'll face. With design, one common place for "low-ball" companies to trick you is in packaging; they quote you an irresistibly low price and then, when you're done, say, "Now, how about if we design the packaging—for another three thousand dollars?" Make sure you know what you're getting!

T2 Design and the "Silver Platter"

One of the better-regarded of the younger design groups in the country is T2 Designs in Santa Monica, California. Headed by Ken Tarlow, whose design work has ranged from the Casablanca fan to those Turbowasher gadgets for washing cars with garden hoses, T2 is aimed at the solo inventor and has developed an interesting service.

The "silver platter" approach attempts to coordinate all the activities involved in turning an idea into a viable product. For one fee (presently about $7,500), T2 will arrange for:

- A "looks like, works like" prototype
- Product packaging
- Basic patent work (through patent attorneys they recommend)
- Product pricing
- Finding an original equipment manufacturer (that is, someone to make the product for you), if you decide to sell it yourself
- Showing the product to store buyers.

In short, they're trying to position themselves as a one-stop center for inventors.

Approaches like "silver platter" designing will likely become extremely popular in the coming years, as the number of solo inventors

---

* Some cutting-edge designers are doing their work on full-color CAD systems, then taking the resulting programs to trade shows and the like. At a recent Consumer Electronics Show in Chicago, for example, a company called Dreadnought Industries lined up more than 100 large orders for its stylish CD racks, from buyers who saw them only as images on a computer screen. Obviously, if you can lock in buyers before you spend any money on models or manufacturing, you're way ahead of the game.

grows. In any case, if you find a reputable design firm in your region whose work you like, try asking them to quote you a price for their version of the "silver platter" approach.

Going Joint Venture

A good design firm can do a lot for you, and its services, as part of a start-up for a venture, are not terribly expensive. But what if you just don't have the $7,000 to $10,000 to get the ball rolling, or if your idea is more complicated and will need, say, $50,000 in design work?

Many industrial designers are willing, even eager, to contribute their skills for a share of the future profits from sales of the product. The usual approach is to trade complete design services for a 50 percent stake in the invention.

This can be an extremely expensive way to go, for a pretty obvious reason: You may be giving up a half-interest in, say, $1 million in royalties to get $10,000 in design work. On the other hand, a top designer will upgrade your standing with potential investors and cut your need for initial capital. Above all, if you have no other options, a half-interest in $1 million is a lot better than 100 percent of an idea that never gets to market.

Probably, you want to joint-venture with a designer only if your resources are very limited, and/or your idea will need a lot of work before it's ready for market.

Whatever you decide, a designer's willingness to joint-venture with you is terrific news, since, obviously, it means he or she believes in your invention.

How Long Will It Take? Image Design & Marketing did the Mattel Power Glove in eight weeks. Most small firms will want a bit more time—say, three or four months if they're busy. During that time, though, you'll have plenty to occupy you: the preliminary patent search if you haven't already done it; meeting with patent attorneys; locating possible buyers or licensees for your products; even scouting manufacturers if you're planning to sell the product yourself.

If you can't find an industrial designer in your area, try contacting:

Industrial Designers Society of America
1142 E. Walker Road
Great Falls, VA 22066
1-703-759-0100

Finally, if your budget is tight, consider hiring a student designer from a local college or university. If you happen to live near one of the country's great design schools, you may have a tremendous opportunity—their students are often available on work/study programs, which cost you very little.

Protecting Your Designs In late 1990 the U.S. government estimated that American firms were losing $40 billion a year in licensing fees to design piracy. A former development and design manager for J. C. Penney told *Business Week* in 1991 that his company expected to see its best ideas stolen "within months."

The problem was that design patent protection (the only design protection available to Americans as of late 1991) is basically unworkable. It takes an average of thirty-two months to get a design patent, and seven out of ten are thrown out by the courts as unenforceable.

Presently Congress is considering a variety of bills that would make designs subject to copyright law. Design copyrights are a better approach and will, at least in theory, save American businesses of every size many billions of dollars in stolen sales.

39

Patent Basics

SHORTLY AFTER you get your great idea, you're probably going to start thinking about getting a patent. That may or may not be the right thing to do. While it's probably never too early to speak with a patent attorney, you can better understand your situation if you ask some basic questions, starting with—

What's a Patent?

That's not a dumb question. Probably ninety-nine people out of a hundred don't know the answer.

A patent, despite the popular conception, is not a governmental grant of the exclusive right to make something; it's a governmental grant of the exclusive right to keep others from making it.

That's an important difference. Here's why:

Suppose you seek a patent for, say, a videocassette recorder which lets the user automatically duplicate videotapes. Your patent claim (grossly simplified, of course), might read something like this:

"My device contains one complete set of read/write VCR heads, and a set of write-only heads. When a prerecorded cassette is inserted into the read/write mechanism, the output of the read/write heads goes either to a television set or to the write heads of the second mechanism, enabling the owner automatically to copy any standard videocassette."

Your patent comes through. Can you start cranking out duplicating VCRs and maybe get the United States back into a huge market?

No! You can keep Sony and Sharp and Toshiba from making duplicating VCRs, but you can't build them yourself unless those big guys license you all the underlying VCR technology, from microcontrollers to record heads. Technically, what you have is an "improvement patent," and it means money in your pocket only if you can beg, borrow, or force the cooperation of the underlying patent holders.*

By the same token, a patent gives you no special right to make a product (say, a dangerous weapon or an unproven drug) that would otherwise be prohibited by law. Furthermore, a U.S. patent provides no protection in foreign countries.

What Does a Patent Give You?

On the other hand, a patent gives you many positive things:

1. The right to keep others from making what you've invented. While we tried to show the limitations to this, it's still tremendously valuable; without it other people, having paid no development costs, would be able to make whatever you've invented, and probably cheaper. Sometimes, moreover, you'll strike gold with a "blocking patent"—that is, a patent which keeps a big company from making an important product. When that happens, they have to settle with you or risk a big lawsuit.

Of course, a patent can also give you the right to collect big damages from people who steal your ideas. In fact, some inventors make large fortunes without ever building anything: they just take out patents, wait for big companies to infringe, and then sue. Again, though, your ability

---

*This example, obviously, is loosely based on the story of Go Video, which actually won a similar patent, then battled for years to get the right to make its machines, after every major Japanese VCR-maker refused to help it. We're not trying to comment on that story, but merely using what we consider a particularly clear illustration of the basic principle.

to collect damages will depend upon how carefully you've documented your work, filed your application, and put others on notice that you own the patent.

2. *It's a bargaining chip.* Let's return to the example of the duplicating VCR. While your patent wouldn't give you the right to compete with the big companies owning the underlying patents, it might give you a shot at either a licensing deal (where they build and sell the duplicating VCRs, but pay you a fee on each one sold), or an original equipment manufacturer (OEM) deal, where they manufacture the machines to your specs and let you sell them. Either deal could make you big money.

3. *It's an asset recognized by venture capitalists.* While the venture capital market has certainly grown more conservative since the go-go days of the mid-eighties, any interesting invention with an issued patent will still get a serious look from venture capitalists and other investors. This may still be too early a stage for you to want to take their money, but at least your negotiating situation will jump notably with a patent in hand.

4. *It deters competitors from beginning production.* Even before your patent issues, you can (as long as you've actually applied) stamp "Patent Pending" on the product. That lets you, if you choose, start manufacture without waiting for the patent to issue, because competitors have been put on notice. If they know anything at all, they know that knocking off a "patent pending" invention means they'll face both an injunction and heavy damages (for willful infringement) when your patent finally issues.

5. *It protects you against "innocent inventors."* If your idea is any good, someone else may think of it fairly soon—and may honestly think he has a right to the market. Your having a patent on record will save you trouble with these "innocent inventors"—and will save them time and grief, too.

6. *It has prestige.* There's a certain distinction to being the holder of a United States patent. It's like a novelist's being published; it means you've arrived, you're for real.

Those are powerful reasons for pursuing a patent, but they also suggest why other people might try to stop you or grab it for themselves. How can you best protect your interests?

Protection Begins the Day You Invent

You should take your first steps to protect your invention the moment you get your idea—or as soon thereafter as you can possibly manage it.

America is virtually the only country on earth to grant patent rights on a "first to invent" rather than a "first to file" basis.* For you as an inventor, that's both good and bad. The good is that, if you keep proper records, you can establish your claim even if someone else has beaten you to the patent office—as long as you can prove you invented the thing first.

The bad follows from the good: Even after you get a patent in this country, you can never be absolutely certain somebody else won't later file an action—called an interference action—claiming he or she actually invented first.

There's increasing pressure for the United States to abandon "first to invent" and move closer to, say, the European standard, partly so the world can simplify the patent-granting process and partly because interference actions are so expensive.

For the foreseeable future, though, "first to invent" is the law, and it means you have to establish, as dramatically as possible, when, where, and how you invented whatever you intend to patent. That in turn means you need to use this simple Action Plan:

1. Keep a written invention notebook. The best sort, probably, is a standard lab notebook, available from any college bookstore; it usually has firmly bound, prenumbered pages. Never tear out a page, and never line out anything so thoroughly it's absolutely unreadable. Don't leave large gaps between entries; these create a suspicion that you might have intended to go back and add "facts" at a later date.

2. Date each notebook entry. Even go so far as to put down the time of any really important thoughts, diagrams, discoveries.

3. Write in ink. As with all the above, you are trying to establish a) permanence, and b) continuity. Do anything you can to make it clear you've prepared your records with absolute scrupulousness.

4. Include diagrams. Pictures showing your invention can have tremendous weight. Do your best, even if you're not DaVinci.

5. Log each disclosure of invention. Keep detailed records of whom you've told what, and when.

6. (Optional). If you have a friend you trust, have him or her read your log and give you a signed, dated (and if you're really thorough, notarized) statement to that effect.

Everyone gets ideas in the middle of the night; lots of people have

---

* Again, this may change; and if America switches to "first to file," you'll need to speak with an attorney, and probably file for a patent, as soon as you can reduce your idea to a workable method.

scrawled bright ideas on napkins at restaurants. That's fine—just make sure you transfer those brainstorms to your notebook as soon as possible.

Deciding Whether Your Idea Is Patentable

In the first rush of excitement over your new idea, you'll probably be busy enough just keeping your notebook in coherent shape while you scrawl down ideas and refinements.

Pretty soon, though, you're going to have to decide whether your idea is patentable. (Actually, there are two questions: Is your idea patentable, and should you patent it. Many unpatentable ideas can still make you money.)

The law sets some relatively simple guidelines for what's patentable. In general, you're on safe ground with:

• A process, machine, manufacture, or composition of new matter.

• A plant, if it produces asexually (that is, without seeds).

• A design. (A design patent goes only to items visible during ordinary use, and it must be a matter of style, not a result of the invention's function. Thus, you could get a design patent for a car's door handles, but not for its piston rings).

• Computer programs and mathematical algorithms. These are patentable if their implementation a) defines a specific structural or physical relationship between elements of the invention, or b) refines or limits the inventive steps.*

Technically, you can also patent a living organism, but if you're working at that level of sophistication, you're probably at an institution well supplied with patent counsel.

If your idea falls within one of those categories, and if it can be reduced to a method, you can apply for a patent. But you still have a large burden of proof to carry. In particular, you must meet:

The General Patent Qualifications

For your patent to receive serious consideration, you will have to convince the Patent and Trademark Office of three things. Your process or product must be:

---

*This definition is just as confusing as it sounds, and several recent software patents (including one to allow advertisements to be incorporated into other programs) have left even the pros scratching their heads. If you have an idea for software, and a copyright won't satisfy you, you should probably talk with a patent attorney early on.

- *New.* (The PTO's term is "novel.")
- *Useful.*
- *Nonobvious.* That is, not an obvious variation on an existing device.

As you can probably imagine, lawyers (and especially patent lawyers) can give you a fight over any of those concepts, for any invention you care to name. Still, the basic ideas are simple enough:

Novel. Establishing the newness or originality of your invention requires searching through the five million-plus U.S. patents issued since 1790 and often foreign patents, too. The system is set up so you can, in theory, do the search yourself, or you can hire a patent search firm to do it for you, at a cost usually of under $500.

Just one warning. In neither case will you get a definitive answer, only an answer good enough to let you know whether or not you should go ahead with the process.

If you do the patent search yourself, behave as an experienced patent investigator would: Seek not only your exact idea but any idea so close to yours that yours would become "obvious" development in light of it.

Should you find patents close to yours, copy down the information. Don't despair. Unless someone else has your invention down to the smallest details, a skilled patent attorney may well be able to draft your claims so that your invention looks distinct enough to merit a patent of its own.

One patent attorney might say an existing invention preempts yours; another might say yours is novel enough. Just remember, ultimately you're paying the bills. You always have the chance to apply for a patent. Listen to the attorney's opinion, evaluate the risk, then make your own decision.*

Useful? If you have an invention and can't think of a use for it, you're probably in trouble as far as getting a patent for it. (Of course, that doesn't mean you can't make money. How useful were Pet Rocks?)

Nonobviousness. This is much tougher, and in fact, is one of the most frequently litigated issues. The basic standard is whether an advance is pedestrian, whether a practitioner *in the field* would naturally have made

---

*This is a warning worth repeating. Even if your patent search, whether you do it yourself or pay for it, turns up no previous patent, and even if the patent office accepts your argument and issues the patent, you don't have an unassailable position. These searches are by their nature only preliminary. If you ever get into a lawsuit, a real patent search (called a "prior art" search) will cost you about another $10,000, and very often it will turn up a previous patent strong enough to overturn yours.

your improvement. One of the best proofs you can have is if other people have used other, less elegant approaches.

An example? Take 3M's Post-its. You might well say that the idea of a piece of paper with a bit of reusable sticky stuff on its back, to allow notes to be stuck to other documents and then peeled of, is fairly obvious. Maybe, but the fact that people have been clumsily stapling and unstapling documents for decades would be a powerful argument of non-obviousness. It would also be a strong argument under the category of "usefulness," since it establishes what the law calls a "long-felt need" for the function fulfilled by Post-its.*

You now probably know as much about patents as the average third-year law student. Congratulations!

As a practical inventor, though, you still need to know more. In particular, you need to know whether getting a patent is in your best economic interests.

1. Can You Pay the Freight? Getting a U.S. patent is not cheap. For a simple patent, you'll probably spend about $2,000 if you do most of the work yourself, and perhaps $6,000 if you use a patent attorney. While most inventors have relatively simple ideas, fees escalate very rapidly as inventions get more complicated.

If the money's not a problem, fine. But if you're on a tight budget, think carefully. That $5,000 you spend to get the patent is $5,000 you don't have to spend on marketing, tooling, promotion, or whatever.

What's the alternative?

You can file for a patent up to one year after you first offer your invention for sale or otherwise disclose it. If you have very little money, many attorneys will tell you to invest what you have in marketing the invention. Then, if the invention starts selling, you still have time to go after a U.S. patent.†

2. Do You Really Want a Patent? This may sound odd, but there are times when you want to avoid getting a patent, even if you're technically eligible and your idea has economic potential. Here are two examples:

a. A patent makes your method public record, and it runs out after

---

* In fact, patentability wasn't an issue for Post-its, but we're using this example because it is more interesting than existing case law, which usually focuses on exciting inventions like automatic manure washers. And you thought patent law wasn't glamorous!

† Remember, though, that putting your product on sale before applying for a U.S. patent prevents you from getting any foreign patents.

seventeen years. If Coca Cola had patented its formula back in 1890, it would have had no protection by 1907; instead, it kept the formula a trade secret and still controls the market today.

b. Sometimes a patent is simply an uneconomic solution.

Thus, the law says you can get a design patent if your invention serves a purely ornamental function. A good example might be a new car hood ornament.

But patents are designed for long-term protection. Can you think of a style of dress that's been in fashion for seventeen years? As a practical matter, most fashion designs are obsolete in six months or a year, while the average U.S. patent takes two years just to work its way through the application process.

That's why the major fashion designers, like Ralph Lauren, very rarely patent their designs. Instead, they make their money by changing fashions every six months or less, and building value into their products by both strong trademark protection and ultra-high-quality construction, so that people will pay their prices even if they can get a pattern enabling them to duplicate the design.

By the same token, while computer programs are technically patentable, they are also copyrightable, and copyrights not only last longer but cost much less. Except in very special cases you probably don't want to patent software.

And here's a last example, probably closer to the average inventor's experience. It shows why sometimes the market makes getting a patent unnecessary, even when it's quite possible:

Not long ago the owners of a pet-supply manufacturing company developed a new sort of bird perch and asked about getting a patent. The perch looked perfectly patentable. Yet this particular manufacturer, while small, had loyal customers and a virtual lock on its admittedly small market. Getting the patent would have been difficult; protecting it worldwide would have been very expensive (roughly $100,000 in fees, over the life of the patent), and most of the customers would have stayed loyal to the brand even if competing models were offered.

The logical answer? Skip the patent and spend the money on developing and promoting the new perch. They followed the advice, and today the perch is a strong seller, with no significant competition.

You now have a general sense of what patents can and can't do for you, and the times when they make sense. If you decide you want to pursue a patent, at least through the first stages, what do you do?

Use a Patent Attorney or Patent Agent

If you really want to make money from your invention, and you're not a patent attorney or agent yourself, hire one to file your applications.

Lots of books and pamphlets will tell you how to file for a patent by yourself and save thousands of dollars in legal fees. We'll even throw in something they usually don't tell you: the PTO says you can file for a patent even if you have no technical vocabulary. If you make up your own terms and use them intelligibly and consistently, you don't have to know a camshaft from a carbonyl. You can literally say, "The whoosis slaps against the whatsis, and then . . ." and you'll be eligible for a patent—and you'll save thousands in legal fees.

Why shouldn't you?

Actually, there are four reasons.

The first is that, unlike trademark or copyright, patent law is extremely (some would say unnecessarily) arcane and complicated. The system abounds with obscure rules and deadlines; miss any of them and your claim can be compromised, in some cases, even totally lost.

The second follows from the first: Missed deadlines and other errors can cost you hundreds of dollars in extra fees.

You may be willing to work through the rules and unconcerned about the expense, but that still leaves the third reason you shouldn't try to get your own patent: Any patent you get for yourself will probably be useless.

Why?

Because the granting of patents (unlike the granting of trademarks or copyrights) is an adversarial procedure. In other words, it's a struggle between you (or your attorney) and the Patent Office, with your side trying to get the broadest possible patent and the Patent Office trying to give you the narrowest one possible. Any patent you win for yourself will probably be so narrow as to be worthless.

Think about it this way. A trademark or a copyright is like a dog license: If you've got a dog and you pay the fee, you'll get a license—and one license is as good as another.

But a patent is more like a land grant: Write it one way and you own ten feet on either side of a mud hole—write it another and you own the Oklahoma territory.

Get the picture?

If so, you'll understand the fourth reason you don't want to do your own patent work: because the pros, the people who'll be likely to invest in your idea down the road, will be betting in large measure on your ability to protect the idea they're investing in. Tell them you did your own patent work and most of them will say, "Thanks very much—we pass," and head right out the door.

What You Can Do for Yourself

While there are strong reasons for getting expert help when you try to patent something you've invented, you can do a lot for yourself.

Even if you never file a patent on your own, you can help your patent attorney or agent to do the work cleanly and effectively, take many steps to strengthen your own legal position, and participate in the business transactions that follow getting the patent—which, after all, are where the real money's made.

40

Patent Attorneys, Agents, and Fees

YOU NOW HAVE a good general idea of how patents work. You may decide to get expert help at the start of your process or you may decide to wait a while. In either case, it's probably worth a minute to discuss your legal options, especially since legal help for inventors is so expensive.

What's a Patent Attorney? A "patent attorney" simply means an attorney registered to practice before the United States Patent and Trademark Office, or PTO. To become a patent attorney requires a) a college degree in science or engineering, b) a law degree from an accredited school, and c) passing a patent bar exam generally considered tougher than any regular bar exam. Every year the United States graduates about 40,000 attorneys and creates only about 400 patent attorneys, so roughly only one attorney in one hundred is going to qualify.

What's a Patent Agent? A patent agent is someone admitted to prosecute (that is, prepare and present) patent applications to the PTO, but who lacks a law degree.

To become a patent agent, a person must have at least five years of relevant experience (usually as, say, an engineer), and must then pass a patent office exam.

Compared with patent attorneys, patent agents are usually cheaper to employ, but generally have far less legal training and may be less prepared to argue your case before the PTO. Unlike a patent attorney, a patent agent will not be able to represent you in court.

Many patent agents are employed in-house by corporations, which have staff attorneys to handle the other legal aspects of intellectual property. Still, some are in private practice, and if you feel basic patent protection is all you need, a patent agent may be an effective economical solution to your problem.

In most cases, though, you're better off with a patent attorney.

How Do You Find a Good Patent Attorney? A large percentage of the country's patent attorneys are already employed full-time by major corporations. Of those remaining, a certain percentage aren't practicing as patent attorneys.

Thus patent attorneys are scarce, and expensive. Expect to pay between $175 and $400 an hour or more for one with good qualifications.

In picking a patent attorney consider the following:

1. If possible, get one with experience as a litigator (that is, one who has gone into federal court to fight lawsuits). Attorneys who have seen how legal documents can go wrong, who have attacked or defended them in legal actions, are often cleverer about drawing them up.

2. Get one with training in your particular field. One patent attorney may have a degree in electrical engineering, another in biochemistry. You want one whose training prepares him or her to represent you effectively. (Obviously, this is less of a consideration if your invention is relatively low-tech. Any patent attorney can probably do a good job with the average gadget.)

3. Try to get one with a business background or at least one who follows business developments. One of the best bits of advice you can get from a patent attorney is a sense of whether or not your product is marketable.

4. Don't necessarily favor the prestige firms. An international law firm with offices on the fiftieth floor of some skyscraper can do a great job for you, but they'll probably also bill you a fortune, partly to cover their overhead and partly because they'll be in the habit of dealing with big corporations, which have complex needs and expect fat legal bills.

If cost isn't an issue, don't rule out using a big firm. The major plus of a big-name firm is that it gains you a measure of credibility at the outset. Bankers and manufacturers will often take you more seriously if you're represented by a major firm.

Clearly, not all these guidelines will matter in every case. Indeed, ultimately the biggest test will be in finding a qualified attorney with whom you can work comfortably.

Meeting with the Attorney Many patent law firms will screen you before you meet with the attorney. The person you talk with (probably a paralegal or a law clerk) will want to know a) whether you can afford to hire a patent attorney, and b) whether you're a real inventor or a crackpot.

Don't be discouraged by the financial qualifying. If you can come across as a serious inventor, with a worthwhile idea, and have at least a small war chest, very likely you will find competent counsel.

In fact, many patent lawyers offer special arrangements for first consultations. Some will give you, say, thirty minutes of phone time for free; others cut their regular fee in half. That's not pure altruism; they know very well that many people have good ideas but not the money to develop them. If you have a really good invention, some patent attorneys will provide services against future revenues from your products.

Make It Clear What You Want The services available from a patent law firm can vary immensely, from an initial evaluation of your chances to a complete program, in which the firm will help you market your invention, cut licensing deals, or even establish a manufacturing program. When you call for your first appointment, try to make it clear what you want.

The Cost of Patents How much money should you budget to obtain your patent?

The numbers can vary hugely. Worldwide protection of a complex invention might cost $200,000 over the life of the patents, exclusive of the costs of any lawsuits. On a much more basic level, probably much nearer to your concerns the first time you seek a patent, we've already said that getting a United States patent for a simple gadget will probably cost around $6,000.

Of that $6,000, only about $1,000 to $1,500 will be in fees paid to the patent office*: The rest of the money will go for patent attorneys' fees and patent searches.

---

*Of course, problems in the application process can result in additional fees. In addition, you will have to spend about another $2,000 to $3,000 in various maintenance fees over the patent's 17-year life.

That may seem like a lot of money for legal work; and it probably raises two questions: What are you getting for your money, and can you do the work for yourself?

Our view is that, especially for your first patent, you are wiser to have the work done by professionals, but to be an "informed consumer" who understands and monitors the process and who contributes wherever possible.

The following chapters will show you both what's involved in obtaining a patent, and ways you can participate. You may decide after reading them that the patent process is something you want to undertake on your own, or you may decide to turn it over to the professionals. Whatever you finally decide, though, it's worth your time to understand what the process involves.

41

Is It Original?
Doing a Patent Search

Patent Searches: An Introduction

LONG BEFORE even thinking about hiring a patent attorney, you've checked the stores and maybe the trade shows to see if anybody is already selling your great idea.

The problem, of course, is that patents exist for many items that either have never gone on sale or are being sold where you'll never see them. That doesn't mean they aren't valid patents.

To find out what's been patented, whether or not it's being offered for sale, you need a preliminary patent search.

Many groups conduct these searches: patent agents, patent attorneys, and specialized search firms. How do you hire one of those firms? How do you do a search on your own?

Even if you've done your own search, most patent agents or attorneys will urge you to have a second one done by a professional firm. We think that's good advice.

Then why try on your own first? Actually, there are several reasons. A search *may:*

1. Save you money (if it shows absolutely someone else has patented your invention).

2. Teach you about the patent system and prepare you to work with patent professionals, and so save you more money.

3. Show you inventions that inspire still more creativity on your part.*

In short, a practice search is a fine hands-on introduction to the patent process.

Still, many people get patents without ever even looking at any patent except the one of their own they finally receive. If you want to spend the money and save the time, then pay for the search at the outset.

You can either hire a search firm directly or have your patent agent or attorney do the hiring. A preliminary patent search from a reputable firm (some are listed in the Yellow Pages of any large-city phone book) will probably cost about $250. Some firms offer prices as low as $79, but don't expect top-grade work. A patent attorney's interpretation of the results might add another $250 to the total.

Finding a Search Firm If you hire a search firm yourself, follow the standard advice for engaging any professional: Seek recommendations from people in the field, then compile a short list of candidates. Make sure any agreement you sign specifies exactly what the search firm is going to do: search PTO records, talk with examiners, send you photo-copies of relevant patents, or whatever—and what it will cost.

Unless you tell them otherwise, search firms will treat you the way they treat patent lawyers. For example, they'll send you letters via over-night service—at, say, $10 a shot—instead of regular U.S. mail. So tell them how you want things done.

Don't expect the search firm to offer a legal opinion on your chances of getting a patent. That's the job of a patent agent or attorney, and even then, in many cases, you'll make the final call.

You'll probably have to pay for the search in advance. As long as you're dealing with a legitimate firm, go ahead. Since they are doing custom work for you, which they'd wouldn't be able to sell to anyone else, they're entitled to be assured payment.

---

*In fact, many people claim to have gotten rich simply by searching the patent records for good ideas that were never marketed, and either licensing them if the patents are still effective or manufacturing them if the patents have expired.

You or your attorney can have a search done with little strain and with modest expense. Still, you may want to do the search yourself, both to learn the system and to get a sense of the kinds of inventions that exist.

Doing Your Own Search: How the System Works

The U.S. Patent system is the world's longest-established and most comprehensive. In existence since 1790, it contains more than five million U.S. patents, as well as full information on patents issued worldwide.

While the system is constantly evolving, it presently organizes U.S. patents issued since 1836 into some 400 classes and 120,000 subclasses. The system thus allows you to find, with considerable speed and fair certainty, whether your invention has been claimed, and (nearly as usefully) what other interesting work has been done in your field.

The PTO maintains a Search Room in Arlington, Virginia, where anyone can study all U.S. patents granted since 1836. The many search firms operating in and around Washington, D.C., rely heavily upon this room; if you're anywhere near the area, you can use it, too.

If you're not near the PTO's Search Room, you can still rely on the nation's *Patent Depository Libraries*. These aren't libraries in the usual sense; they're collections of materials kept in other libraries. There are sixty-four such collections, located at university and public libraries across the country. Each PDL has at least the basic materials for conducting a patent search, although only a few have the complete collections (extending all the way back to 1790) that might be important for scholars.

If you can't conveniently reach a PDL (Wyoming, for example, doesn't have one), then hiring a search firm may be unavoidable. If you can reach a PDL, here's how to begin your searching:

1. Get a Copy of **General Information Concerning Patents** Published by the PTO, this not only lists all the country's PDLs; it gives a clear, if not terribly detailed, introduction to the whole patent process. It also includes copies of the forms to be filed with a patent application.

You can get this pamphlet for $2 either directly from the PTO or (usually more quickly) from the nearest Government Printing Office store. Check the phone book of the nearest big city.

Along with reading *General Information Concerning Patents*, you need to decide the type of thing you've invented. Come up with all the synonyms you can; A solar cell, for example, might also be called a "photoelectric cell." You want to make sure you're going to search under every likely name.

Once you've done that, head to the nearest PDL. You'll probably find it in the Science and Technology section of the designated library. You'll also probably find at least one librarian who's an inventions buff, so don't hesitate to ask for help and advice. Many libraries have also written their own support materials, to help guide you through the process.

Basically, though, your first stop should be:

2. The *Index to the* Manual of Classification This is a relatively thin loose-leaf publication, listing all the classes and subclasses alphabetically.

In our case, then, if you look up "solar cell," you'll be given Class 136, Subclass 243+ (the "+" means "and following"). (If you looked up "photoelectric cell," you'd find about thirty-five subclassifications listed, including everything from "analogous rectifiers" to "stereoplotters"— and the 136/243+ listing for "generators, solar cells.") You might also decide to look at 136/292* (the "*" means a cross-reference), for "space-satellite applications." After all, many space satellites are powered by solar cells.

With your short list of likely classes and subclasses in hand, you're ready to move on to:

3. The Manual of Classification This is a much thicker, two-volume set which lets you confirm and clarify your search list. One patent research guide calls the *Manual* "complex, technically detailed, and very finely reasoned." All that's true—it's a masterpiece of technical thinking—but don't worry. You are unlikely to invent something more complicated than your own technical background. If you know enough to invent, say, a "copper oxide analogous rectifier," you'll know enough to search for comparable products.

The *Manual* also has a built-in checking system. It contains complete definitions of all categories and subcategories. If you're not sure whether you've checked the right areas, just look up the definitions of the resulting categories and subcategories.

Once you're comfortable with your list of categories and subcategories, move on to—

4. The U.S. Patent Classification Subclass Listing This is a part of the system in transition. At most libraries you'll probably find it on microfilm (hard on the eyes!), but it is gradually being supplanted by the CD-ROM-based CASSIS ("Classification and Search Support Information System").*

You may well find all the patents for the previous six to twelve months on the CASSIS (which is easy to use), and all earlier patents on microfilm.

In either case, the method is simple. Just look up the class(es) and subclass(es) for patents that interest you, and CASSIS and the *Patent Classification Subclass Listing* will give you the numbers of all issued patents that fall under those classes and subclasses, as well as the dates of the issues of the *Official Gazette* in which they appeared. That, in turn, sends you to the:

5. Official Gazette The *Gazette* is the Patent Office's weekly publication. It lists all the patents granted by the PTO in the previous week (the material is then reorganized for easier use in the quarterly and annual editions). The *Gazettes* are a snap to use. You have the date(s) for each issue you need; within each issue the patents are listed numerically by class and subclass.

Remember, however, that the *Gazette* publishes only an abstract and one drawing of each patent. If the material in the *Gazette* makes it seem like your idea is at all close to any abstracted patent, you'll need to examine the complete patent itself. So now you ask the librarian to point you toward—

6. The Patents Themselves These are held in PDLs on microfilm, but you can usually get printouts for 15¢ or so per page. Most PDLs will have the patents you need; otherwise, they can get photostats of them via interlibrary loan. Finally, of course, you can order any patent you want from the PTO itself for $3.00 per patent.

How Long Will It Take? Patent searches are actually more difficult to describe than to accomplish. If you're fairly familiar with library research, and if the facilities aren't in demand when you're there, you can probably complete a preliminary patent search for a relatively simple gadget in, let's say, half a day.

A Few Last Tips Keep in mind that design patents are always col-

---

*Since October 1992, a few PDLs have also offered APS, the same on-line search system the PTO's own patent examiners use. APS is a powerful system, but at $70 an hour, it's also expensive.

lected separately. For example, you'll find them in the back of the *Gazette*.

Hot advice. Patent search firms don't really like you to know this, but if you're having trouble with a search, you can actually get the PTO to help you for free. Just send them a letter explaining as best you can how your gadget is constructed, how it works, and what it's supposed to do. Include the best sketches you can manage, showing your gadget from all sides (with the parts all labeled), and send the information to:

> Commissioner of Patents and Trademarks
> Attn: Patent Search Division
> Washington, D.C. 20231

They'll help you determine, on a time-available basis, what class(es) and subclass(es) cover your intended invention. They are, however, giving you only guidelines, based on your submission—they are not warranting their work. When you add in the fact that they can rarely respond as quickly as one might wish, you may well decide that a private patent search (if you can afford it) is money well-spent.

Summing Up Patent searches, at least basic ones, can be done by the individual inventor. All you need is a methodical approach, access to a PDL, and about half a day of solid working time.

Once you get serious about your invention, though, you probably should hire a professional to do the work for you—again, usually for between $250 and $500. This professional-quality search will probably be money well-spent in helping you and/or your attorney decide whether or not to apply for a patent.

42

Applying for a Patent

Just the Basics Even though we think you're wise to get professional help, at least when applying for your first patent, it makes sense to understand the application process. If you decide to file your own application, consider one of the books in Recommended Reading. You can get the Patent Application forms from either the PTO or any Government Printing Office store for $2.00. The forms come in a booklet with basic instructions for filling them out.

Drafting a Patent

A patent has three basic elements:
1. A written specification of the invention, which contains
   a. The background of the invention
   b. Summary of the invention
   c. Brief description of the drawings (if any)
   d. Detailed description of the "Preferred Embodiment"
   e. The claims
2. The drawings (if necessary)
3. The oath or declaration of the inventor(s)

Background and Summary The "background" sounds simple—it's merely a discussion of the problem your gadget solves and of existing inventions in the field.

Just bear in mind that the law says patent applicants have a "'duty of candor"—you're bound to list and discuss every existing invention or patent, granted in the United States or elsewhere, that may invalidate your claim. Of course, you're also supposed to show why your invention still deserves the patent, but failure to give the PTO full information can invalidate your patent. It can even, in certain circumstances, leave you open to charges of defrauding the Patent Office. So take this seriously. (Yet another reason to leave the job to professionals.)

The "summary," of course, is the simple, straightforward explanation of how your invention works and what it accomplishes.

These two sections, if properly done, are your chance to make a psychological pitch for the importance of your invention (which, at least in theory, will make the examiner look more kindly upon it), and to stress its originality and uniqueness.

Description of Drawings and the "Preferred Embodiment" These are pretty straightforward: You explain the drawings you provided and show the best possible version ("best mode" in PTO parlance) of your proposed invention.

The Claims Every part of the patent process is important, and all of it is rule-bound. But "The Claims" are the meat of your application. Your patent, if it's granted, will protect only what you claim (or rather, as many of those claims as the patent office chooses to grant). If you don't claim it now, it's lost forever. So before you fire off your patent application, take time to think through your claims carefully.

The basic logic of claims drafting is simple: Draft the broadest claim possible, without infringing prior art, then draft progressively narrower claims to ensure that some survive the prosecution process. (Again, "Prosecution" is the process of applying and defending your patent application before the Patent Office.)

Be meticulous. It's vital that you make no significant errors or omissions. You cannot add new material to your application once you've filed it, so any important omission will mean starting all over again.

The Drawings You aren't required to include drawings, but if you do include them, you need to follow the detailed instructions in "General Information Concerning Patents," the $2.00 PTO handbook. Again, the PTO is extremely fussy about the rules, which range from the kind of paper and ink to margins and kinds of shadings permitted. Hiring a drafts person with patent experience is probably a good investment.*

The Oath The oath is simple enough, but make sure you read it carefully and understand it fully. In your oath you declare that you are the first and sole (or joint) inventor of the invention claimed, and also that you know of no facts of any sort that would invalidate your patent.

You have to be careful here; it's in your interest to be both honest, and thorough. If any part of your idea came from someone else, you'd better find out where he or she got the inspiration. Otherwise, you may end up like the people at software manufacturer Ashton-Tate, who lost their most important piece of intellectual property after it was discovered that part of it derived from a public-domain program developed by the Jet Propulsion Laboratory. Nobody did anything morally wrong; it just happened that one of their researchers had used a bit of the JPL program, and nobody from the legal department thought to ask him about it before they applied for protection.

Filing Fee Along with your application, you'll be required to send in the application fee, which for "small entities" (that is, nonprofit groups, individual inventors, and small businesses), is presently $355, with increases likely very soon. There is no provision for hardship waivers.

---

*You may, if you prefer, submit informal drawings; the examiner will criticize them and will require formal drawings before the patent issues.

There are additional fees for special circumstances, such as applications listing more than twenty claims.

That's a brief introduction to the application process. Some sources for more complete information are included in Recommended Reading. But we'll stand by our idea that working with a patent attorney or agent is the way to go.

43

What Happens Next

YOU'VE CHECKED YOUR FORM, paid your fees, and sent in your papers. Now what?

Overall, the patent issuance process takes about two years, but once your idea is "patent pending," you can move on toward commercializing it.

Statistically, the odds of getting a patent are very good. Roughly two out of three patent applications are finally approved, although few are approved without challenges and changes. Those challenges, usually called "Office Actions" by the PTO, will probably shock you the first time you run into them. Not only will the PTO search foreign patents, which were probably beyond your reach, but the examiner will be trying to knock out as many of your claims as possible.

The result? The first office action will probably disallow many (perhaps all) of your claims and leave you feeling pretty sick. Don't panic— it's all part of the game.

Responding to "Office Actions" When you get your first office action letter, you'd better (if you haven't already) bring in a patent attorney, because as a rule you get only one chance to respond. After that, your options get increasingly expensive.

Your lawyer, then, will try to reverse the action. This will involve changes in the application wording, redrafted claims, and written arguments, to convince the examiner that his or her interpretation is wrong.

Be ready to help by explaining to your attorney precisely why your patent differs from those cited by the PTO. Most good patent attorneys will expect you to help with the revised application, but if you aren't asked to, speak up.

Roughly two-thirds of the time, the modified patent will be accepted. When that happens, congratulations! You've joined a very select society. All that remains is to mail the patent office your issuance fee—presently, $585 for sole inventors or small companies—within 90 days. Once the PTO receives your money, it will have your patent grant printed and mailed to you. It will also open your patent file to the public, and begin making copies available to interested investors and others.

If you're rejected a second time, though, you're probably in trouble, because second rejections are usually made "final." Technically, you can appeal "final" rejections to the PTO's Board of Patent Appeal and Interferences, but you'll need a pretty sound case—and it's probably too expensive for the average invention to justify.

If your patent is still rejected, you can technically take the PTO to court, specifically, to the Court of Appeals for the Federal Circuit, or to the U.S. district court for the District of Columbia. Both of these approaches, however, are extremely expensive, and make sense only if you have a lot of money on the line. For the average inventor, it makes more sense just to admit defeat and to drop the patent process. Remember, though: if no one else has relevant patents, you probably can still exploit your idea, even if you don't have the limited monopoly a patent would have given you.

But for now let's assume you're in that top two-thirds of all applicants whose patents are granted. And let's move on to the good stuff: making money from your invention.

44

Should You License or Sell?

ONCE YOUR IDEA has been reduced to a workable method (and, ideally, patented) and designed into a salable product, you have to decide whether to manufacture the product yourself or to license it.

If you haven't decided this earlier in the process, you have to do so now, because this is where you begin to turn your idea into real money.

The pluses of manufacturing yourself include absolute quality control, maximum profit, and the control of future add-on products. The minuses are equally dramatic: You need (1) considerable start-up capital, (2) a variety of business skills, (3) a large commitment of time, and (4) willingness (which any business owner must have) to run a considerable financial risk.

In contrast, licensing is much simpler. You, with your lawyer's help, grant someone the legal right to manufacture your idea, in return for which you receive a cash payment and/or royalties on each unit the licensee sells.

The first appeal of licensing, of course, is its simplicity.

Licensing or Selling: Let's Consider Some Examples

Obviously, we cannot tell you categorically whether you should license or manufacture your idea.* But here are a pair of examples that might help you choose.

Licensing: Barbara Arner and the Fast Track Tie Rack In 1985, when Barbara Arner got her great idea, she probably seemed an unlikely inventor. Although she'd intended since girlhood to find "one great idea," she'd never before tried commercializing anything. And her background, as an organizing specialist, with some work in accounting, was not exactly technically oriented.

But at an anniversary dinner in July 1985, she was struck with a simple idea: to reduce the sort of motorized rack you see in dry-cleaning stores to a motorized desktop tie rack to help men organize their closets.

Ms. Arner was no engineer, but she was smart enough to approach a friend, who happened to be industrial designer Ken Tarlow, of T2 Design. With his help, the idea became a workable method, which they named the "Fast Track Tie Rack." She contacted a patent attorney of his recommendation and, for about $3,500, started the patent process.

Meanwhile, Arner and Tarlow developed not only the technical drawings but a working model to show potential investors or licensees.

---

*When we say "manufacture," we're including two possibilities: either you actually build your own goods and then sell them, or else you contract out the building (to what's called an "O.E.M.," or "original equipment manufacturer"), and then handle marketing, sales, service, and the like yourself.

They also contacted OEMs for quotes on manufacturing. The news was good: The estimates came in at about $6.50 per unit, which meant the racks could be sold in the stores for about $30 or $35 apiece. That was an ideal price for a gift item, especially in the flush 1980s.

But Mrs. Arner decided against manufacturing the product herself, especially after she accidentally met a man named Alvin Finesman, who'd helped build both Salton and Cuisinart.

Mr. Finesman became interested in the Fast Track on the basis of drawings Mrs. Arner sent him, but to advance the process, she flew from Los Angeles to speak with him at the Chicago Housewares Show. That was in April 1986, some nine months after she'd first had her idea.

She took with her to Chicago the prototype Fast Track, and that was enough to clinch the deal. The following weekend, via long-distance telephone, their attorneys worked out the deal, giving Mr. Finesman exclusive rights to the product, in return for a 5 percent royalty.

Alvin Finesman was the right man for the job, as events would soon prove.

The good and the bad. How did the licensing deal work out? Financially, just great: The Fast Track sold 200,000 units in its first year, and over a million in its first five. There was never a problem with the royalty payments, which have long since topped $1 million.

But licensing does have its drawbacks. For one thing, the late Mr. Finesman was strong-willed and brooked no interference with his running of the business. Mrs. Arner thought (very reasonably, in our opinion) that as a woman inventor she would have been a valuable lead personality for the product. She even hired her own publicity agent—but Mr. Finesman rejected her efforts.

In 1991 Mr. Finesman's company, P.N.I., was bought by Dansk, which was in turn bought by Brown-Forman, a big-board company. P.N.I. has become something of a corporate orphan, and Mrs. Arner is trying to buy back her licenses. If it works, she may well move into OEM manufacturing. She is developing several new ideas, and now, thanks to her Fast Track experience, she has the experience, the confidence, and the war chest to support them.

Licensing, in short, was a great way for Barbara Arner to get her great idea profitably to market.

Manufacturing: Budd Wentz and the WentzScope If you wanted to pick model credentials for a solo inventor, you might describe someone like Budd Wentz, inventor of the WentzScope.

Mr. Wentz, an avid tinkerer from boyhood, started his adult career by getting an engineering degree from Berkeley. He followed that with a law degree from Hastings. After passing the bar, he went to work for a patent attorney. His plan was to become a patent attorney himself, "but in the back of my mind," he admits, "I always planned to be an inventor/entrepreneur."

Just out of law school in 1975, he published two children's books, one of which let kids cut out and construct Victorian animation toys. He served as an idea person for children's software programs and worked in a Berkeley science museum. He designed experiments for *Mr. Wizard's World* on the Nickelodeon cable television channel. And he kept looking for an invention that could become a business.

One of his inventions was a toy microscope with unique optics that made it fun and easy for children to use.

His original plan was to try to sell the microscope as a toy, but he found his first, unexpected market when the New York Museum of Science, for which he was a consultant, needed a microscope to let children enjoy one of its exhibits.

He made the first model out of plywood; when that began to draw attention, he built several more. Soon, enough people were asking for the microscopes that he started looking for a way to build larger batches.

At that point Mr. Wentz decided to patent the WentzScope. Interestingly, despite his patent law background, he hired an attorney to do the work, although with input from him. With the patent pending, he needed to decide whether to license or to manufacture his invention.

He decided to contract out the manufacturing, then do the assembly himself. Then he expanded production by a systematic program that let him keep full control. That meant both high-quality work and the maximum potential for profits. Specifically, he ratcheted up production in three stages:

1. The first few units he made himself.

2. As volume grew, he shifted to a highly skilled home machinist, who made the parts sets in runs of ten to twenty units.

3. As volume grew still higher, he switched to a larger machine shop with computer-controlled equipment, which could handle still larger orders.

During these first three stages (up to, roughly, the middle of 1991, or eighteen months after starting business), Mr. Wentz did all the final assembly himself. And he also made a point of contributing ideas to the manufacturing process. His suggestions steadily lowered manufacturing costs and raised quality. Again, he feels that while his engineering degree was of some help here, the parts of his background that helped him most were his lifelong practice of tinkering and his willingness to get out to trade shows and the like and ask questions.

The Wentz approach was based on certain key principles:

• He had the skills, both legal and technical, to advance his idea into the manufacturing stage.

• Despite having those skills, he made use of both legal and manufacturing experts, while providing input that helped them work more effectively.

• Once he decided to manufacture, he scaled his production to the size of his market, so that he never had to tie up money and effort in inventory. He also contracted out all his manufacturing, which kept his capital costs extremely low.

Summing Up Yes, you can make the most money by turning your invention into a business, but, as Barbara Arner's story shows, you can still make a million bucks or more simply by licensing your invention, sitting back and letting others do most of the work and take most of the risks.

45

Licensing Your Invention

LICENSING IS almost always the simplest, cleanest approach to profiting from your idea. It's a fine approach for first-time inventors, or for anyone who wants to profit without turning an idea into a full-time business.

On the other hand, licensing does have some risks. So let's start by running through the problems you may encounter, and the ways to avoid them.

Remember What You're Promising Here's a minor point, but you need to consider it. Whenever you sell anything, you're promising the buyer he or she will enjoy the "quiet use" of it, free of legal hassles.

Where patents are concerned, that means you're probably going to be at risk of legal action if your licensee gets sued for patent infringement. To guard against that, you have to be sure both that your patent was professionally searched and prepared and that you have insurance to protect you in case of a legal dispute. Your attorney can advise you about insurance—it's not hard to get, but you do need to get it.

Once you're comfortably certain that you've protected yourself legally:

Know What You're Giving Up People with inventions often cheat themselves by yielding valuable rights before they become valuable. Often they throw in these rights when they could have cut the deal without them. Even the most skillful licensers can fall into this trap.

One of the champion licensing organizations of the 1980s was Japan's Nintendo, the videogame company. No firm could make Nintendo-compatible game cartridges without Nintendo's approval of its whole operation.

That control was so tight that licensees frequently complained of unfair competition, and there were even some antitrust questions raised by various state governments. Fair or not, Nintendo's licensing program was unquestionably a brilliant success—

Until Nintendo cut its deal with Sony in 1988.

The two companies were going to co-develop a new, more expensive game machine. The key would be a more sophisticated central processor, with enhanced sound and graphics. All Sony wanted was one little detail: the right to make compact-disk-based versions of all the Nintendo games that ran on the machine.

In 1988 the home market for CD-based games was essentially zero, while Nintendo's cartridge-based games were generating billions of dollars in sales. Nintendo agreed—Sony got its license.

Suddenly three years go by; it's 1991. CD-ROM players are getting cheaper by the day, and big companies are starting to sell CD-based videogames, which are strikingly more complex and, by some accounts, more appealing than the older cartridge-based games. Nintendo is still selling a ton of game machines, but it no longer owns the rights to put its newest games on CDs, which is probably the fastest-growing part of its market. As one analyst told the *New York Times,* Nintendo "gave away the store."

Watch those giveaways! Before you try to license your idea, sit down with your attorney and figure out all the rights you have to sell—and which ones you're selling, which ones you're keeping for yourself.

Research Your Potential Buyers

Let's say you're ready to take your idea to market. One way or another, your first potential licensee appears. This can be a very exciting time, but you still need to do your homework before cutting any deals.

If your potential licensee is an individual or small company, watch his or her financial stability as well as track record. You need to see financial statements and credit reports.

Okay—that's pretty obvious. But, sadly, people who would proceed very cautiously with a small licensee will fall all over themselves if a big company takes an interest. That's a *big* mistake. You need to—

Research Those Big Companies, Too! This can be crucial. Some big companies work quite well and honorably with small firms; some will take advantage of any blunders you make but still stay within the law; and some will swipe anything they can get and then tell you to sue them if you don't like it.

Do They Really Want to Make Your Product? It sometimes happens that companies with competing products may want to license or even buy your patent just to eliminate it as a competitor. That may be perfectly okay with you as long as you get paid adequately. With a flat-purchase agreement, you're probably fine; you'll know at the outset what they're offering.

But what if they offer you just a royalty, then never put the product into production? That's one reason we stress minimum royalty payments when we talk about contracts. It's a relatively minor danger, but licensing can get a lot nastier than that.

Here's an example, still being litigated, of the kinds of problems you can have with licenses:

The Great Jet Ski Rip-off

About thirty years ago an American inventor named Clay Jacobson came up with the idea for the jet ski. In 1971, after getting a U.S. patent, he cut an exclusive licensing deal with Kawasaki Heavy Industries of Japan.

That deal included Kawasaki's right to view all Jacobson's designs. So what happened?

The day after Kawasaki engineers viewed those designs, Kawasaki filed in Japan for Japanese patents on the jet ski—and listed its own engineers as the inventors. Even worse, it got those patents and used them as evidence when it applied for further patents, back in the United States (it got at least one). Within four years Kawasaki was so secure it ditched its deal with Jacobson.

At that point Jacobson sued Kawasaki for patent infringement. He settled for $3 million, and Kawasaki's U.S. patent was voided. But the other Japanese jet ski manufacturers refused to deal with him, either as licensees or suppliers. Since those companies collectively owned the market, Jacobson was effectively out of the game.

The nastiness went on. The Kawasaki-backed U.S. Jet Ski Boating Association banned Jacobson and his son from the racing circuit. Kawasaki ran radio and TV ads praising itself for inventing the jet ski.

Finally Jacobson sued Kawasaki again. In July 1991 a jury in Los Angeles awarded him $21 million—an amount Kawasaki intended to appeal. (*Business Week,* August 19, 1991)

We're not trying to pick on any one company or nation. The point is simply that licensing your invention is a serious step, and you need to proceed carefully.

Licensing, especially to big companies, has its risks. The first way you manage those risks is to investigate carefully your potential licensees.

Beyond that, how do you structure your deal?

Licensing Basics: What You Want in a Contract

You obviously want to hold onto as much as you can and to receive as much as you can for what you do surrender. The counterpoint, of course, is that if you try to make the deal too one-sided, the other party will walk away. It's just plain business sense that a good contract is one that's fair to both sides.

Actually, as legal documents go, license agreements are fairly simple. Of course, the big issue is:

Royalties Again, the normal range of license fees varies from 3 to 10 percent of sales, with 5 percent by far the most common figure.

Much of that needs to be negotiated competitively. For example, you may give favorable terms to a first licensee (those terms to be kept secret as a condition of the license), both to get the ball rolling and to build yourself a war chest, in case you need to defend the patents or otherwise to expand your activities.

Your license may, of course, be different in any number of ways. You might, for example, be giving a license to use your patent in exchange for the right to use the other party's patent.

Beyond that, any basic licensing agreement will have to cover at least the following:

1. Introduction. The introduction simply states that this is a licensing agreement, between a willing licenser [that is, you] and a willing licensee, for the rights embodied in specific patents or patent applications. The introduction also states that the licensor is legally entitled to dispose of those rights, whether the license is exclusive or nonexclusive, and the term it is to run [normally, for the life of the patent, unless earlier terminated by agreement].

2. The license. The license repeats the terms of the license as mentioned in the introduction [that is, exclusive or nonexclusive, and the term it is to run] and adds details: usually, the countries in which the patents are held, and those for which the license is granted.

The license also usually includes a clause in which the licensor agrees to inform the licensee if he or she issues license(s) for the same patents to anyone else.

3. License fee. Usually just one sentence, this specifies how much money the licensor is to receive as the fee for granting the license. This is a lump sum, not the royalties you'll be receiving once manufacture and sale of your product actually gets under way.

How much are you going to receive?

Basically, three main factors are going to determine this: how quickly your patent can be put to profitable use, how profitable it is likely to be, and how desperate you are to cut a deal (or, putting that another way, how many other bidders there are).

As a practical matter, of course, this is going to depend upon the size of the players involved and the value of the invention. If you've invented a gizmo that's going to be built by a small company and sold at roadside fruit stands, you might not get anything for a licensing fee, or you may get a little, say, from $5000 to $10,000. If, on the other hand, you've developed something with immediate commercial value and licensed it to a big company, they might give you a large licensing fee (in the hundreds of thousands of dollars, or even more), particularly if they want an ongoing relationship and think money in your pocket will make you a more stable working partner.

Try for what you can get. If you're dealing with a big company but they won't pay a licensing fee, try for an advance against future royalties. If they won't let you get your hands on any of their money, look out: They may be preparing to stiff you.

4. Royalties, records, reporting. Now we're getting to the meat of the license. Basically, this section must, in whatever format, provide four things:

a. The royalty rate. This can be either a flat rate (say, $2.50 per widget), or a percentage of the selling price (usually 5 percent) received by the licensee.

b. Keeping of records. The licensee shall keep full and accurate accounts of anything affecting the money owed to the licensor.

Normally, these records are to be kept for a minimum of five years and are to be available for audit at any reasonable time. (Normally, you pay for the audit; sometimes, costs are split; and sometimes you pay only if discrepancies are found.)

c. Payment schedule. Normally, royalties are paid quarterly: say, in January, April, July, and October. This, of course, is only custom; it can be changed if there's any reason to do so.

d. The minimum annual royalty. This is one way you can enforce minimum performance. Suppose someone licenses your invention and then loses interest in it or simply fumbles the ball? Or suppose (as sometimes happens) they want an exclusive license just to keep your process/product off the market, so they can promote their own?

Minimum annual royalty is basic protection for you. It says that the last of the year's quarterly payments must be at least large enough to bring the year's total up to an agreed minimum amount. Thus, if the agreed minimum annual royalty is $30,000, and the January, April, and July payments have totaled only $10,000, the October payment must be at least $20,000, even if the licensee hasn't sold a single widget.

If the licensee doesn't make that payment by the due date, you can unilaterally pull the license without further discussion, any time within (usually) the following 30 days.

5. Termination. This lists the ways you can get your license back, usually if the licensee goes bankrupt or breaches any of the other conditions of the license. If case of breach or default, you'll probably be obliged to give 30 days' written notice of termination by registered mail. (Whatever the details of your contract are, be sure to observe them to the letter.)

Often, the licensee will have the right to terminate the license— usually on six months' notice.

6. *Assignment.* The licensee has the right to assign the license to anyone to whom he or she sells his or her entire business.

Not an unreasonable clause, but try to have it modified to read "with approval of licensor, said approval not to be unreasonably withheld." Why should you have to give a license to just any bozo who buys your licensee's business?

7. *Infringement.* You agree to protect the patents from infringement. Ideally you want to have the final say in this matter. Remember, patent lawsuits cost a fortune. You don't want to have to start one just because your licensee says there's a problem. Ekstrom (a classic text on licensing law; see Recommended Reading) suggests this phrasing:

The LICENSOR agree[s] to protect its patents from infringement and [to] prosecute infringers when in its sole judgment such action may be reasonably necessary, proper, and justified.

That says it pretty well. Just remember that litigation is expensive: you need both a war chest for launching suits, and insurance for defending them.

8. *Nonuse of names.* A minor clause: Licensees agree not to use your name in any advertising or sales literature without your written approval on each occasion.

This is a reasonable right to reserve if you can. Why stake your reputation on anybody else's work, to any greater degree than is necessary?

9. *Schedule of included patents.* This is not a clause, technically, but rather an attached listing of all the patents included in the license. At a minimum, the license schedule should include patent number, country, issue date, title, and inventor(s) of record.

Licensing contracts range from much simpler than outlined to far more complicated. More complex contracts include: interest charges on past-due royalties; releases (either for infringements which occurred before the license was granted or for infringements of other patents the licensor may have or subsequently receive in the same area); and "validity and scope" clauses, which, in simple language, say that if any subsequent court challenges shrink the scope of your patents, the licensee will still be bound to pay on the license for any surviving patent rights.

Summing Up The contract law behind a basic license is not very complicated; it's not nearly so complicated, for example, as the law behind the patent itself. Probably any decent business attorney can draw up a license—and again, you yourself can always examine the model contracts in Eckstrom.

Much of what you'll be paying a top licensing attorney for, as on so many other occasions, will be negotiating savvy: the money you get up front, your royalty rate, and your annual minimum payment (if any). That in turn requires a working knowledge, not so much of the law as of the business you are in.

You can best help your attorney if you assemble the following:

1. A list of uses for your patent.
2. A list of likely licensees. (Remember, think globally.)
3. An estimate of your market. Be realistic. If you can't do anything more sophisticated, try to find out the annual sales of the product nearest to yours—perhaps the product you think yours will replace.

But suppose you want to make your product. What then?

46

Manufacturing Your Invention

RUNNING A BUSINESS is a huge subject. Here we simply want to cover briefly a few issues that are especially important for inventor/ entrepreneurs.

Business Plans

The key to turning an idea into a business is a detailed business plan. The plan should itemize not only your products and where you intend to sell them, but how you intend to make them, the kinds of experts and staff you'll have, and, especially, how much money you'll need and how you'll spend it.* Your plan will not only guide you through your start-up, but, along with your personal financial statement, be crucial to attracting money from lenders or investors.

Where the Money Goes You probably won't have devoted much time to your business plan before you realize that manufacturing is very expensive.

How to Spend $70,000—or $3 Million—for the Same Thing When Budd Wentz set out to build the WentzScope, he kept quality high and costs low by contracting for manufacture and doing assembly himself. In fact, he estimates he spent, during his first eighteen months, only about $70,000, including living expenses.

But at the same time Budd Wentz was starting his business, he was able to follow the start-up of a similar firm, one making optical equipment of roughly the same complexity for the U.S. military. These people chose to gear up big-time at the outset. Their start-up costs? Roughly $3 million, or more than 40 times the cost of the Wentz start-up!

Sure, there were many differences between the two companies, but the key was the amount of manufacturing they chose to do in-house. Running a manufacturing operation takes tools, machinery, real estate, trained workers, lots of insurance.

That, in turn, leads us to:

A Cure for High Costs: The Original Equipment Manufacturer (OEM) If your goal is to build, rather than license your invention, bravo! But when you discover how expensive it is to do your own manufacturing, don't panic.

Instead, think of manufacturing as being a range of possibilities, from something as fully integrated as General Motors, which makes almost every component it uses, to the so-called "hollow" corporations, which do design work and sales, but contract out all their manufacturing to OEMs.

You can think of using an OEM as being halfway between licensing and full-scale manufacturing. You are running a business and you can be involved in the manufacturing, but you don't take on all the burdens at once.

At this level, an OEM probably calls itself something more modest,

---

*For more on this, see the books in Recommended Reading or get the free "Checklist for Going into Business" from the Small Business Administration. Call the SBA at 1-800-368-5855.

like "machine shop," but the idea's the same: somebody who makes your product to your specifications, at an agreed-upon price.

The advantages of using an OEM are probably obvious. You don't buy any manufacturing gear, you don't have to learn manufacturing, and your time and money are mostly focused where you can use them best—in the process of selling your goods.

Drawbacks? First, you're trusting someone else with part of your work; if he fouls up an order, you'll be the one dealing with irate customers. Second, if you choose an overseas manufacturer, there'll be a long lag time between orders and deliveries. That makes it hard to keep pace with changes in your market. If a new color, say, becomes hot, but your supplier can't get it here from Taiwan in less than eight weeks, you'll lose a lot of sales.*

Still, OEMs (especially those based here in the States) are one of the best ways to build a business without a huge capital outlay.

How do you find an OEM? Start with your phone book, ask anyone you know with business experience, visit trade shows, or contact your local inventors' association. You can also call a local industrial designer for some suggestions; most will help you with a name.

Or you can take a more systematic approach.

Pati Hillis and Gadgets To find the best and nearest manufacturer(s) for your product, the most common place to start is with *Thomas's Register,* a massive set, available in most libraries, listing virtually every manufacturer in the United States.

That's where Pati Hillis started when she decided to put into production her own idea: an "updated version of a classic French turn-of-the-century corkscrew." The register gave her a list of "cast-makers, die and stamping experts, platers, and screw-machine operators" near her home town. It took her eighteen months (and 22,000 miles of driving) to visit all those people, line up the ones she wanted to work with, and get the first batch of parts in place for her own small company to begin assembling.

That may sound like a lot of grief, but the care helped turn an idea into a going business with a prestige product. Today her $50 "Pullman" corkscrew is available at upmarket shops across the country. (*New York Times,* April 22, 1991)

One good tip. The 1990s are seeing a rapid scaling-down of American

---

*There's also a real danger of counterfeiting by foreign OEMs.

defense manufacturing. We read mostly about the big firms, but there are literally thousands of small defense subcontractors who formerly worked under the big companies, but now are scrambling for other kinds of work. Many of these shops are hungry enough to give you bids competitive with any foreign offer, especially if your product is not labor-intensive. And their skill level is very high.

Action Plan—OEMs

If you want to manufacture or use an OEM to manufacture your own invention, you need to:

1. Do a thorough market study so you know what people will pay for your invention (that is, the retail price).

2. Set your manufacturing cost target at no more than 20 percent of retail price.

3. Get adequate industrial designs, from your industrial designer or elsewhere. (You can just take your idea to a machine shop, and sometimes they can reduce it to workable instructions, but that's risky).

4. From your designer, an inventors' association, *Thomas's Register,* or similar sources, get a list of manufacturers. From your lawyer (or, if you don't have one, from your designer or inventors' association) get a sample *nondisclosure* form: these require that anyone signing them agrees to treat what you tell him as a trade secret, and neither to use it nor to share it with anyone else.

5. Interview manufacturers. After having them sign a nondisclosure form (this is a must), get their references, as well as their price quotes. Can they deliver your gadget for your target price? How long will it take? You have to trust your instincts as much as their claims: Does the place look modern and efficient? Is the work force stable (turnover in small shops can be horrendous), and does it appear sober and committed?

6. Finally let them know you intend to be involved in the manufacturing process, and find out if that bothers them. If it does, keep looking. You need to be able to have input.

7. With numbers in hand, contact likely buyers. Once you have their commitments, even tentative ones, you can draw up production contract(s) with the shop(s) that are going to do your work. Use a lawyer. (You may want to switch to a regular business attorney; your patent lawyer may be too expensive to use on a simple contract.)

8. Like Budd Wentz and most other successful inventor/entrepre-

neurs, stay involved in the manufacturing process. Don't just place an order, then disappear.

You may need to deal with more than one shop. That's fine as long as you take the time to develop solid working relations to the point where you can count on them to deliver on time.

Field Testing: Getting Your Good Idea Dirty

So far we've spoken as though you can go directly from design prototypes to mass production. For many gadget-type inventions, that's so. But there can be a lot of development work between your great idea and a great salable product. To take an extreme example:

Irvine Sensors, an eleven-year-old semiconductor company, is developing a remarkable idea. Today, all semiconductors are etched onto flat surfaces. Irvine Sensors wants to build "stacked" or three-dimensional semiconductors.

Many experts think I.S. leads the world in this emerging technology and might well dominate what will shortly be an $18 billion market.

A great and worthy idea—except that, so far, Irvine Sensors is still in the R and D stage. The company has spent $30 million (mostly in federal grants) to solve manufacturing and design problems.

Typical problems? To name just one, they've had to try more than 1,000 different glues to hold the circuits together. As a company executive told the *Los Angeles Times,* "I don't think anybody else was crazy enough to do it."

You're probably not trying to revolutionize an industry. But simple gadgets have their problems, too. When the California drought of the 1980s became so bad that people were stealing water, two San Diegans, Alan Parchman and Mike Stoddarts, decided to design a lock for outdoor faucets. They had a working model of their Waterguard in three or four days.

Great—except that water thieves are tough customers. The first Waterguards were smashed with everything up to and including sledge hammers. So it was back to the drawing board.

It took another year to turn the Waterguard into a workable, salable $15 gadget. Today's model apparently holds together no matter what hits it.

Such practical problems are pretty rare—you don't need to agonize over them. On the other hand, if your invention will either push the limits of any existing technology or be used in any sort of hostile environment (including outdoors in bad weather), budget the time and money for field testing.

A Last Bit of Cheer, and an Action Plan When you first set out to build your invention, you may feel daunted by your lack of technical background. Don't let it worry you. A background in manufacturing or engineering can help, but no one has ever said it's crucial, especially for the sort of low-tech manufacturing most ideas require. In fact, we asked Budd Wentz how useful his engineering and law degrees were in manufacturing the Wentzscope.

His answer?

"One day walking through a trade show is worth three months in college."

So if you want to learn to manufacture, just get out there like Budd Wentz and Pati Hilis, and hit those trade shows and small O.E.M.s. You can do it!

47

Funding Inventions

Everybody's Favorite Question: Where's the Money?

PROBABLY the most common question asked of business advisers is: "I've got a really great idea and want to turn it into a business. Where do I get the money?"

As you've probably guessed by now, that's the wrong question. What you need to ask is:

"I've got a great invention and a detailed business plan. Where do I raise 'X' dollars?" You can't realistically expect a loan until you have a solid plan, nor should you spend much of your own money until you have it.

Once you have that plan, your prospects are much brighter.

You Don't Need a Fortune Successful invention-based businesses have been launched for as little as $500.* Almost 70 percent of the *Inc.* 500 (the fastest-growing American small firms) during the 1980s were launched with less than $50,000 in start-up capital. Of course, not all were invention-based businesses; still, that does give you a ballpark figure.

If you expect to attract investors—in fact, if you expect to survive past your first year—you'd better do whatever you can to squeeze out extra costs before you start. We're talking about such things as cheap rents, used equipment, cutting your salary to almost nothing.

But, however much you reduce costs, you're still going to need money. Where do you get it?

Your Own Resources Like it or not, your own money, either liquid assets or funds raised from mortgaging real estate, will probably be your main source of early capital. Add in loans from friends and family, and you have the primary financing means of some 75 percent of all the businesses on the *Inc.* 500.†

Even if you can get formal outside financing, be prepared to put up some of your own money. Most investors will expect it as a sign of sincerity, if nothing else.

If you can't raise that start-up capital, licensing deals are probably a better bet. Then, once you have a war chest from royalties on your first invention, you can try manufacturing your second great idea.

Once you go outside friends and family, the money becomes more costly and more difficult to get. Here are a few possibilities:

Bank Loans Roughly a third of all *Inc.* 500 start-ups got corporate loans from banks, while another 23 percent got personal bank loans.

For a bank loan, you'll probably need at least three things: a business plan, a track record, and some personal contacts.

But don't hesitate to improvise. One of the country's largest black-owned companies got its start when its inventor/founder was turned down for a small business loan. So he went back to the same bank a few days later and asked for the same amount as a vacation loan. They gave it to him—and that was how he launched his company!

Venture Capitalists Venture capitalists provide money in return for part ownership of your business and (often) a large say in its operation.

---

*Actually, if you'd accept ice cream novelties as "inventions," the record is much lower. Tom Carvel launched his company with a $15 personal loan.

†Don't just take the money out of your account. Have the bank lend you the money against your passbook. The interest will be a deductible expense, and you'll build your business credit rating as you repay it.

They make most of their money by taking the business public once sales grow to a certain point; accordingly, the money available from these people will depend largely on the overall market for initial public offerings of stocks in new companies. When the market goes flat, venture capital tends to dry up.

You give up a lot to get venture capital, but if you deal with a *good* venture capitalist firm, you'll get not only money but first-rate management assistance in exchange. Be prepared for a rigorous going-over before they commit any money.

Government Funding Both the federal government and most state governments make money available in various ways for start-ups that will either create jobs or advance technology. There are also special loan categories for veterans, minorities, and women. Government-backed loans will normally have the best interest rates available.

The people at the Small Business Administration are generally helpful, but rather than trying to navigate your way through the SBA thickets, you might contact a Certified Development Corporation. There are 450 of these federally chartered nonprofit organizations across the country; they exist to help you prepare and package your loan application.

About Investors: A Warning It's really romantic to be able to say, early on, "I got a venture capitalist to put up half-a-million bucks. I didn't use a penny of my own money."

Fine, but getting capital that way means giving up control. Bringing in a venture capitalist or private investor(s) early on, when your business isn't worth much, will mean giving up a very large amount of control for a relatively small amount of money.

Let's return to Budd Wentz. From his earliest days, he was approached by venture capitalists attracted to the idea of a (relatively) hi-tech, hi-margin, American-made product. But he turned them all down.

The result?

He may have missed a chance for quicker growth or a higher personal salary, but today he owns 100 percent of his business.

And that business is growing more valuable every day. He may well need venture capital in the future, but when he goes after it, he'll have to surrender a far smaller part of his business to get the money he needs.

Big Companies You probably should not take your idea, at an early stage, to a big corporation. They're likely to say, "Thank you very much," help themselves to any unprotected parts of your ideas, and go into business as your competitor. Unless they've signed a nondisclosure/noncompete agreement (which they almost certainly won't), they can do this perfectly legally, as happened after the Go Corporation showed its proposed pen-based software system to Microsoft Corporation.

Even after you have a going business, be cautious about dealing with big companies. Even if you do get a deal to buy your corporation, you probably won't be happy; the odds against a genial buyout of a small company by a big one are extremely high.

On the other hand, a big brother can be extremely helpful if it will a) benefit from your product, and b) be unable, for whatever reason, to become your competitor.

For the last eight years, a San Diego firm called IVHS has had most of its R and D costs paid for by Allstate Insurance.

Why?

Because IVHS (it stands for "intelligent vehicles / highway systems") was studying electronic ways to prevent highway collisions. Allstate, which took an equity stake in IVHS, was obviously the perfect big brother; it had the cash, stood to benefit if the system worked, and clearly had no interest in turning itself into a manufacturing company.

If you can find a big backer meeting those conditions, by all means consider a linkup. Otherwise, be cautious.

Overseas Groups More controversial funding for ideas (especially hi-tech ones) comes from foreign corporations.

Between 1986 and 1991, according to the American Electronics Association, Japanese companies alone bought stakes in 153 American electronics firms. "American" start-up companies, from Next Computers (which got millions from Japan's Canon), to Poquet, the maker of notebook computers (owned now by Fujitsu) have depended upon foreign capital from their early days. So you certainly have to look seriously at this possibility.

With a low-tech idea, of course, foreign investment is probably much less likely, although it does still happen; and here's one new source which may become significant in the 1990s:

Would-be Immigrants Following the lead of a very successful Canadian program, the United States has begun giving citizenship preference to wealthy foreign immigrants willing to establish businesses here. Inevitably, many of these prospective immigrants, especially from strongly entrepreneurial societies like Hong Kong, are interested in investing in invention-based companies. The laws are still evolving, but this is something to watch.

Mortgaging the Property While it's not nearly as well-known as bringing in investors—who get an equity stake (that is, an ownership position) in your intellectual property—you can also try to get an *intellectual property mortgage.*

As with any other mortgage, you are borrowing money, using the property (in this case, the patent) as security for the lender. If you make payments on time, the property remains yours forever. Only if you default on the loan does the lender have a chance to seize your property.

Any competent business or patent attorney can help you arrange the proper paperwork. Of course, a patent attorney will probably have a clearer idea of the value of the property.

Royalty Financing One new and interesting twist on venture capitalism is the royalty financing agreement.

The idea is simple enough. Investors give you money, to be invested in developing a new product, and are repaid out of royalties earned once that product actually goes on sale.

Royalty financing has three large pluses: First, it's sometimes available when other forms of financing aren't. Second, because it's technically neither a loan nor a capital investment, it neither loads your balance sheet with debt (which would make it hard for you to borrow money), nor dilutes your ownership share. The third main reason may be the best of all: You don't have to pay it back until you start earning money from the invention.

What's the downside?

If your product becomes a hit, you can end up paying out a lot more in royalties than you would ever have paid in traditional financing. At that point you'll have to choose between buying back the royalty agreement with cash (which is expensive), or converting it into an equity stake in your company.

Royalty financing is a new concept and only slowly growing in popularity. It really hasn't been around long enough to have been thoroughly evaluated, but it definitely seems worth considering. If you'd like to know more about it, you might contact the man generally credited with inventing it:

> Mr. Tom Nastas
> 4700 S. Hagedorn Road
> East Lansing, Michigan 48823
> 1-517-332-6246

The original fund Mr. Nastas created is now fully invested, but he is serving as an adviser to large institutions and says he would be interested in hearing from entrepreneur/inventors.

A Closing Note Entrepreneurs are susceptible to financing scams, which usually involve someone offering to put you in touch with a neglected or hard-to-reach source of money. The scam artists usually want an up-front fee to put you in touch with lenders or investors, who can range from "Asian billionaires" to "Mid-Eastern oil money" to (in a new and particularly nasty variant) alleged church or religious groups wanting to make ethical loans.

There are legitimate loan finders or brokers. Just remember:

1. Don't pay any up-front fees to be "put in touch with lenders." If you absolutely have to pay a fee, pay only after the loan goes through and you receive the money.

2. It's illegal to pay "finders' fees" on federally backed loans.

Summing Up You can go after financing at any stage in the idea-to-business stage. Just remember two things:

• Most serious investors or lenders won't talk with you until you have a detailed business plan in hand, and—

• The earlier you seek money, the more people are going to expect in the way of a track record and detailed business plans, and the more of the business you'll have to surrender to every dollar raised.

Keep your "dot" firmly in mind. The further you move toward it on your own, the more of it you'll own when you get there!

48

Promoting Your Inventions

HERE'S A FACT OF LIFE that persuades many inventors they'll be happier just licensing their invention and leaving the business to others:

You can't just make a product; you have to sell it.

Selling a product is hard work and, if you hire professionals to advertise and/or market it, amazingly expensive.

How expensive?

Wayne Jervis, Jr., a marketer who has launched products large and small (from Coca Cola's Sprite to the recent, entrepreneurial, VCR Plus), estimates an entrepreneur would need at least $40,000 just for a preliminary professional marketing study. That's merely to decide whether the product is worth promoting. The campaign itself would use "as much money as you can lay your hands on"—a million dollars is not a lot. In fact, as you'll see in Part Four, when a meat-packing company went to the pros to build its brand name, it spent nearly a million dollars for a six-month-long campaign in one city.

Suppose you don't have a million dollars handy. What can you do on a shoestring?

Actually, with imagination and verve, you can do a lot. In fact, you can even get things like TV advertising for free.

"Perceived Advantage": The First Basic Principle of Selling

The first principle of selling is to tell the buyer what you're going to do *for him or her.* This is what marketers like Mr. Jervis call the product's "perceived advantage." If your buyer doesn't clearly perceive that your product's going to benefit him or her—never mind its other virtues—you may as well go home.

Moreover, you'd better be able to explain that advantage to the buyer quickly.

Here's a way to start:

Get a friend with a stopwatch to give you 30 seconds to make your sales pitch. Keep giving it until it's absolutely irresistible.

Then have him give you 25 seconds to make the same pitch. Don't talk faster—just whack out 5 seconds of extraneous material.

When you've got that version polished to perfection, cut another 5 seconds off the time limit. When that version works, cut 5 seconds more.

And so on. When you've got the whole pitch down to 5 seconds, that's your sales pitch—that's your "perceived advantage" in a nutshell. Never forget it, no matter how you may decorate it in the coming years.

The Second Principle: Know Your Markets

We've stressed this before, but now it has a new importance, because every dollar or minute you spend trying sell to people who aren't buyers in the first place is a dollar or a minute wasted.

Where do you find the people with the strongest built-in desire for your product?

Obviously, that's going to depend upon whether you're dealing with a consumer or an industrial market. Industrial markets are relatively cut-and-dried; you'll know the (relatively few) buyers, and either call on them yourself, hire a salesperson, or engage a manufacturers' representative.*

So let's concentrate on the consumer markets, where the majority of first-time inventors begin.

The Name Retailers Your first thought will probably be the big chains, from Sears and K Mart to Bloomingdale's and Neiman-Marcus.

That's a fine idea on the face of it—these firms move a huge mass of goods.

Unfortunately, these days the big retailers are giving inventor/entrepreneurs the cold shoulder. In fact, most major retailers won't risk the costs of stocking a new product unless it's a) offered by someone with a strong track record, or b) backed by a million-dollar or better ad campaign.

That's a harsh business, and many buyers will tell you they've had to pass on some great products, but most traditional American retailers have gotten absolutely hammered by the economy over the past ten years. They simply can't afford to gamble on new products.

That doesn't mean getting into the big stores is impossible, just that it's very hard. And it's getting harder. In December 1991 Wal-Mart, for example, announced it would no longer deal with manufacturers' reps, those commission salespeople who historically have done the selling for new companies that can't afford their own salaried salespeople.

Two notes. First, if you *do* try the big guys, you should still focus on your market. Thus, after midwesterner James Arner patented a shovel-like snow clearer called a Snaug'R, he pitched it to True Value hardware stores. They tested it and liked it so much they agreed not only to carry it but to manufacture it for him. In the winter of 1991, its first season, Snaug'R sold 4,600 units at $50 each, and for 1992 True Value planned to increase the advertising. (*Wall Street Journal,* August 27, 1991)

Second, while Barbara Arner's Fast Track Tie Rack got its first deal

---

*For manufacturers' reps, try the Manufacturers' Agents National Association. Their Directory of Manufacturers' Sales Agencies is available in most libraries, or from the Manufacturers' Agents National Association, 23016 Mill Creek Road / P.O. Box 3467 / Laguna Hills, CA 92654-3467. Telephone: 1-714-859-4040.

with the prestigious Bullock's department stores, that doesn't really contradict what we've been telling you.

Remember that Ms. Arner had licensed her product to Alvin Finesman, who was already well known because of his role in creating Cuisinart. As fine a gadget as Fast Track was, it was Mr. Finesman's involvement that clinched the Bullock's deal.

A big name, in short, can bring you both skills and instant credibility—which is a terrific selling tool.

Licensing is one way to get that credibility. You can also hire a big name to run your company, but for all but a handful of start-ups that has proved ruinously expensive. Too many big names simply cut themselves in for a big salary, then cut out when the going gets tough.

A better plan is to offer someone who has a strong track record and who believes in your product an equity position to get him or her to join your operation. If the person likes your idea enough to invest in it, even better.

Big retailers are tough for newcomers, but if you have unusual resources, give them a try. Just don't stake your future on them.

What else should you try?

Special Markets for Inventors The great surge in inventions during the 1980s has lately spawned an assortment of new marketing opportunities for inventors. Some of these, like stores that exclusively feature new inventions, are themselves so new as to be hard to judge, but they seem promising. Thus at New Products Showcase in Irving, Texas, you'll pay $350 plus a percentage of sales to have your new product on the shelves for three months. That's a much better deal than most trade shows and so an idea definitely worth considering. (*Wall Street Journal,* August 27, 1991)

By the same token, some established but creative retailers are trying to get an early lead on promising new ideas. Thus, Richard Thalheimer, founder of high-end gadgeteer Sharper Image, now runs semimonthly open houses for inventors with ideas meant to help the environment. Even the PTO runs an annual showcase for inventors; technically, you cannot sign deals there, but the contacts can be terrific.

And here's a relatively new idea:

Free Television! Using Infomercials You've probably seen "infomercials"—those 30-minute commercials that masquerade as informational programs. Actually as old as TV itself, they've been revived by cable.

Why are they good for new inventors?

Because many of the companies that make infomercials will make and show them for you for free. (Of course, nothing's absolutely free; they take a profit out of sales, but your up-front costs are zero.)

Tony Hoffman, whose Maui Productions is a leading infomercial maker, offers these tips on using them:

- They work for any product that has visual snap, something that will show well on TV. (Although one fellow used them to sell eighty million dollars' worth of subliminal audio tapes.)

- You have to be able to deliver the product to the infomercial producer for 20 percent of what it will sell for. (That's a tougher deal than some other routes. As you know, the normal rule is that you have to *make* it for that percentage.)

- If Maui likes a product enough, they'll even do the manufacturing. They'll also look at products still in the design stage. (Don't worry about making a fancy pitch; that's their job.) They (or comparable companies) will give you a yes-or-no answer within a week and will have a commercial on the air within 90 days. Commercials that "test" well are run until they stop producing sales; some have run for two and a half years. Many products move from infomercials to traditional retail markets.

- Technically, you can make your own infomercial from scratch. The problem is that the established companies have locked in the best showing times. You'll have a hard time getting even a good slot for your test marketing.

That's an "industry" view. The truth is, there are no absolute rules. Talk to some of these companies and see what kind of deal you can cut. Presently about eighty companies, spread across the country, make infomercials. For an information packet contact: The National Infomercial Marketing Association, 1-202-962-8342.

Those are some likely sales channels, both new and traditional. Here are ways you can sell more effectively:

Make Yourself the Spokesperson

Sometimes your best tactic will be to act as your own spokesperson. In its most dramatic form, this forges a strong identification between you and your product. For example, any product from the Peter Norton Computing Company contains not only the founder's name but his signature and photograph.

You may never go that far, but it's still hard to top an inventor/ founder's personal involvement in those early sales.

Khanh Dinh came to the United States as a refugee in 1975. He worked as an air-conditioning repairman but wanted more from life. So in 1978 he invented a solar collector—and collected royalties for several years. In 1983, Mr. Dinh started his own company to perfect an air dehumidifier he'd invented. After five years of shoestring development, he approached nineteen U.S. air-conditioner makers—and got fourteen rejections and five polite responses, which produced no notable orders.

So how did he proceed? "He pitched his product at meetings of architects and building engineers. He wrote articles for trade magazines." (*Wall Street Journal,* August 27, 1991) In short, he got out and promoted himself directly to his most likely buyers, and he didn't stop to worry that he was dealing with a new culture, a new language.

The orders started arriving. By 1991, Mr. Dinh's Heat Pipe Technology, Inc. was doing roughly $1.5 million in sales, growing fast, and discussing large-scale deals with at least two major companies.

Direct Mail Direct mail is just what it sounds like: You approach selected customers directly through the mail. The key to it lies in building or buying a mailing list that focuses on exactly your target customers.

Charles Wilkeson was in many ways a classic inventor/entrepreneur. He invented a useful product, a special dog brush that applied flea repellent or medicines while it combed a dog's coat. Unfortunately, as the *Los Angeles Times* described him, "Wilkeson spent thousands of dollars on prototypes to perfect his invention. He spent hundreds of thousands of dollars on manufacturing equipment." In fact, by the time he had a patented, workable product, he had nearly run out of money for marketing.

And pet supplies is a terribly crowded market, usually calling for big ad budgets. The business was in trouble, with a swelling inventory and few sales.

Then a marketing consultant named Ronald Safier put up money for the worldwide distribution rights to the product. More to the point, he found the right market for the product: veterinarians.

By vigorously direct-mailing to 50,000 veterinarians, Mr. Safier launched Brush-ettes for real. Eighteen months into the campaign, he had sold 200,000 units, and business was booming. Veterinarians were not only great customers, they were automatic salespeople. Pet owners who saw Brush-ettes in the vets' offices wanted to buy them for home use.

The Brush-ettes campaign worked because it was both aggressive and well-focused. However aggressive and well-focused your campaign is, though, don't expect huge returns from any one mailing. Even the best rarely score orders from more than 2 or 3 percent of people on the list. Still, with the right list, direct mailing can be highly effective.

Veterinarians were model consumers; potential buyers looked up to them as people who knew the right products to buy. If you can, try to get your product to these model consumers, whether professionals, champion athletes, or film stars.*

That's an overview of some basic markets and methods. Now let's look at something more elusive and more valuable: creativity.

Tripledge Wipers: How to Sell Smart Tripledge windshield wiper blades were a classic start-up product: the inventors spent four years in a garage perfecting their design and manufacture, then began selling them through ads in such magazines as *Popular Mechanics.* The product sold well, especially considering the modest advertising. In its best year, 1987, the Tripledge Wiper Corporation sold one million dollars' worth of wipers.

Unfortunately, the owners were determined to break into the big retail channels. According to the *Wall Street Journal,* they spent nearly a million dollars trying unsuccessfully to persuade companies like K Mart to carry Tripledge. With no brand-name recognition, no ad budget remaining, no big names on the board of directors, they struck out—and Tripledge went into Chapter 11 bankruptcy.

Enter Ms. Jennifer Runyeon. In 1988, she and a partner bought Tripledge Corporation out of bankruptcy for under $500,000. Then they began to make it a big business.

They didn't touch the product, which was fine. They redid the marketing. First, they arranged to put their ads in the monthly bills sent to oil

---

*These days, of course, even slightly famous people generally want large fees for their endorsements, and even getting your product used in a movie (a "product placement") can cost thousands. Still, inventors do sometimes get lucky: A stuffed toy called a F.R.O.Y.D. appeared on the TV show *Designing Women* simply because one of its stars thought it represented positive values. You need something special to get a freebie endorsement, of course, but if you have the goods, try for the words.

company charge card holders. That was smart: They were direct-marketing potential buyers who drove their cars a lot of miles.

Revenues rose quickly, but then Ms. Runyeon and her partner hit on their real strategy. They began advertising on cable television—a strategy that boosted sales of Tripledge wipers twentyfold, to more than $20 million a year, in less than two years.

But we're supposed to be talking about low-cost strategies, right? Well, how about zero cash? That was the way Ms. Runyeon did it. She cut deals with the cable syndicates where they ran her TV ads in return for a royalty on each sale resulting from those ads (a matter easily tracked, since the ads gave distinct toll-free phone numbers and P.O. boxes).

By 1991, Tripledge was ready to try cracking the mass-retailer market again. Expensive move? No—an immediate income earner, because Ms. Runyeon sold the rights to sell Tripledge products through mass retailers. Now it was another company's job to persuade K Mart and Wal-Mart to carry Tripledge products. By late 1991 both had agreed to do so.

Toys: Launching Abalone on the Cheap Want another example of smart selling? Consider the game market, one of the toughest markets in the country.

According to the *New York Times,* Hasbro, Inc., the largest American toymaker, also controls 75 percent of the U.S. market for games; among other things, it makes sixteen of the country's top twenty. That means fantastic clout, especially in a market owned by a few giant retailers like Toys "Я" Us. Most of these retailers won't even consider your product unless it's backed by a multimillion-dollar ad campaign. Consumers, the reasoning goes, are so saturated by ads for the "top-twenty" games that they won't even notice a new game without big promotion.

Now consider a game called Abalone, created by two French artists and built into a success by an entrepreneur named Jan Travers, who calls himself "a big believer that you can do things without money."

Abalone is a simple game, where players move large marbles to control a hexagonal board. No microchips, no video screens.

And virtually no advertising budget. But by substituting inventiveness for cash, Mr. Travers managed to sell 100,000 copies of Abalone worldwide in just two years, between 1989 and 1991.

How did he do it?

He decided Abalone's market, at least initially, would be fashionable folk with leisure time, people who probably would never be caught dead with, say, a Nintendo set.

So Abalone gave away the games, to places where fashionable people might gather in their leisure time. The idea was that the owners of ski resorts, quiet cafés and the like would leave the games out for the customers to try. The customers would play Abalone, like it—and buy sets for themselves.

"Ah," you're probably saying, "but where did these eager customers find Abalones to buy? I thought the big stores wouldn't carry it without an advertising commitment."

That's where the real cleverness came in. Mr. Travers approached hundreds of small specialty stores, with a promise that if they stocked Abalone, they'd never find it selling at the Toys "Я" Us down the street for half the price.

Sure, Toys "Я" Us would have refused the game. Mr. Travers's offer was still honest, and he soon had a long list of specialty stores as dealers. Small shops are desperate for exclusive merchandise; they just can't afford to compete with the high-volume discounters. Abalone's offer was irresistible.

Approaching all those small shops, even while games were being given away to "model" locations, kept Abalone Games in close touch with its customers. That in turn let the company solve problems before they cost sales. Abalone came in a six-sided box, matching the game board inside. Stylish—but customers were having trouble gift-wrapping it. In almost no time Abalone had a six-sided gift box on the market. Problem solved—and sales continued upward.

Of course, cleverness will take you only so far. In mid-1991 Abalone licensed its star product to Galoob, the big toy company, for a royalty on the high side of 5 percent. You might see that as a defeat, since Travers and friends wanted to stay independent, or you could see it as a dramatic victory, since Abalone Games succeeded where giants like Mattel flopped: in launching a new, successful board game.

Today Abalone is backed by the sort of media campaign that puts products into the big leagues. But it all happened because its owners knew how to improvise at the outset, and took the time to understand and to reach their market. (*New York Times,* July 4, 1991)

Brochures and Manuals and Why They Matter

There's one part of selling that many inventor/entrepreneurs overlook, to their regret: brochures and manuals. Most new products need brochures to introduce people to them, and manuals to explain how they work. It's pretty obvious how brochures can help with selling, but why are manuals sales tools?

Because you don't really have a sale when somebody buys your product—you have it when they decide to *keep* it.

That's where manuals come in. True, very few people read manuals before using products, but most of them do turn to the manual when they have a problem. If your manual solves the problem, you've probably clinched your sale. If not, the buyer will throw the gadget in the trash and tell everybody he knows it's a piece of junk, or else return to the store and demand help or a refund. Those returned products will kill the store's profits (they not only lose a sale; they have all the costs of restocking, processing refunds, placating the probably irritated consumer). Too many refunds, and they'll cancel your deal, even if the product is selling relatively well.

So take the trouble to write a good manual—it will make you money in the long run.

P.S.: The Litigation Danger Here's another key point: Even if your product is so simple that people don't need a manual to make it work, including one will reduce your chances of getting sued.

One of the most common grounds for a lawsuit is called "failure to warn." Even if people get hurt by misusing your product in wildly stupid fashion, they'll still probably be able to find a lawyer to sue you, but by including a warning you'll neutralize one of the suit's most powerful claims.

Summing Up Advertising is the key to establishing a successful new product. While the experts will tell you there's no substitute for money, the truth is you can probably succeed in your early days just by hustle and creativity.

Wherever possible, use brains, not bucks!

49

Patent Litigation

WITH ANY LUCK, your issued patent will guarantee you the quiet and successful ownership of your invention for many happy years.

Sometimes, though, your patent leads you straight into legal complications. What happens when problems arise?

Using the courts to protect ideas is becoming an ever-larger part of the inventor's life. As Charlie Hall, the inventor of the modern water bed, told us, "A patent is a license to sue to protect your ideas, nothing more or less."

We're going to try to show you how to be an effective litigant should the need ever arise. But first we want to give you the downside of litigation and to show why sometimes you're better off not suing at all.

The Bad News: Time and Money

To call patent litigation expensive is to understate matters wildly. Most major patent firms expect, in the active phase of a patent lawsuit, to bill even smallish clients $50,000 or $100,000 a month. *Total* legal bills, especially to fight a big company, can easily run between $4 and $5 million.

Those are only the cash costs of litigation; they don't count the stress and the loss of time as key managers and employees are dragged into the process, which can last for years. Major corporations engaged in patent lawsuits generally estimate time lost by key personnel as adding roughly 50 percent to total legal costs.

The Good News

That's the grim side of litigation. The good?

1. It's going to cost the other side just as much, which may force them to give up.

2. If you win, you can collect on all your legal fees, plus damages (assuming, of course, that the other side has the money to pay), and you often get lots of lucrative licensing deals, to boot.

• Gordon Gould, inventor of the optical laser, spent over $4 million on legal fees, most of it raised by a litigation syndicate. After his patents were upheld in 1987, the licensing money began pouring in: almost $18 million in the first two years, with (according to the *American Bar Association Journal*) nearly $200 million expected over the life of the patents. Before the suit was settled, Mr. Gould was earning $40,000 a year and living in a small New York apartment.

3. Above all, you often have to sue, whatever the cost, to protect your rights—especially your right to stay in business and to profit from your ideas.

The Two Main Kinds of Litigation

The two main kinds of patent lawsuits are infringements, and interferences.

Infringements you probably understand. Somebody holds a patent, and somebody else makes a product which allegedly uses that patent without permission. The patent holder sues the infringer.

Interference is a strictly American action, resulting from our "first to invent" system. Someone gets a patent, then someone else claims he actually invented the thing first, but couldn't get to the patent office soon enough. Or else a patent examiner simply notices that an application claims the same invention as some already granted patent, but with an earlier claimed date of invention. In either case, the examiner declares an "interference" action to determine which of the patents should be validated.

Unfortunately, you can be hit with an interference case at any time, even years after your patent issues.

How bad are interference actions?

In 1991 top interference attorney Danny Huntington told a legal conference in San Diego that he urges clients to forget about fighting an interference action unless they have at least "a couple of hundred thousand dollars" for legal fees. After recounting a case in which 637 papers were filed in one interference, he declared he personally favors elimination of the interference process, which he called both "crazy" and "a form of intellectual greenmail."

Interference cases are filed with the PTO itself, infringements in federal district court. Both kinds of cases can be appealed to the Federal Circuit Court of Appeals, a special court created to hear intellectual property cases. In either case you'll need attorneys who are specialists.

If you get into litigation, expect the opposition to attack you on any or all of the basic grounds for the granting of a patent. They'll try to show your idea was unoriginal or obvious or even useless. They'll very likely discover patents missed in the original patent searches; they may even, as happened in some of the water-bed litigation, argue that your idea first appeared hundreds of years ago. And, of course, they may even get much nastier than that, by trying to prove you defrauded the PTO or even stole the idea outright. The fact that patent litigation can be nasty, brutish, and long means you'll want to consider carefully the big question:

To Sue or Not to Sue?

The first time someone challenges your patent, either by suing you, or making a product your patent protects, you're going to think you know what you want. You're going to want the villain hung in the town square—for openers.

Instead, use an economic, not an emotional, model in deciding what to do. That means calculating (1) how much you're losing from the infringer—which tells you, too, roughly how much you are likely to be awarded in a winning lawsuit; (2) how well-heeled the infringer appears to be, which will tell both how likely he or she is to fight and how likely you are actually to collect your award; (3) how long you can afford to fight.

Once you've answered those questions as best you can, you're ready to:

Choose an Attorney You want an attorney who is:

• A patent litigator. If your patent was prepared by either a patent agent or a patent attorney who does not go into court regularly, you need other representation.

• Aggressive and a winner, but willing to listen to your input. Get recommendations, check records, but also ask yourself, can you work comfortably with this person? It's probably going to be a *long* association.

• Willing to evaluate frankly both the strengths and weaknesses of your case. You need not accept the first opinion you hear, but you want straight talk.

If you're doing the suing (especially if you're suing a big company), you may be able to get your attorney to take the case on a contingency basis, which means he or she collects a portion of any eventual winnings instead of billing you at an hourly rate. Many of the best attorneys never take contingency cases, but it doesn't hurt to ask.

Do What You Can for Yourself You can cut your bills and improve your results if you make efforts to help yourself. When you go to any attorney, have your documentation ready. Be ready to explain why your patent doesn't infringe or why the other fellow's does. Have sample products with you and be ready to walk the attorney through the key points. In short, pitch in—why pay some patent attorney between $200 and $400 an hour to do the simple things?

When It Comes to a Fight While we're urging you to stay out of court if possible, if you do go into court, play to win. This is hardball; you want to make matters so difficult and expensive for the other side that they'll see reason quickly. Go after them not only for patent infringement but for every other valid cause of action. If there are valid criminal charges, go after those, too. (Don't go after them capriciously, of course, but if you have a case, take it to the D.A.)

Just remember, once you sue somebody for infringement, they'll almost always try to get your patent(s) invalidated. So don't start unless you're prepared for the fight.

Small Opponents As a practical matter, you're often going to deal with small players. You'll probably want them either to leave the business (perhaps after paying you for sales they've cost you), or to cut a licensing deal to pay you royalties. You may also seek damages, but any damages will be proportional to your lost income. You can recover triple damages only if you can show the infringer willfully ignored your patent.

In any case, before you file suit, your attorney will send the infringer a letter, stating your claim and demanding that the infringer immediately either quit business or buy a license from you. Sometimes that will be enough; sometimes you'll actually have to file the suit before they come to terms; and sometimes you'll actually have to fight out the whole case, which is when things get expensive.

If you are seeking large damages, your attorney will try to frame the charges so as to engage the other side's business liability insurance. Even a shaky business may well carry several hundred thousand dollars' worth of such insurance, and if you engage it, there's a good chance of actually collecting some real money for your losses. (There's also an excellent chance of having to fight the insurance company's attorneys for the next five or so years, but that's part of the game).

Generally speaking, if your problem is with small-time infringers, your goal will probably be to force them into being reasonable. But what if a big corporation is infringing on your idea and making big money at it? Can you fight them and win?

Believe it or not, yes. Even better, you can sometimes get people to pay for the fight. Here's how:

Going after the Big Guys A patent doesn't have to be high-tech to interest a big company or to produce huge revenues. One major manufacturer was hit with an over-fifty-million-dollar judgment for taking an inventor's idea for a toy car improvement. In 1990, to take an even more dramatic case, inventor Robert W. Kearns won a $10.2 million payment from Ford, and in late 1991 he won another judgment against Chrysler. When his other suits, against virtually every major car company in the world, are resolved, he (and his attorneys) may well walk away with $100 million. That's all for the invention of a relatively simple but extremely useful device, the intermittent windshield wiper.

Those kinds of numbers make capitalists start drooling—and that's why, in recent years, something new has been created:

Getting Someone to Help You: Forming a "Litigation Syndicate" Patent lawsuits involving big companies and valuable patents have two main characteristics: They take a lot of money to prosecute and they can pay off hugely. As a result, companies are increasingly being formed to find and invest in infringed patents.

If you hold a patent that looks solid, and other people seem to be making a lot of money by infringing on it, and you don't have enough money to fight them by yourself, you might well be a candidate for one of these "litigation syndicates."

Basically, in a litigation syndicate, people buy shares in your lawsuit. These investors understand they're taking a risk. If you lose the case, you don't owe them anything. But if you win, they share in your winnings.

At this stage, such litigation syndicates (which go by a variety of names) are highly controversial, partly because most people are tired of

America's litigation glut and partly because some of the early ones ran afoul of an obscure legal principle called champerty—which is the process of investing in another's lawsuit strictly for profit, and which is illegal in most states.

The jury, in short, is still out on litigation syndicates, but unquestionably they have helped some inventors.

Blazing Water Beds: An Example In 1968 a San Francisco State College design graduate student named Charlie Hall invented a thing called the water bed. Mr. Hall, a notorious straight-arrow, tried to establish the water bed as expensive furniture. Meanwhile, competitors, playing on the bed's spicy image, built innumerable cheap knockoffs and finally drove Mr. Hall's company out of business by 1975.

Rather than give up, Mr. Hall started another company, to sell innovative camping gear. By 1985 he was once again wealthy.

And by 1985, water beds were a big, stable business, with many profitable companies, virtually all of them apparently infringing (knowingly or not) Charlie Hall's patents.

By now, though, Charlie Hall had the two key ingredients for successful patent litigation: enough money to hire lawyers, and infringers with enough money to be worth pursuing.

So he began the way you should: trying to force infringers into paying royalties without a long, nasty court fight. This part of the program worked fairly well; in short order he had signed agreements bringing him about $400,000 in royalties.

Then somebody decided to get tough. As Mr. Hall was filing a complaint with the ITC to stop an outfit called Intex from importing water beds from Taiwan, Intex countersued to invalidate his patents.

The cost of fighting Intex was likely to exceed what Mr. Hall could afford. To pay for it, he and an investor friend formed a partnership, called WBX, to raise money. By selling interests in the litigation, WBX raised $750,000. With that money Mr. Hall pressed his lawsuit, and in July 1991, he and his WBX partners were awarded $6.4 million.

Also in 1991 Mr. Hall and associates formed a new partnership, the Patent Protection Institute, to invest in patent cases. That is, they'll put up the money to litigate the case in return for a (large) share of any ultimate winnings.

Should you engage a litigation syndicate? They make good sense, provided you understand that they are taking a large risk with their money and expect proportionately large returns. You have to compensate not only the investors but the syndicate's management, which will expect generous salaries for all the years the lawsuits may last. That's fair enough, but it's just as fair that *you* should keep those large returns if you can raise the money yourself.

Overall, you might do better raising your own war chest, even if it means creating your own litigation syndicate. If you can't manage that, though, and can't raise the money any other way, by all means consider one or more of these new litigation syndicates.

Above all, though, 1) always investigate any patent-related group carefully before acting, and 2) never enter an agreement involving any of your intellectual property rights without consulting an attorney. Finally, watch the champerty issue: Make sure any group you join intends not only to fight for the patent rights but to use them once they're won.

Persistence: The Key Whatever else you decide to do, you need persistence to succeed in patent litigation. Jerome Lemelson was on his fifth set of attorneys when he finally won a verdict in his toy track suit against Mattel. Robert W. Kearns, inventor of the intermittent windshield wiper, got his first patent in 1969, but didn't win his first money until 1990.

If you decide to fight a major company, expect it to be a career. It may not be, of course—if inventors keep winning these big cases, big companies may rethink their strategies—but you have to be psychologically prepared.

Indeed, you'd better be psychologically ready to fight any and all challenges to your patents. But remember that many inventors enjoy the rewards of their inventiveness for their full seventeen years without ever stepping inside a courtroom.

50

Case Study: Peter Norton and Norton Utilities

"What advice would you give to people with ideas?"
"I don't think people with ideas should be given any advice at all."
—*from our interview with Peter Norton*

How do you make $100 million in seven years as an inventor?
Well, if you're Peter Norton you go through public schools as "a loner," attend (and drop out of) a small college in the Pacific Northwest known for "brilliant and unstable" students; get drafted and spend two years teaching combat first aid; spend five years in a Buddhist monastery in Northern California; bounce from job to job in computers; return to college and get your degree; and work for CalTech's Jet Propulsion Laboratory. Then, when you're pushing forty, you plunk your life savings into a company to sell some computer programs you invented while fiddling with the first IBM personal computer.

And that's all there is to it.

Oh, we forgot to mention: You ought to study calligraphy, as much as possible.

How do the pieces of this puzzle fit together?

Fitting In Peter Norton describes his growing up in Seattle in the 1950s and early 1960s as an "Ozzie and Harriet" existence, white picket fence and all. Yet he felt himself a classic outsider, who kept to himself and, without ever really breaking out, never really fit in.

A good student, he chose a school long favored by gifted outsiders: Reed College in Portland, Oregon, some two-thirds of whose students drop out before graduation. Majoring in math and physics, Norton found himself working hard for the first time. He did passably well, but couldn't really break through to excellence; as he puts it, he could do math, but he couldn't figure out "what math was." In particular, he couldn't grasp the mathematical concept of "elegance."

Meanwhile, like many creative people, he felt his "inner spirit fighting" the restraints of schooling.

What he enjoyed most at college was calligraphy. Indeed, he was among the ten or so students active in the art. But even there he found a problem: He was "extremely sensitive to rankings" and knew exactly where he ranked as a calligrapher. Moreover, he decided that people in all fields fell into three groups: those who knew little and cared little; those who worked hard, but had no gift for the craft; and those who both worked hard and had the gift—who were, in short, artists.

That led to the key insight: that to be remarkably good at anything, you need some kind of special engagement with the material. Lacking that almost mystical element, you'll never be more than competent at what you do, and what you do will never make you particularly happy.

Where did that leave Peter Norton? In math, physics, even calligraphy, he seemed always to fall in the middle group: He worked hard and was smart enough to do passably, but could never find the thing he loved, where he could distinguish himself. He could never discover the *art* of what he was doing.

Then a summer job changed everything.

A Duck to Water His first summer after college, Peter Norton took a job with a firm that prepared statistical data for insurance companies. In those years the work was done on adding machines—until one day his supervisor took him to a room filled with whirring electronic gear, pointed to it, and said: "Kid, we bought a computer and we don't know how to use it. There's the manual; see if you can figure it out."

Peter fell instantly in love with programming. It was a passion aided by the absence of chaperones: nobody in the company understood computers, so nobody bothered him. For someone who savored being left to find his own way, it was virtual heaven.

Soon he was writing programs at a blazing pace, and it was then that he began to understand the elusive "aesthetics of math," and especially the notion of "elegance." "Elegance," usually applied to mathematical proofs, is a hard concept for nonmathematicians, but it means both "cleverness" or "intelligence," and "economy": A proof is "elegant" if there can be no more concise or brilliant way of proving the same thing. In programming, the same aesthetic ideal existed—but as a practical demand, because a program was simply more efficient and affordable if it had elegance.* The passionate interest that had eluded Peter Norton elsewhere hit home here. Now he had the talent he had lacked for calligraphy, and the privacy he needed to teach himself the craft. Unambitious and extremely private, he found computer programming almost a perfect escape.

Enjoying Himself Here's an important point: Even before he was self-employed, Peter allowed himself plenty of time to savor his own achievements. He'd reread his own work for the pure pleasure of it: whenever he came upon a particularly elegant bit, he felt a sensation akin to "taking the creamy top frosting off the cake."

For a worker in a big corporation, this might have been merely an adjunct: big outfits have built-in systems of rewards. But for someone who was eventually to become an entrepreneur, it was a crucial habit of mind. Enjoying the process is one of the best things you can do for yourself.

On His Own But a programmer's life, solitary as it was, was not isolated enough for Peter, especially because, with the computer industry booming, most of his friends were striking out on their own, either as free-lance programmers or as consultants.

Peter simply "lacked the guts, the gumption" to make the move himself. He felt "like a puppy" watching all the big dogs strike out on their own.

Finally, after several years of listening to him lament his lack of nerve, one of Peter's friends handed him a contract job and told him "to put up or shut up."

Peter put up: He handled the job easily. But when the job ran out, late in 1981, he was back in the same old bind. He simply didn't have the nerve to make "cold calls" to drum up another free-lance job for himself.

It might have been back to the same old grind except for one curious coincidence. He'd been playing with a newly released product: the first IBM personal computer, which appeared in the fall of that year. To learn the system, he'd written a set of small programs that made the computer both easier and safer to use. Now that he faced the prospect of taking a regular job, it occurred to him that he might bundle these programs together and try to sell them. He called them:

---

*When Peter Norton started programming, "elegance" was desperately needed, because computer memories were so small and computer time was so expensive that inelegant programs either wouldn't fit in the machines or ran too slowly to be workable.

The Norton Utilities

In 1982, when he decided to go into business for himself, Peter Norton had no debts, no family, and about $30,000 in savings. From his point of view, it took no particular courage to risk that $30,000 on an invention: he was responsible only to himself, and would have had no real trouble getting another programming job.

Still, any business is a gamble. Peter told himself he'd be cautious and reasonable; if the business wasn't paying its way by the time his savings ran out, he'd fold it rather than go into debt.

Peter nearly did fold. After its first year the company, despite having sold almost $60,000 in software, was still losing money. Less than $5,000 remained in his bank account and, good as the software was, Norton Utilities had no money left for promotion. He'd told himself from the outset that "he wouldn't walk over the edge of the cliff," but now the cliff's edge was in sight.

Becoming a Trade Name Just in time Peter had an insight worthy of the best of professional marketers. He realized that the very technological glitter of computers had left an opening for someone who could humanize them. A "clumsy, klutzy, ill-speaking person" would make the ideal spokesman for a computer software firm. He would become what Frank Perdue was to chicken, or Tom Carvel to East Coast ice cream—a spokesman who was transparently not a professional, who appealed precisely because he was an ordinary Joe.

Does Peter Norton's idea of making himself the centerpiece of a massive advertising campaign seem contradictory for a self-described "shy person"? It probably does—until you realize that the "Peter Norton" writing the books and appearing on the software packages is largely a persona, a public image which perfectly preserved the private man.*

The advertising clicked swiftly, especially after Peter began writing newsletters dispensing exactly the sort of homey, trustworthy computer information his advertising promised. He gave the brochures for free to user groups and computer stores, and that led to another big break:

A publisher asked Peter to write an introductory text on the increasingly popular personal computer.

---

*Interestingly, despite Peter Norton's success as inventor, businessman, and patron of the arts, we could find only one published article about him—and that dealt mainly with the workings of the Norton Foundation.

Not many computer nerds would have felt comfortable writing for a generalist audience, but Peter had decided as an Army first-aid instructor that he had a talent for communicating. That was enough: *Inside the IBM PC* was the first of a series of Peter Norton books which, working symbiotically with the success of the Norton software, helped make him one of the half dozen or so best-known people in the PC world. In this, he seems to highlight one of the true gifts of the most-gifted idea people: He makes a strength of whatever he possesses.

Growing a Company

While books are written about the anguish of growth, Peter Norton managed the process with scarcely a hitch. Peter says the growth process went smoothly for three reasons:

First, he ducked the "start-up stress" problem entirely, simply by deciding it would be neat to have a "play room" with gadgets like postage meters and multiline phones. He enjoyed the process, though he was later methodical enough about it to attend the Harvard Business School's Smaller Company Management Program.

Second, by the age of forty, Peter was feeling "over the hill" as a software inventor. He places great stock in studies showing that scientists and mathematicians do their most creative work before thirty. Whether or not that functioned as a self-fulfilling prophecy, it certainly made him willing, even eager, to find bright young programmers and "urge them to wear the laurel wreaths"—to take the lead and the glory in designing new software.

Above all, Peter says his lifelong habit of avoiding or downplaying anything at which he could not excel (what he calls "the arrogance of shyness") made him avoid the sorts of entanglements which, while they help companies grow, often end up with their founders kicked out onto the streets.

That approach worked well. In its seven years as an independent company, Norton produced a string of well-regarded, successful products, with very few management glitches. Unlike many entrepreneurs, moreover, Peter Norton kept complete control of his company, and kept the overwhelming share of the wealth created when the company was bought, for about $70 million, by the Symantec Corporation in 1989.

Some analysts at the time argued that the sale was inevitable: The software industry was consolidating, and Norton was too small a company to stay independent and privately held. In fact, the company was preparing to go public when the Symantec offer materialized.

That's a matter for business theorists to debate. For our purposes, though, *this* is what matters:

Two years after the sale of the company, Peter Norton's fortune, including royalties on Norton products now sold by Symantec, had topped $100 million, and he was free to pursue his cultural/philanthropic interests almost full-time. He had gone from free-lance computer programmer to centimillionaire in seven years.

Obviously, there's much to be learned from Peter Norton's approach. But we were particularly drawn to three more general ideas:

1. Don't waste time trying to conform to social norms or agonizing about quirks in your character. "Quirks" can be quite as much strengths as weaknesses; it all depends upon how contented you are with them and how skillful you are at applying them. Put up with mainstream ways as long as you have to, then use your desire for independence as an extra spur to putting your idea into action, so you can then live the way you want.

2. Don't agonize over supposed flaws in your background, training or opportunities. What the heck kind of training is two years teaching recruits to bandage bullet wounds, followed by five years in a Buddhist monastery, for a guy who wants to build a software empire? It's perfect training if he has the imagination to put it to the right use.

3. Enjoy the process. You can make life as miserable as you want to, but why bother? Books are written on surviving the stress of being in business for yourself. Peter Norton's office is decorated with highly playful, colorful modern art, and he often greets visitors with customized, computer-generated placards, and answers his correspondence on oversize postcards with full-color pictures of himself playing with his children.

In short, if you have the capacity for creativity—and nearly every human does—delight in it. The rest will follow in time.

Part Four

THE BUSINESS
OF *IDEAS*

———

TRADEMARKS, TRADE SECRETS, AND FRANCHISING YOUR GREAT BUSINESS IDEA

51

What's the Good of a Business Idea?

IF YOU ASKED a hundred people on the street to name someone creative, probably most would name artists, a few would name scientists or inventors, and almost none would name businesspeople.

That's a shame, because business can be at least as creative as any other field. Indeed, many businesses begin with creativity in the arts or sciences, then grow by adding layers of creativity in sales, marketing, financial infrastructure, or any other part of the business process.

In this section we're going to show you how to run with a business idea, how to define, protect, and exploit the underlying ideas of your business. We're also going to show you how itemizing your ideas, your intellectual property, will prepare you for perhaps the most important way you can profit from them: franchising.

Finally, we'll profile the man who created one of the most significant business ideas of the 1980s, Sol Price, whose idea of the membership discount warehouse allowed him in just fifteen years to build a seven-billion-dollar-a-year operation and a personal fortune of well over $300 million.

52

The Toughest Job Around: Protecting a Business Idea

HOW DO YOU PROTECT a business idea?

The short answer, of course, is that you can't protect the idea itself. Fast food restaurants, membership discount stores, mail order retailing—every great business idea is cloned, and usually very quickly.

Actually, that's a good thing. A monopoly on an entire business idea would be totally anticompetitive, and so, unfair to consumers and to the country.

But what creative parts of your business *can* you protect?

Actually, quite a few.

"Submethods" and Trademarks

We've said that businesses are special because they often contain many levels of creativity. To put that differently, they contain many "submethods" which, together, make your business succeed.

Basically, there are two parts to protecting your overall business idea. You try to protect all the submethod ideas of your business—any inventions, copyrightable materials, or trade secrets—and you protect the sum of all those things: your products and / or your business name, as embodied in your trademark(s) and trade name(s).

Most of this part will be devoted to trademarks and the ways (especially, franchising) to profit from them—but first, let's talk briefly about ways to collect and control those submethods:

The I.P. Audit: Finding Your Business Submethods

In the 1980s, intellectual property law firms began offering a new service: an "Intellectual Property Audit."

An "I.P. Audit" means that a team of lawyers, sometimes backed by accountants, searches your business for all your original ideas, sees how well you've protected them, and then assigns them a cumulative value. Professional I.P. Audits have two main uses: to prepare a business for any major financial event, especially its sale or merger, and to show the owners ways they may better protect valuable intellectual assets.

Doing It Yourself Obviously, you can't match a professional audit. But you can adopt the basic idea to help you understand your business much better—and to locate those valuable, protectable submethods within it.

Just get a large notepad and go through everything in your operation. List how you do it; describe your methods in detail. Don't jump to the "important" ideas; follow goods and supplies from the time they reach your premises to the time they leave. What kind of machinery do (or will) you use? Where do (or will) you buy supplies? And so on: Even small ideas can be valuable, whether it's a recipe for a tasty hamburger topping, or a special salespitch that gets your people in to see major buyers.

Your audit should bring you these advantages:

First, it can inspire immediately useful ideas about improvements, dangers to correct, even tips to pass from one department to another.

Second, a mere habit of being analytical about your business will prepare you to grow through either franchising or opening new branches. Whether you're selling franchises, or simply training new managers, you can't really teach your business until you understand it.

Most important, your homemade audit of a going business will alert you to submethods (from computer programs to employee manuals) that can be protected by patents or copyrights. In particular, be alert for:

Unnoticed Inventions It's by no means unheard of for small businesses to invent, almost accidentally, useful machinery. Thus, the country's largest maker of madeleine cookies actually made its equipment by adapting other people's castoffs. With much of the machinery re-engineered to fulfill entirely new functions, the company's as much a technical as a culinary marvel. More often than you'd suspect, the machinery you create or modify is original enough to deserve a patent.*

If you use some original-seeming gadget, tell your attorney. You

---

*That is, a patent on your inventive contribution.

may well have a patentable invention on your hands.

What about Everything Else? Your I.P. audit may well leave you feeling uneasy, because unless you're running an arts- or a technology-based company most of your valuable ideas won't fall directly under either copyright or patent protection.

What about those ideas? Can you protect them?

53

Trade Secrets

YOUR I.P. AUDIT will give you a list of the submethods in your business. With a lawyer's help, you can then protect everything that can be patented, copyrighted, or trademarked.

But what can you do if you have useful ideas or information—strategies, customer lists, or other kinds of business intellectual property—that don't qualify for a patent, trademark, or copyright?

Keep It a Secret! Few people realize that if you take certain basic steps, the law will protect you against the theft of things you cannot, or would rather not, protect by other means.

While "trade secret" has something of a high-tech ring, it actually means any method or information that a) has economic value because it isn't generally known, and b) you take steps to protect. Trade secrets can include things as simple as your formula for bidding on contracts or the place you buy some rare line of merchandise.

You protect these secrets by a) declaring them trade secrets and b) taking consistent, formal measures to keep them confidential. While the definition of a trade secret varies from state to state (check with your lawyer), in nearly every state you'll gain important protection from those two basic steps.

Now, the great weakness of a trade secret is that anyone who discovers or develops the method or information independently has just as much right to it as you do. But trade secrets aren't simply "better than nothing" protection. In some cases, they're the most powerful protection you can get.

Coca Cola and Wrigley's:
Two Great Trade Secret Programs

Perhaps the best known of all modern trade secrets is the formula for Coca Cola; for over a century the company has kept it a virtually perfect secret. The formula is something of a legend, with reports (true or not) that only three people in the entire company know it, that it's kept in a massive vault in the company's Atlanta headquarters, and so on.

An even more trade-secret-intensive operation, though, is Wrigley's chewing gum. Wrigley's is a major player worldwide in gum, partly because it holds a technological lead over other manufacturers. Despite that investment in technology, it keeps not only its recipes but its machinery as trade secrets, not patents. Here's a description of one of the company's thirteen plants:

Wrigley's sprawling red-brick compound in southwest Chicago . . . is guarded by security cameras and tall barbed-wire gates. Were it not for a small, brass nameplate and the smell of mint hanging in the air, the factory would be a complete mystery in the mixed-use neighborhood of warehouses and modest old houses. Uniformed security guards patrol the compound in Jeeps. Their "GUM" license plates are another clue to what goes on here. . . . It is best that nobody else knows anything about them at all, Wrigley figures. —*Wall Street Journal,* May 25, 1991

It's no accident that Coca Cola and Wrigley are both food companies. Food recipes tend to remain constant over time, and (as we mentioned in Part One) a trade secret, properly managed, can give far longer protection than any patent or copyright.

Less Obvious Trade Secrets You may not have a formula as valuable as that of Coca Cola. You may never want a program as rigorous as Wrigley's. Can you still benefit from trade secret law?

Absolutely!

In Los Angeles in 1991, a jury awarded a janitorial service $2 million from a competitor who planted a "mole" inside the company. This mole slipped the competitor information about the firm's clients and what they were paying, and even worse, hired relatives of his to work for the firm but to sabotage each job. Then the competitor could swoop down and capture the business. The dishonest competitor was found guilty of both theft of trade secrets (the client lists and contract information) and unfair competition (the sabotaging of jobs). (*Los Angeles Times,* April 19, 1991)

Basic Trade Secret Methods In short, even the simplest business can have valuable trade secrets. To protect yours, start by following these simple steps:

1. *Make your employees sign trade secret agreements as a condition of employment.* Standardized forms are available from many sources. Consult an attorney for your specialized needs.

2. *Make sure your employees know what is a trade secret.* Your company manual (and training program) should explain not only the general idea of trade secrecy—but what parts of your business must be kept confidential. Any documents containing trade secrets should be clearly stamped (traditionally, in red ink) "Confidential Trade Secrets."

3. *Train your employees in protecting secrets.* The worst thing that can happen is for your people to give away secrets innocently. Salespeople are often the worst offenders—they want to impress potential buyers, so they give away your secrets to make themselves and you sound important.

4. *Restrict access to trade secrets.* See that valuable materials are kept by only a few people—and far away from any copying machines. Keep an "access log," so you know who's seen what, and when.

What else should you watch?

Trade Secrets: Keep Them Safe from Lawyers Another way trade secrets leak is through attorneys during legal disputes, even if you're not a party to the basic dispute.

What do you do when somebody official-sounding wants information?

Unless it's your own attorney asking—never tell anybody, attorney or otherwise, anything about any trade secrets, especially if there's a legal dispute involved. Some attorneys will try everything, from threats, to plays for sympathy, to outright lies, to get information. Once you've provided it, you've seriously compromised your trade-secret protection. They're threatening to sue you if you won't talk? Or promising your help will save the spotted owl? Tough! Just repeat the following:

"I'm sorry, but you'll have to talk to our attorneys."

You don't have an attorney? Then say:

"I'm sorry, but we consider that privileged information."

If they want your information badly enough, they'll go into court to get it. That's not pleasant, but it's smarter than giving away your most valuable secrets.

Watch Those Consultants and Independent Contractors Make anybody who does contract work for you agree in writing to treat anything they learn about your operation, or develop on your behalf, as your trade secret. Otherwise, your competitors may well use your consultants to get your secrets.

That happened to Lamb-Weston, Inc. In 1990, they won patents for curlicue French fryers. Meanwhile, they discovered, a competitor had hired their main engineering consultant to design a duplicate system.

Lamb-Weston was lucky: Because it had signed the consultant to a confidentiality agreement, the court barred the competitor from selling its French-frying system anywhere in the world for eight months. An eight-month lead was a tremendous advantage for Lamb-Weston, but the judge ruled that that was what they would have had if their secret had not been stolen.

Trade Secrets and Formal Security To protect secrets, you need not only legal documents, such as nondisclosure forms, but concrete security measures.

Don't go overboard. Basic precautions should make you quite safe and establish your court case for secrecy should that ever become necessary.

For moderately important secrets, you should consider paper shredders, computer security programs (simple programs for PCs cost about $100), multi-strike ribbons on your typewriters, and a safe for important documents. If your secrets are more valuable, consider hiring a security consulting firm to review your systems. Also keep in mind two modern sources of leaks:

Faxes. Establish procedures for transmission of trade secrets. In 1991, a major law firm lost three months of intensive jury-selection work in a national class action suit when a temporary clerk accidentally loaded a stack of confidential information into a fax machine and hit a speed-dial button—automatically sending all the information to the other side's lawyers! (Aside from any malpractice lawsuits that might arise, the lost legal time alone was probably worth $250,000 or more.)

See that only qualified people handle your trade secrets—on every level. And consider adding a brief confidentiality statement to your fax cover sheet.

If you have really valuable trade secrets, consider a fax machine that encodes transmissions. Today, hi-tech companies buy most of these machines, but with the gear getting cheaper, it's becoming a reasonable option for anybody with important trade secrets.

Cellular phones. Technically, anybody with a cellular scanner can eavesdrop on your cellular phone calls.

Again, the concern is not so much that somebody will be out there intentionally spying on you (most people with scanners are probably just amusing themselves), as that some attorney in a court case someday will ask, "You call these trade secrets? Then why were you blabbing about them over a broadcast system like a cellular phone?" A little discretion is all you need to solve the problem—although, if you absolutely must discuss secrets over the airways, encoding phones are available.

Remember the overarching principle: To establish that something is a secret, you have to show that you've treated it as a secret.

Trade Secrets: The Penalties

How much cash compensation can you get for a stolen secret?

In 1985, John Stegora, a 3M contract worker, mailed samples of a forthcoming 3M medical product to four of 3M's competitors.Three of those competitors simply ignored the offer, but the fourth, Johnson & Johnson, apparently used it. Mr. Stegora was caught by the FBI, convicted and sentenced to prison, but at Stegora's trial a J & J official denied under oath having studied the sample Stegora sent him.

Actually, J & J did use the sample—and so brought its own competing product to market three months ahead of schedule. But only after 3M filed a patent infringement suit was the use by J & J accidentally revealed.

The result? On May 1, 1991, a Minnesota Federal Court fined Johnson & Johnson $116.3 million for patent infringement and theft of trade secrets. (*Business Week,* May 5, 1991)

Yes, you can win big if somebody steals your trade secrets.*

Trade Secrets: Going After a Big Company A big company, with big lawyers, can collect big money when there's an outright theft. But what if you're a *small* company—and what if you provided the secrets, in expectation of future business? Are you sunk?

Not at all!

In the mid-1980s, the Harley-Davidson motorcycle company made an oral promise to a company owned by Christy J. Dello: If Dello would develop a new muffler for Harley-Davidson, Dello's company would get

---

*If somebody offers you a competitor's trade secrets, you should simply: (1) call the competitor and tell them what's up, and (2) call the FBI. The FBI can't act unless a federal law has been violated—but they will put you in touch with the right agencies.

the exclusive contract to build the mufflers for H-D. On the basis of that promise, Dello borrowed $500,000 to expand his factory.

Instead of giving Dello the contract, H-D took his plans, modified them somewhat, and gave the contract to another company. Dello lost his home and business, and filed for bankruptcy. He also filed suit— against H-D for fraud, malice, and misappropriation of trade secrets.

In its defense, Harley-Davidson argued that Dello was too slow to deliver the needed mufflers, and tried to alter the contract H-D had offered.

The result? The court ruled H-D had no right to the trade-secret information, and was responsible for Dello's financial collapse. And H-D had to pay roughly $1.2 million in compensation, $5.5 million in punitive damages, and $400,000 in legal fees.*

So trade secrets can be a powerful tool, even for a small company facing a large one. Use them wherever you properly can.

What You Can Take from a New Employee

Now, let's reverse the trade secret question, and ask briefly what you can honorably do if you're on the other side of the trade secret question.

Of course, you're not going to accept anything that's obviously stolen: documents, formulas, and the like. But what about the more common situation, where you hire somebody who knows a lot about a competitor's operation?

Frankly, that's a gray area in the law. Your lawyer will probably look first at the new employee's old employment agreement, to see how many of its restrictions will stand up in light of your state's trade secret laws. Often, the old contract will have provisions unenforceable in law (for example, if it says the employee can *never* contact old clients).

Overall, though, the choice will come down to your decision about how much information to take from that new employee. Here's our best general advice:

If you use too much information too obviously, you can very well expect to get sued for theft of trade secrets, and also (since you and the new employee were both involved), to be accused of conspiracy.

Probably the safest advice is this: If you happen to come across a

---

*In fairness to Harley-Davidson, we should point out that the company has excellent relations with many small suppliers.

competitor's method which seems better than yours, don't copy it; use it to inspire you to something better. After all, you don't want to match the competition, you want to *beat* them—right?

Remember, too, that what goes around tends to come around. Once you start pushing the boundaries of what's considered fair play in your field, your competitors will surely do the same.

Trade Secrets vs. Patents: The Down Side While trade secrets are powerful, we don't want to mislead you into thinking they're more powerful than patents. Where inventions are concerned, a patent allows you to sue any infringer—even if he was unaware he was infringing. If you can prove the infringement was "deliberate and knowing," you can collect big-time: all his profits, plus triple damages and attorney fees. This kind of wallop tends to deter people from cheating you.

By contrast, to prevail in a "theft of trade secret" lawsuit, you must prove that the secret was unlawfully taken or received—and that's a tough standard of proof.

In short, for most inventions you want a patent. On the other hand, you may choose to protect some inventions (generally, those that have either very short or very long economic lives) via trade secrets. More importantly, trade secrets can help protect other parts of your business, such as customer lists, which are otherwise unprotectable.

Summing Up A sound program of patents, copyrights, and trade secrets, designed with your attorney's help, will give you the best possible protection for your business's submethods.

Now let's discuss the really good stuff: what you can do to protect your overall great business idea.

54

Picking Your Trade Name and Trademarks

IF YOU'VE READ THIS FAR, you know about patents, copyrights, and trade secrets. Congratulations! One more topic, and you'll know all the basics for protecting your business ideas.

The topic is trademarks and trade names.* Here are the basic rules:

1. Trademarks are words or symbols used to identify goods or services in commerce.

2. Trademarks can be claimed for use as long as priority (that is, first use) can be established, even if they are later registered by someone else. But only by registering them can you block all subsequent users. If a search shows you have a valid claim on a mark, you can accompany it by the ™ or ᔆᴹ (for service mark) symbol. However, you can use the more powerful ® symbol only if your mark is registered with the Patent and Trademark Office.

3. Trademark rights are created and preserved by use. In this regard, trademarks are distinct from all other forms of idea protection. You can write a novel and throw it on the shelf, and the rights are still yours for your lifetime and another fifty years. Patent rights go to the first person to invent, whether or not he actually builds the gadget. But trademarks must be put and kept in commercial use to have force. Any name that goes out of commercial use will, after a short time, be tossed back into the pool of available trademarks.

On the other hand—

4. If properly protected, trademarks are forever. As long as you take the proper steps to protect your mark and to use it in commerce, it can keep its value virtually forever.

Trademarks: The Legal Value Here's the odd thing: Even though the value of the trademark derives from the products that bear it, the law gives extremely strong protection to the trademark itself.

Accordingly, even though trademarks are theoretically protected to keep consumers from being cheated by imitation goods, such marks provide a kind of blanket protection for all the otherwise unprotectable submethods of your business: the materials you choose, the way you control quality, and so on. No rip-off artist can make an inferior version

---

*Technically, trade names are words that identify your business in commerce, while trademarks include both words and any other marks or designs (like Apple Computer's multicolored apple-with-a-bite-out-of-it) used to identify *goods*. Words can be trademarks only if they appear on products as primary identification: thus, "Xerox" is both a trade name (for the company) and a trademark (when it appears on the machines).

Different laws protect trade names and trademarks. Trade names are protected only in state and common law; trademarks are also protected by the federal Lanham Act. To get a general grasp of the issues, though, you can overlook that distinction; for the sake of readability, we're going to use trade name and trademark interchangeably. Ditto for service names and marks (which technically protect business services) and certification names and marks (such as the Underwriters Laboratory "UL"), which certify goods as having special characteristics.

of your product or service, stick *your* name on it (or even something very similar), and make a quick buck at your expense.

Trademark, in short, is the umbrella protection for your business—and that's why big companies will spend tens, even hundreds of millions, to develop and protect their marks.

The Magic of a Name

The right name, after all, has tremendous value: "Rolls-Royce," "Ferrari," or "Tiffany" immediately evokes a whole series of powerful, positive images. These (and many others) are legally protected trade names that have become universally known brand names.

As your company name becomes recognized—as it reaches a point where consumers will buy your product at least partly because of it—it becomes an increasingly valuable piece of intellectual property.

So the idea of creating and protecting a valuable future mark should be foremost in your mind when you name your company and its products.

You want, in short, the perfect name, the one that's as exciting as your business idea itself. You want to use flair and imagination—but you also want to choose a name you can protect.

The Law of Marks—Our Short Course

Basically, the law will keep others from using any properly registered trade name, or any name confusingly similar to it, no matter what other claims they may have.* For example:

"Gallo," the wine-making company, is among the best-known names in the liquor business. So it's probably no surprise that when a Guatemalan beer maker named Gallo wanted to sell in the United States, it was forced to pick another name. The brewers didn't even argue; they just changed the name to "Famosa 1896" and went about their business.

But when a member of the Gallo (wine-making) family wanted to use his own name on his cheese, the brothers who owned the vineyards said no and went into court to stop him.

---

* Technically, federal law also prohibits *dilution* of existing trademarks, which means using anything too close to a registered trade name, even if no reasonable person would probably be confused by it. Thus, even though nobody would be likely to believe that a "Xerox" candy bar was made by the copier company, the courts would prohibit your making one.

The result?

The court backed the wine makers. Not even the claim of a birthright is strong enough to overcome the rights of ownership of people with a trademark.

We'll show in the next chapter how to check to see if a name's been claimed; for now just remember that the governing rules for rejecting a trade name are those questions of *confusing similarity* and *dilution*.

Prohibited Categories What other factors should shape your choice of a trade name or mark?

Superficially, you can register any unclaimed name or mark. In practice, the PTO will reject trademarks found to be:

• Mere ornamentation, not helping to identify "the goods or services as coming from a particular source."

• Immoral, deceptive, or scandalous.

• Insulting to "persons, institutions, beliefs, or national symbols," or fraudulently suggesting any connection with the same.

• Re-creations of the "flag or coat of arms or other insignia of the United States, or a State or municipality, or any foreign nation."

• Evocative of any living person who has not given his or her written consent; or of "any deceased U.S. President during the life of his widow, unless she has given her consent."

Those are the PTO's guidelines. In addition, you need to:

Keep It Legal This may sound too obvious to mention, but the mere fact that you can register a trade name does not mean you can ignore all the other laws governing trade.

Aside from the few rule-outs mentioned above, the PTO is checking only to see whether anyone else has claimed the name you want. Registration of your name doesn't give you any warranty that it's otherwise legal to use it.

For example, it's a federal crime to misrepresent the country of origin of your products. If you're making Widgets in Taiwan, they should say "Made in Taiwan." If the parts are made in Taiwan, but the final product is assembled in the USA, they should say "Assembled in USA of Parts Made in Taiwan."

Despite this, attorneys regularly hear from too-clever entrepreneurs who've decided they can register a trade name like "Widget USA," then make the widgets in Burma or somewhere, leave off the country of origin, and let everyone think they're selling an American-made product.

In fact, all this does is open you up to other charges, from false advertising to unfair competition.

The same holds for health claims. Just because the PTO accepts the trade name "Superlowfat Fudge" doesn't mean you won't be sued by either the federal government or individual states for false advertising if your fudge is, in fact, fatty. Indeed, you can even be at risk if you imply health benefits you can't really prove; one major company was challenged by the FTC simply because its cooking oil used an electrocardiogram chart as a logo, thereby (supposedly) making an implied claim of healthfulness.

By the same token, you can't use the image of any public person who died less than fifty years ago, because their "rights to publicity" survive. Hence, no "Elvis" chewing gum or "Albert Einstein" volleyball shoes, unless you get permission from their respective estates.

Call your company whatever you like (as long as the PTO and your state authorities agree), but don't assume a trademark gives you any extra-legal authority to misrepresent your product's ingredients, healthfulness, country of origin, or anything else.

Be Socially Responsible In 1991 G. Heileman Brewing found itself in trouble after it named a perfectly legal high-alcohol malt liquor "PowerMaster" and focused sales efforts on the urban black community. Heileman argued, with a certain logic, that it was only responding to a strong existing market, but the idea of associating alcohol—and so, drunkenness—with "power" and mastery, touched a sensitive nerve, especially in a community already hard-hit by alcohol abuse. Soon community leaders were on the attack; Heileman was on the evening news, and very quickly the Bureau of Alcohol, Tobacco and Firearms was asking for a name change.

A little forethought in making up your name list can save you a lot of trouble. Why risk being irresponsible?

Some Names Are Easier to Protect Than Others

Some marks are either unavailable by law or else simply unwise. What else counts?

Over the years the courts have granted some kinds of marks more protection than others. When you pick your name, you might want to watch:

The Levels of Strength The courts have recognized four levels of strength for trademarks and names, and have granted protection accordingly.

The four levels depend upon the distinctiveness of the mark. Since the point of a trademark is to help consumers tell your goods and services from someone else's, the more distinctive your mark, the more protection the courts will award. These aren't ironclad categories, but they do offer some guidelines.

The four levels of distinctiveness, in order of decreasing protection, are:

Coined or fanciful names. These, the most distinctive, are given the strongest protection. Examples would be Xerox, Exxon, or Sanka.

Arbitrary names. These include words with dictionary meanings, but without any clear connection with what the company does or what the product is or how it's made. Examples would include Chevron or Shell, when applied to the petroleum retailers.

Suggestive names. These imply something about the company or its products—most often, of course, its strengths or virtues. Examples would be "Ever-ready" or "Die-Hard" batteries.

One fairly common tactic is to take a suggestive name and give it an exotic spelling—"Lok-Tyte," for example—that pushes it closer to the "Coined or Fanciful" category.

Descriptive names. These explicitly describe a characteristic of a product or company: for example, "Nickel Cadmium" batteries. These names, as you might expect, are the weakest of all; the courts aren't going to let you claim as your exclusive property some part of the English language which your competitors would normally have to use to describe their own products. Competitors would make what's called a "fair use" defense of their actions, the courts would almost certainly support them.

Indeed, the courts usually protect descriptive names only if they have attained "Secondary Meaning"—that is, if the public has come to associate the name with the particular product. Thus, "General Motors" is probably merely descriptive (even though, technically, cars are powered by "engines," not "motors"), and "International Business Machines" is certainly descriptive, but both have demonstrable secondary meaning. Most people think of particular products and a particular company when they hear the names "IBM" or "GM"—hence the names are strongly protected.

Also in this category are surnames. Thus "Jones" is probably an unprotectable name, since when most people hear it, they don't think of any particular product. On the other hand, "Gallo," "Ferrari," and "Armani" all probably bring to mind particular companies, with distinctive products—so, again, the courts have protected them.

Those are the basic legal considerations. What about the *art* of choosing a name?

Choosing a Name   A choice business name is so desirable that plenty of consultants are ready to help you find the right one—for a nice fee, often well over $10,000. A stylish logo to go with it can add another $25,000 from a top graphic designer.

Are these people worth the money?

Maybe—and maybe not. There's a good chance you can do as well as the naming experts, especially if you start early, when you're first excited by your great idea.

You already know that different types of names have degrees of protectability: a made-up word, like XYZLBLOP Corp., would have the greatest degree of protectability. Unfortunately, such words have the smallest degree of natural charm and the least ability to inspire strong feeling.

So your first job is to decide whether you want maximum protectability or maximum meaning. If you decide at the outset that you want protectability, by all means make up a word. If you want maximum meaning, try this:

As part of your basic business plan, write a brief statement of what distinguishes your business—its most original, exciting feature. Boil that down to a handful of words, then go to a thesaurus and look up action-packed synonyms. Don't forget the classical (and, if you're respectful about it, biblical) images, and consider using slang names if you have the right kind of product: Burger King's "Whopper" was certainly a good choice.

If, at the end of this simple procedure, you decide you want to hire a consultant or to name the company after yourself, that's fine. At least you won't end up paying some consultant $10,000 to tell you to name your new one-minute car wash "Jiffy-Wash."

Those high-priced consultants will use basically the same method: they'll get you to describe the "core idea" or "core value" of your business, then try to find words and symbols which capture that in exciting ways. They also provide some secondary services, such as running the names through computer lists, to make sure they don't provoke negative images in foreign languages.*

Apples & Rainbows: Why Names Aren't Decisive   Above all, before you agonize about names, consider the following tale of two computers.

Naming "experts" (often connected with advertising agencies) often cite Apple Computers and its rainbow-colored apple logo as perfect examples of trademarking. Students give apples to teachers, and Apple wanted the school market; the multicolored design was friendly at a time when computers were still thought of as strange, cold, and daunting; and the apple has been associated with the power of knowledge since biblical times.

Fine—but now consider this: About the time Apple was taking off, DEC, a vastly larger company with a terrific reputation, also introduced personal computers. Their logo? A bright multicolored rainbow. Pretty similar, eh? A rainbow is a symbol of joy, of reward (the pot of gold), and even of peace—also dating to biblical times.

Yet the Rainbow computer was perhaps the only complete flop in the distinguished history of DEC. Why? Mostly because the machine itself didn't deliver on any of the features implied by the bright, cheerful logo: it wasn't particularly easy to use or particularly friendly. It also used a nonstandard microprocessor, which knocked it out of the general business market. DEC lost nearly a billion dollars on the project.

Artistic, creative trademarks are great. If you have lots of money, you might even hire a professional designer to produce something gorgeous. Indeed, one sound reason for hiring a designer as you get bigger is simply to create a mark distinctive enough that people infringing it will be easily beaten in court.

Just remember: At day's end, products make the name, not the other way around.

What a Name Can Really Do for You

Actually, the best early use for your trade name is as a way of focusing, for yourself and your investors, workers, and customers, what

---

*And bear in mind what happened to the world's largest grower of popping corn after he decided to sell a new breed of corn under his own brand name. He hired some snazzy Chicago consultants; after grilling him for hours, thinking about it for a week, and billing him $13,000, they told him to name the new brand after himself. So he did—he called it "Orville Redenbacher's."

exactly you want your company to be. If the folks designing the first Apple computers were reminded by their name that they were supposed to be making friendly computers, terrific. If consumers got the message, better still.

Do try to pick a name meaningful to you and to others. Be aware, though, that even the most appealing name will quickly fail if the products don't support it. There are plenty of boring names out there attached to great products and wildly successful companies. IBM, AST, ALR, NCR, and other alphabet companies sell a lot of computers, too.

So don't agonize over your name. Pick it—protect it—develop it. But above all, remember that the most important issue will be making the name you pick mean something.*

A Final Note You will *lose* your trademark if you let it fall into ordinary English usage, as a generic term, a verb, or an adjective. Of course, this is a rare occurrence, but it's interesting to know that famous trademarks that have fallen into common use include "Kerosene," "Escalator," and "Shredded Wheat." ("Heroin" actually was another, and its initial sales were so strong that they forced the parent company, A. G. Bayer, to delay by many months introducing still another trade-named product. The delayed product? They called it "Aspirin.")

55

Protecting Your Trademarks

YOU'VE THOUGHT THROUGH the laws and the real core of your great idea and found the perfect name (and perhaps logo or mark) for your business.

How do you protect it?

---

* Sometimes, you can simply buy a great trade name that's no longer in active use. Thus, in 1985 Mr. Benny Alagem bought the Packard Bell name from Teledyne for about $100,000. With the slogan, "America grew up listening to us. It still does" (and some great products), Alagem made the new Packard Bell into the third-largest U.S. PC maker in just six years. (*Business Week,* January 27, 1992)

Introduction: Why DBAs Aren't Enough

Most people who start small businesses never even think of registering a trademark or trade name. The few who do design a logo for their company simply use it—and most merely get "public domain" logos from their local print shop. As for trade names, they normally just file the standard "fictitious name" or a "Doing Business As" (DBA) form at their local city hall.

For a small business with no growth plans, a DBA might serve: It meets the usual legal requirements for a going business by merely making the company's ownership a matter of public record.

But a DBA, while a necessary step, is extremely weak legal protection, and no good at all if your great idea is going to grow into a good-sized business.

Anybody whose *registered* trade name is either the same as your unregistered name or even confusingly similar to it can force you to change yours. If you're stubborn about it, they can then sue you for willful infringement and seek big damages.

It doesn't matter if you've been doing business for twenty years; if they registered their mark even one day before you started business, they can make you change. Even worse, whether or not you have priority (that is, earlier use of the name), anyone who has registered that name federally can stop you from ever doing business under that name across state lines.

Your great idea, in short, will never be a great business unless you properly trademark your business name.

How bad is a name change?

Think for a minute how much you'll have invested in stationery, labels, advertising, and signs. Add in the number of people who know your product by name and won't be able to find it anymore. Include the time lost in making the change, and factor in a bit for the consumers who'll (wrongly) think you had to change the name because of criminal wrongdoing. And don't forget the legal bills.

Colliding with someone else's registered trade name can ruin a business. How can you avoid it?

The Bare Minimum If you're starting a new business, you should at least search the trademark registries to make certain nobody else has claimed the name or mark you want. Then, if you register for just a DBA, that registration will establish your prior use and probably make you relatively immune from attack.

If you have any intention of building that business into anything big, though, you should absolutely take the next step and register your trademark.

Who Regulates Trademarks?

Because the federal government technically regulates only interstate commerce, you need, unfortunately, to deal with at least two regulatory bodies: your state government (usually the office of the Secretary of State), and the U.S. Patent and Trademark Office.

Then, of course, if you're ever lucky enough to sell your products overseas, you'll have to get international registrations. At that point, you'll probably need an intellectual property law firm to monitor your marks and see that the renewal fees are paid on time worldwide. These days, many American start-up companies find themselves exporting before the end of their first year in business. If you think that might happen to you, day one is not too early to ask your attorney about international trademark registration.

What Does a Search Cost and How Long Does It Take?

The simplest approach to searching is to have an intellectual property attorney do it for you. A basic search of state and federal registries and common law usages (that is, names used by going businesses but not registered as trademarks) normally takes 7 to 10 business days, and costs about $250–$500 per name, including the attorney's interpretation of the search results.

That's not a fortune, but if the search shows the name is taken, you'll have to pay a like amount to search your next-choice name. The process can get expensive if (as often happens) you need to try six or seven names before you find one you can claim. You can save yourself some of that money by eliminating as many bad choices as possible before ordering professional searches. Here's how:

Start by checking with trade associations, trade directories, and local chambers of commerce for existing users of the name you want, or of names similar to it. If you don't find any existing users (and you're willing to invest a little more of your own time to save legal fees) you can then do your own preliminary federal trademark search.

Most libraries which have the PTO's CASIS patent search system also have the CD-ROMs for the federal trademark registry. To use the system, simply identify which of the 42 product and service categories your mark applies to, then look up the name.* For example, if your mark is "Bunny Snugs" for baby clothes, you'll search category 25: "Clothing, including boots, shoes, and slippers." If your search reveals that "Bunny Snugs" or, say, "Bunny Snuggly" or "Bunny Rabbit Snuggies" is already registered, strike the name off your list of possibilities.

If your preferred name survives your preliminary search, it's wise to invest in a formal search and analysis by an intellectual property attorney. While even a professional search won't absolutely guarantee your mark will never be challenged, it's affordable, sensible protection. In the event of a future dispute, it will show you made a good-faith effort to find names you could legitimately use.

Moreover, an attorney can help you decide whether an existing name is too close to the name you want to use—and that can be important if you have a particular stake in the name. Suppose, for example, you've already spent $10,000 on a Bunny Snugs logo—and then discover that a tiny company halfway across the country has registered "Bunny Snugglies" for shoes. Can you risk using your name? In such situations, an attorney's advice is essential.

We think the money for an attorney's opinion is well spent. If, however, you are willing to settle for merely the search without the analysis, you may want to consider hiring a professional search firm to assist you. These are the same firms used by many attorneys for their searches. Top search firms provide splendid research but no analysis or interpretation. For a basic state, federal, and common-law search, they'll normally charge about $250–$300. Two of the largest search firms are Thompson & Thompson (1-800-692-8833), and COMPUMARK U.S. (1-800-421-7881).

---

*Don't be daunted! Trademark searches are vastly easier than patent searches. Remember, too, that the librarians are there to help.

Registering: When and Why

If you're serious about protecting your business idea, you should register your marks with your state government as soon as state law allows—immediately, if you're already in business.

If you're already in business interstate, you should apply for a federal mark as soon as possible. Even if you have no plans to go national on a big scale for several years, it may still be worth your trouble to pursue a federally registered mark. The moment you sell or advertise out of state, you're involved in interstate commerce and so eligible for a federally registered trademark.* That simple ® beside your mark gains you a number of valuable rights, including:

• The right to sue for infringement in Federal Court.
• The right to sue infringers for triple damages, plus attorney fees.
• The right to display a notice of registration (the ® symbol). This symbol is constructive notice to any potential infringer that you have claimed the mark. In plain English, they can't plead ignorance when you sue them.
• The right to seek criminal penalties against anyone counterfeiting your mark.
• The right to record your mark with U.S. Customs, and thus to prevent entry into the U.S. of any goods bearing an infringing mark.

In addition, registration can help you in at least three other ways. First, the simple fact that your mark appears in the register means that you won't have problems with the great majority of businesspeople who are honest and conscientious: They'll find your mark in their search of the Federal Registry, and simply pick something else. Second, Federal registration is often a precondition for registration in foreign countries, something you'll certainly want if you intend to sell overseas. And third, a mark that remains in the Federal register for five years becomes an "incontestable" mark. Incontestable marks are extremely difficult to challenge; as long as you take the ordinary steps to enforce them, they should be yours exclusively, forever, for all the United States.

Doing the Paperwork Whether or not you hire an attorney to apply

---

*Technically, in fact, you can apply for federal registration up to six months before you intend to start business interstate. Once your plans are firm, you may as well apply; nothing's gained by waiting.

for your trademark, you'll be glad to know the forms are much simpler than those for getting a patent.

Should you use an attorney? The forms are certainly manageable by the average person, but attorneys' fees for doing the paperwork are also proportionately cheaper. If you want to make sure things get done right the first time, and especially if you have complicated artwork, an attorney's help is worth the money.

If you want to apply on your own, get a copy of *Basic Facts about Trademarks* from the PTO; it has both the necessary forms and fairly detailed instructions.

Meanwhile, in brief, here is what's involved:

The application has three parts: (1) a written form, (2) a drawing of the mark, and (3) the filing fee. In addition, if the mark is already in use, you will need to submit three specimens of its use: labels, business cards, or whatever. (If it's not already in use, you'll need to submit the specimens, along with another $100 fee, when you do start using it.)

The Form Here you tell the PTO what words appear in your mark and whether or not it includes artwork. You tell them who owns the mark (you, a partnership, a corporation, or whatever). You tell them what kinds of goods the mark will protect, and why you are claiming rights to it (either because you have been using it, or because you intend to).

You need to file a separate application for each mark you want to register, even if they're all for the same company.

Don't forget to complete the back side of the application, which has your declaration (under penalty of fraud) that you own the mark—plus your phone number and other details. The PTO invites you to use photocopies of any of its forms, but many people forget to photocopy the backside of the application.

Also remember that if you hired someone to design your logo, your contract with him or her must clearly give you all rights, for all time.

The Drawing At least for those of us with limited graphic skills, the drawing seems pretty demanding. In fact, unsuitable drawings are a main reason for the rejection of applications.

Drawings are either *typed* or *special*. If you're really only trademarking something verbal (say, the name "BoolaBurger," without any special graphic features), you simply type it, in capital letters, on the center of a sheet of "pure, white, durable, nonshiny" 8½″ × 11″ paper.

If your trademark is going to be more elaborate, though—if, say, the word "BoolaBurger" will be topped off with a couple of palm trees, a pair of Polynesian dancers, and some special curlicues—you need a "special form drawing." These drawings do have special rules (no larger than $4'' \times 4''$, no "fine or crowded lines," no photographs). If you don't follow these rules to the letter, your application will be returned; so, if you don't have at least some aptitude for the graphic arts, and a knack for following detailed instructions, you're probably better off hiring a pro to do the work. While a top graphic designer will charge you thousands for a really snazzy package of designs, you can probably get a competent free-lancer to do something nice for a couple of hundred dollars.

Here's a tip: The PTO will generally take camera-ready copy of the sort prepared by a graphics shop, as long as it meets the other criteria (proper labeling and so on). Any good graphics shop should know the requirements, so you might well economize by having them prepare the whole package for you at one time.

After You File Again in contrast with patents, the trademark review process moves very quickly.

1. The form gets a quick review for basic correctness (Did you sign it? Did you include the proper fees?). If everything appears in order, you should receive a serial number and a filing receipt, which tells you that your forms are "in the mill."

2. About 90 days after you get your filing receipt, an examining attorney will let you know whether or not your mark is registrable. He or she may also return the forms on grounds of "procedural informalities"— while a filing receipt generally means your paperwork is okay, it doesn't guarantee it.

If you have any problems with the application or if the examining attorney thinks your mark doesn't meet the legal guidelines, you must respond within six months or your application is automatically dropped. If the examining attorney doesn't buy your amendments (and/or explanations), you can then appeal to the PTO's Trial and Appeal Board, or you can simply drop the application and try another mark.

As always, you want to appeal only if you have a substantial monetary stake in the trademark, and if you think your case is strong. You definitely need legal representation for the appeal.

On the other hand, if all goes well, the end of that 90-day period should bring a letter from the examining attorney saying your mark is approved. At that point, the mark will be published in the PTO's weekly *Trademark Official Gazette*.

3. Now comes another wait—because, for the next 30 days any in-

terested party has the right either to file an opposition to your trademark or to request more time to do so. While few businesspeople read the *Gazette* themselves, many hire trademark search firms to do it for them, for a relatively small monthly fee. As your mark grows more valuable, you'll probably want to arrange for the same service; eventually, if your business prospers, you may well have to hire people to watch your trademark worldwide.

A Trademark Opposition is much like a court hearing, although it's heard by the Trademark Trial and Appeal Board. Again, you'll almost certainly want to have top legal support if you think your mark is valuable enough to fight over at this level.

The losing party in an Opposition can carry the matter over to Federal court—but again, we're talking about very valuable trademarks; when you reach that stage of business, you'll have plenty of in-house counsel to advise you on the proper course.

4. If, as most often happens, no opposition is filed, then, about 12 weeks after your mark was published in the *Trademark Gazette,* the mark will officially register. From then on, it's yours to use—and to protect.

If You Still Haven't Started Using the Mark If the mark is approved, but you told the Trademark Office it isn't yet in use, you'll now receive a "notice of allowance," which gives you six months to begin using your mark in trade. If something plausible arises that delays your start of business, you can get an extension for six more months—but at the end of that, if you haven't begun using the mark in business, you'll lose it. Switching from "intended use" to "actual use" requires the filing of more papers and additional fees, presently $100 per form.

That's your time frame: You want to protect existing operations immediately, and you probably want to start protecting anticipated marks about four to six months before you expect to need them.

Summing Up Overall, if you do your homework, registering your trademarks should be clean, simple and (relatively) inexpensive. So don't hesitate—do it!

And don't waste half the value of registering: Once you've registered your mark, make sure people know it. That "®" should accompany every use of your mark. Even if you have only a state registration or a clear claim to an unregistered mark, use that ™ symbol. Those symbols put people on notice, and make them liable for triple damages if they infringe. So, use them!

Now let's talk about making that mark even more valuable.

56

Building Your Trade Name: Advertising

THUS FAR we've been writing as if great products and a great organization were enough to make your name famous. In a perfect world that would be true. In this world, however, you often need to take steps to bring your name to the public's attention. And that, of course, means advertising. And advertising means money.

How much money?

For the last half century, Americans have approached advertising with the same philosophy we used to win World War II (or, for that matter, the Gulf War): Line up all the guns this side of heaven and blast away until the other guy quits.

Advertising that way can cost a fortune. In 1991, Procter & Gamble spent about one billion dollars advertising its U.S. brands.

Obviously, that's vastly beyond the range of a new company, no matter how great its idea. Still, small companies, increasingly afraid that even their best ideas can get lost in the crush of an overcrowded market, are forever taking the big risk: betting the store on snazzy ad campaigns.

So let's look at what can happen to a fine small company that tries to advertise like the big guys. And then let's glance at some other ways to play the game.

Coleman Steaks: A Gourmet Trade Name
Tries Going National

Suppose you've got a much-admired product but sell in only a small area. You want to build a national reputation. How do you go about it?

Consider this story from *Inc.* magazine:

Coleman Natural Meats (CNM) was started by a family that had raised cattle on the same Colorado land for five generations. It began 1990 as a well-run $23 million-a-year purveyor of beef raised without hormones or antibiotics.

In the health-and-environment 1980s that was a choice market, and Coleman grew steadily. But it was still a relatively small company, selling mostly to small chains of health-food stores.

By the late 1980s, though, big chains were asking to carry the product, provided Coleman could back it with a professional-grade promotional campaign. In other words, provided Coleman could make itself into a "brand" name.

Very few of us have ever bought beef with a brand name. It usually comes plastic-wrapped with the supermarket's name, a price, and little else.

So Coleman, with the help of some venture capitalists (who invested about $2.5 million, in exchange for more than half the company), decided to make its name known.

First, it hired a former executive of Perdue, the company that turned its chickens into a national brand. That executive, Mack H. Graves, proposed building Coleman into a $100-million-a-year company in five years. He also warned them that building a brand name in just one city might cost $1 million.

He wasn't kidding. Here are some of the expenses just to break into the Boston market:

• $266,000 to create TV ads. They used the director of Chevy's "Heartbeat of America" ads, and shot on location in Colorado. (These are production costs. You can figure between $75,000 and $125,000 to create a fancy one-minute commercial. Top-grade commercials are, minute-for-minute, roughly as expensive as the average feature film. And that's without celebrity endorsers, who often get $1 million and up to represent a product. To all those costs, you then add the cost of air time to have stations or networks actually run your ads.)

• $10,000 for a signature tune, done by the composers of music for Buick and other national accounts. (This wasn't a whole song, just "a few bars" of background music.)

• $25,000 for a top graphics designer to do their logo and basic brochure.

• A top ad executive to guide the campaign: $7,500 a month.

They hosted three separate dinners to get Boston notables associated with their product. They ran two-page ads in Boston papers and hired public relations firms to get their name before the press.

Overall, the campaign cost nearly $650,000 for about five months of advertising in one city. Those are just the itemizable expenses. They don't count the time and energy of company executives, or the stress, or the control over the company the founders sacrificed to raise the money for the expansion try.

Was it worth it?

Two months into the campaign, the few chains that had stocked CNM beef from the outset were reporting sales had doubled, but no other major Boston markets had signed on to carry the product. The failure of a key piece of local wrapping equipment had management scrambling to fix a spoilage problem and prevent damage to CNM's image.

Perhaps even worse, other cattlemen's groups decided that CNM's ads, by stressing the healthfulness of natural beef, were implicitly slamming ordinary beef. The National Cattlemen's Association then started a Boston-area counter-campaign, implicitly attacking CNM—even as CNM's meat packer, apparently influenced by the dispute, tried to cancel CNM's packing agreement. (*Inc.*, July 1991)

A year later, though, Mel Coleman, CNM's patriarch, told us that, while the ads did not work as planned, they taught CNM much. Today CNM has dropped the television ads in favor of more modest print ads aimed mainly at retailers, not consumers. Retailer ads (run in trade papers) work more cheaply and effectively than do consumer ads. Above all, the company is focusing on its niche market: Health oriented retailers and consumers—including, perhaps surprisingly, vegetarians.

The new approach seems to be working: even in the recession year of 1991, sales grew a solid 10 percent. The company's products are now carried fresh in twenty-six states, and frozen in all fifty. Mel Coleman speaks often before groups of ranchers and others to promote CNM's use of natural rangelands and natural beef, and newspapers cover his speeches as straight news. As he puts it, CNM was a pioneer in the business— "and when you're first, you're news."

That seems like sound advice for anyone with new products. Before you try an expensive campaign, consider how far some organizations have gone with building their trade names *without* big advertising campaigns.

Alliance If you can form a marketing alliance with a better-known company, you not only cut your initial capital costs but get a tremendous amount of free "association" value attached to your trademark.

Take Joan & David shoes.

For the first quarter century of its existence, the company relied heavily on its tie-in with the fashionable Ann Taylor women's clothing stores; at one point Ann Taylor was selling over $40 million a year of Joan & David shoes. Perhaps as important as the retail outlet, though, was the chance to build a valuable trade name without massive advertising.

The downside to an alliance, of course, is that you are, in large measure, at the mercy of the larger company. As co-founder Joan Helperin told the *Wall Street Journal,* "It's like being a guest in somebody's home." In the late 1980s, a new owner of the Ann Taylor chain wanted Joan & David to drop its trade name and become a private-label supplier to Ann Taylor. By 1991 the two firms were in a lawsuit, which settled with an agreement to end their relationship by February 1993. That left Joan & David with the daunting job of building a new retail network, virtually from scratch.

Note: This is strictly a marketing arrangement; you're not inviting the bigger firm to buy into you or to run your operation, although often it will try to do both.

Marketing alliances, though increasingly popular, are still fairly rare.

But here's a tactic open to anyone with imagination:

Having "Character" No matter how great your company, you're going to get a lot more free media attention if you give the media something with a human flavor. As journalist-turned-computer-entrepreneur Adam Osborne once observed, journalists don't describe things, they tell stories. Give them a story and they'll pay attention to you.

Ben & Jerry's How interesting is ice cream? Sure, everybody likes it (statistically, Americans are the world's largest ice cream consumers), but ice cream is hardly front-page news.

Unless of course, the ice cream is made by Ben and Jerry, the two ex-hippie masters of free publicity.

How much free publicity? Well, in June 1991, the company's annual meeting made the front page of the *Wall Street Journal.* Sure, the tone was joking; the heading was, "Oh, Wow, Man: Let's, Like, Hear From the Auditors," and it referred to the company's investors as "Woodstockholders." But the article also pointed out that Ben & Jerry's annual sales zoomed from $9.8 million to $77 million in just five years. Those numbers are no joke.

How does a shareholders' meeting for a small business make the front page of the nation's premier business newspaper? Especially when lots of big companies spend a lot of money on their annual meetings and either get roundly ignored by the press or else roundly criticized by their shareholders for squandering the company's money?

How come, in short, everybody loves Ben & Jerry's?

The answer, of course, is that they've built a strong image around the story of the company's founders. The story is that two counter-culture guys are trying to build a big business without betraying their principles.

What principles? Well, they're pro-environment, pro-peace, pro-something-like-industrial-democracy, and so on.

And Ben & Jerry's promotes them the most sincere way possible: with money. Seven and a half percent of the company's earnings is earmarked for charitable causes. Nobody in the company can make more than seven times the pay of the lowest-paid worker. And so on—whatever one thinks of the company's values, they're at least willing to put their money where their politics are. (Yes, lots of major companies give money to charities. But Ben & Jerry's gets maximum mileage because they tie the charity to the convictions of two real human beings—again, they give the press a story.)

For Ben & Jerry's, the human image and the business idea coalesce into effective promotion:

Ice cream, obviously, is supposed to be fun, and these guys are having fun, big-time. Ice cream evokes simpler times and America's rural roots, and these guys never let consumers forget they're a small firm from Vermont, not some label of a conglomerate owned by a still-more-faceless conglomerate from overseas. Finally, consumers feeling guilty about slurping down superpremium ice cream probably find a certain consolation in knowing some of the proceeds from their purchases are being donated to help save the Brazilian rain forest and otherwise doing good.

In short, the company has made itself and its founders into a story as much as a product. It was that story—of fun-loving entrepreneurs having a blast, doing good, and making a fortune—that got Ben & Jerry's on the *Wall Street Journal*'s front page, and the front cover of *Inc.*, and Heaven knows how many other choice free-advertising opportunities.

What's that sort of publicity worth? The day that article appeared, the *Wall Street Journal*'s rate quote for a full page in the national edition was $105,352. Ben & Jerry paid zip.

With deals like that, you can afford to let folks laugh.

It's no secret we think small firms should use more imagination and fewer dollars to build their trade names. Still, traditional advertising will become important to every firm at some point; when you start using it is up to you.

Action List—Traditional Advertising

If you are going to try to crack a bigger market with a fancy campaign, pay attention to the following:

1. Be sure you've got the infrastructure in place to deal with the growth that will follow. Coleman Natural Meats did a better job in this regard than ninety-nine firms out of a hundred, but their one glitch with a defective machine cost them heavily. Details count.

2. Set aside a war chest—the bigger, the better. Professional campaigns cost a fortune.

3. Research the people who are going to help you. Hire people with specific experience in launching or expanding smaller companies.

4. Bring on board someone who can deal with high-level agencies. This may be the toughest acquisition you ever make. You need someone who can both guide you toward big-time growth and understand your present limitations.

You'll probably need your first truly professional ad campaign about the time your firm outgrows your management skills in many areas. So this might be the time to start overhauling your entire team, and to start thinking about getting yourself more business training.

5. Be frank with the pros you hire. You or your new executives have to get through to the ad agency and creative people you hire that you're not General Motors. Anything they can do, without sacrificing quality, to save you money will dramatically up the chances that you'll survive and grow—and so become a bigger account in the future. If they can't get the message (and many hotshots can't), look for another agency.

6. Be prepared to work harder while the campaign's running than

you've ever worked before. As Coleman Meats showed, a big ad campaign is going to cost you stress two ways: when it works and when it doesn't. If it develops problems, you'll be watching your hard-earned money go down the tube while you scramble to correct the glitches. If it works perfectly, you'll be scrambling to capitalize on the attention by converting interest into sales, long-term contracts and even longer term name recognition and prestige—in short, into a more valuable trade name.

Think of yourself as being at sea without fresh water. Suddenly a rain squall comes by, and you've got about ten minutes to drink or store as much water as you can. That's roughly what a big ad campaign is like for a small firm.

Action List: Getting Promotion on the Cheap

As good as professional advertising can be, it's usually too expensive for even successful small companies. If you want to do it yourself, remember the tips we provided in Part Three about establishing new products. And above all:

1. Consider forming alliances with better-known companies. Also consider "cross-advertising": using prestige items in your ads to build subliminal associations in buyers' minds. (If you're referring to anyone's products by name, get their permission. People rarely refuse, since they're getting free press.)

2. Find your own story—and remember that the best stories have a theme. (Ben & Jerry's "story" is "two ex-hippies build growth company"; their "theme" is more like, "If your heart's in the right place, you can make money *and* uphold your social values.") If you know what you and your company are about, you can make that into a story that will attract attention and influence buyers.

57

Trademark Litigation

YOU'VE GOT A GREAT BUSINESS IDEA, and you're executing it well. What happens then? You become popular and start making money.

And what happens *then?*

Far too often people start imitating you.

Except for the parts that are copyrighted or patented, you can't protect your business idea. You're going to have competition, and you can't stop it.

What you can stop is anyone trying to fool the public into thinking he or she is you.*

Trademark Litigation: What Is It Good For?

You may think only jumbo corporations have to fight trademark infringers. In fact, anybody with a good business idea had better be prepared to go into court fast and often—or the clone artists will be picking their bones.

99¢ Only Stores are a Los Angeles–based chain of small, off-price outlet stores; they sell close-out merchandise and the like at very low prices. In fact, nothing in the store costs more than 99¢, and most things sell in multiples of that price: such as 2 for 99¢, 5 for 99¢. The stores are bargain hunters' delights, and the chain grew rapidly through the 1980s. In mid-1991 it opened its twenty-fourth outlet.

So how many infringers have the 99¢ Only Stores had to sue in their first seven years in business?

Would you believe *165?* That works out to filing roughly twenty-four

---

* Actually, this happens in two different ways: People start businesses that look too much like yours, or they sell counterfeit copies of your goods. We'll discuss business clones here and counterfeiting in the next chapter.

lawsuits a year. And that, of course, doesn't count the infringers who quit after getting a first threatening letter.

The 99¢ Only Stores are unusual. Not only have they been remarkably successful, but they have low entry costs and tend to operate in areas with many immigrant entrepreneurs, who are unlikely to be schooled in the nuances of intellectual property law. Still, the point is clear:

Trademark infringement cases are common enough these days for you to need to be ready to fight one whenever you see someone infringing your name.

How It Starts   You can find yourself in a trademark fight in one of two ways, neither of them pleasant. If, for example, you were running that fast-growing (imaginary) restaurant chain, BoolaBurgers, Inc., the trouble might strike as follows:

1. You're on your way to work one morning, and you see a construction site with a big sign out front: "Future Site of BoolaBurger." You gasp and turn pale, realizing you haven't signed any contracts to build a BoolaBurger on that location. Maybe you pinch yourself to make sure it's not a nightmare—then, gnashing your teeth, you pick up your car phone and dial your lawyer.

Or—

2. You arrive at work one morning, and find a blazing letter from the law firm of Ruff, Tuff & Gruff warning that you are infringing on a federally registered trademark owned by BoolaBurgers, Inc., of Poughkeepsie, New York, and that if you don't desist within forty-eight hours, they are going to sue you for five million bucks. With cold sweat running down your face, you remember you decided to skip all those trademark details and to register just in your home state.

Well, those examples are pretty much stacked decks. In the first case you probably have an easy win, and in the second, you're probably going to have to buy a license or else change your name.

But what about the more common and more difficult situations? Suppose that, on your way to work, that sign had read "Future Site of Boola Bernie's Polynesian Snack Shop"? Or suppose the angry letter from the attorney had referred to an East Coast company called "Boulé Burgers: The Finest in Franco-American Cuisine"? Then what would have been your position?

In either situation, you and your lawyer are going to have to estimate the strength of your case and, from that, your chances of winning a lawsuit.

Of course, you can never be certain what a court will decide, but in general there are nine guidelines used to decide whether two marks are confusingly similar:

1. *Similarity of marks with respect to appearance, sound, connotation, and impression.* Do the marks use the same colors? Rhyming sounds? Words with similar connotations? ("Dove" and "Angel" for example, might both be said to connote mildness or gentleness.)

2. *Similarity of goods and services.* Would a reasonable person assume the two products were made by the same firm? "Gallo" wine and "Gallo" beer would likely cause confusion. "Gallo" wine and "Gallo" cheese, maybe. But "Gallo" wine and, say, "Gallo" transmission parts? Probably not.

3. *Similarity of trade channels.* Are both products sold through mail order? Advertised on television?

4. *Conditions of sale (impulse versus considered purchases).* The more likely people are to buy the product at a quick glance, the wider circle the courts will draw around its mark. They don't want to allow marks that could be mistaken by someone unwilling to devote effort to the decision.

Thus, the Ferrari horse and the Ford mustang might be visually confusing symbols, but very few people are likely to get home from the car dealer, look closely at their $200,000 Ferrari, and say, "Damn! I meant to get the Mustang."

5. *Strength of mark.* We've already mentioned that certain classes of marks (completely arbitrary ones, for example) are considered stronger than others (those that are merely descriptive, for example). The court will factor these into its calculations.

6. *Actual confusion.* Are there cases on record of consumers who were tricked by the trademark into buying?

7. *Length of time of concurrent use without actual confusion.* Clearly, the longer the questionable product has been on the market without recorded cases of confusion, the less seriously the issue will be taken. (A good reason, of course, for you to act as quickly as possible if someone else seems to be infringing on your trademark or name.)

8. *Number and nature of similar marks on similar goods.* Are we talking cheeses, where almost nobody can tell one wax-and-dye mark from another? Or computers, where the Apple logo, for example, is importantly distinct?

9. *Variety of goods with which the mark is used.* If the mark is widely

used, the chances are greater that consumers would expect it to turn up on still more products—hence a greater chance for confusion or deception. "Disney" appears on thousands of products; consumers would be quicker to assume anything marked Disney was from the entertainment company than they would be to assume, say, that a toaster marked "Boeing" was made by the aerospace company.

Those are general legal criteria. You can match your situation against the list to get a rough idea of the likelihood that infringement exists, but always keep the idea of confusion foremost. If Boulé Burgers operates only white-tablecloth restaurants in fancy hotels, there's not much likelihood of confusion. On the other hand, if you can find an architect's drawing of Boola Bernie's future snack shop, and it looks just like your place, you might have grounds for an action.

(You're not trying to be your own attorney—just to get a general idea of your situation. Of course, you'll get a better estimate from your attorney, but if you want a more detailed discussion of the nine criteria, try the *Nutshell* guide we list under "Recommended Reading.")

When Somebody Sues You If you ever get a cease-and-desist letter, check first with your attorney, and then with your insurance carrier to find out who will be paying for your defense and how much coverage you have.

If you've followed our advice in the previous chapters, your position should be solid. The other side may ultimately file its lawsuit, but if you have a valid trademark registered with the PTO, the chances of their succeeding are very small.

When You Sue Somebody Else If you think someone has infringed your name and/or mark, you need to:

• Make certain your trademark is properly registered.

• Document your losses, as far as possible, so you know what losses you can reasonably claim and what remedies you can realistically expect.

• Check your own insurance, just so you're ready in case you're countersued.

• Make sure you have access to money for the bond you'll probably have to post, to help compensate the other side in case you lose. You'll also, of course, need the money for legal fees.

If you and your attorney then determine you have a reasonable case, send the other side a cease-and-desist letter.

After the Letter If the other side is fly-by-night, they'll probably just go quietly out of business. If they want to buy a license or otherwise compromise, you can judge that like any other business proposition.

If the other side resists, get ready to spend money in a hurry. Like most intellectual property litigation, trademark suits have their costs "front-loaded." You'll be paying big bills at or near the outset. Here's why:

If you want an injunction to make the other side cease business until the case is heard, you'll almost certainly have to post a bond.

The bond is money you'll forfeit to the other side if they prevail in the lawsuit. The amount of the bond will be based on two things: the losses they will likely suffer from having to take their products off the market, and what you can realistically afford to pay. (Obviously, an international company could claim losses far greater than any bond you could possibly post.) In December 1991, when Sideout Sport sued Nike and forced them to take $5 million in products off the shelves, the bond was $100,000—not nearly equal to Nike's potential loss, but probably the most a small company like Sideout could afford.

You don't need to have all that money in cash; there are companies that will post bonds for a fee. The fee will normally be a percentage of the bonded amount, and will depend upon the bonding company's estimate of the strength of your case.

When Someone Attacks Your Trademark

It's not a common problem, but sometimes, instead of trying to imitate your product, people will try to discredit it.

That's what apparently happened in a 1990 incident. A small New York soft drink company, whose hot new beverage was clobbering the big brands in the few neighborhoods where it was sold, suddenly found itself the subject of vicious rumors apparently started by sales reps from one of those big companies. Within months, the small bottler's business, according to the *Wall Street Journal*, "went to nothing."

The situation got so bad that the mayor of New York actually appeared on TV to drink a bottle of the company's beverage to prove it wasn't at all toxic. Despite such actions, the small company still lost some 40 percent of its market and virtually all of its momentum. Not until late 1992 did the company fully recover.

Those horror attacks are extremely rare. But what can you do when a competitor starts running down your product in a dishonest way?

A little rough-and-tumble business competition won't kill anyone. You certainly can't file a lawsuit just because a competitor says his product is better than yours. Still, if someone crosses the line of fair competition, and especially if you can document losses, then:

Legal Recourse You can counterattack on various legal grounds, including *Unfair Competition, Advertising Injury, Libel or Slander,* and *Product Disparagement.* Realistically, these are tough lawsuits to win, both because free speech gives people a lot of latitude and because evidence is hard to find. Still, enough people do win these so that they make a credible threat if all else fails.

If you have a problem with a nasty competitor, consider this:

Action List—When Someone's Damaging Your Trade Name or Trademark

1. *Isolate and document the rumors or attacks.* Find out who has heard what and when and where they heard it. Once you have the evidence, talk with a lawyer. Know your legal options.

2. *Confront the perpetrators.* When you do, stay calm—and don't start by threatening a lawsuit. Just one overeager salesperson may be behind the problem, and a simple phone call may resolve matters. Be polite; don't force the other side to fight.

Whatever response you get, send a follow-up letter, recapping the discussion—so you have the start of a paper trail.

3. *Take your case public.* If the rumors or accusations are serious enough, make sure your side of things gets heard. This may be as simple as answering a letter to the editor, but it may mean hiring a public relations firm, running counter-advertisements, or meeting with community groups.

4. *Talk with private investigators.* This helps if a particular competitor is clearly behind the problem. Investigators don't have much luck chasing rumors; that New York bottler never found out who printed the lies about its products.

5. *Document your losses.* Any financial recovery will depend upon proving your business actually suffered.

If all else fails, you have to threaten a lawsuit. Since lawsuits are expensive for all parties, this may be enough to stop the problem. If it isn't then go ahead and sue.

Summing Up Few companies ever have to fight anything slanderous. Still, you know how to respond if you ever need to.

Trademark infringement actions are, on the other hand, increasingly common; but again, you know what to do, and if you've followed our advice about searching and registering your marks, you'll be in fine shape.

So let's talk next about the other half of the problem—when somebody's knocking off your products.

58

Knockoff and Counterfeit Goods

HOW DO YOU KNOW your great idea is a hit?

When somebody else rips it off.

In 1991 *Fortune* magazine estimated that counterfeit goods in just four industries (PC software, pharmaceuticals, recordings, and films) were costing American business a minimum of $15.5 billion a year.

Everybody knows that prestige products like Rolex watches get knocked off. But how real is the danger to you?

To get the scoop on the problem and how to solve it, we went to two experts: intellectual property attorney William Steffin, of the Los Angeles firm, Lyon & Lyon, a specialist in anticounterfeiting law, and Bill Ellis, perhaps the country's best-known private investigator of counterfeiting crimes.

What Gets Ripped Off? Anything with a high differential between manufacturing cost and selling price. Take computer software: A program can cost millions to develop, and sell for hundreds of dollars a copy, but copies can be made for a couple of dollars. However, counterfeiters are just as happy to go after, say, T-shirts with hot logos or characters.

How Soon Can the Rip-offs Appear? Almost instantaneously. According to Bill Ellis, if you take samples of a promising product to Taiwan or Korea and spend a week or two showing them to potential manufacturers, you can expect that "knockoff copies will be in the hold of a ship, bound for America, before you get on the plane for home."

How Do the Rip-offs Work? That would take a whole book to describe. Sometimes the counterfeiters just make cheap knockoffs in their garages. Sometimes all they counterfeit is one of your licensing agreements, then they show that to legitimate manufacturers, who do the manufacturing for them. With electronics, they often buy legitimate goods, then repackage them as more expensive models: In 1990, crooks bought Intel 286 microprocessors and replaced the shells with fake ones reading "Intel *386*"; a $100 processor was suddenly worth $600.

How Do You Discover You're Being Ripped Off? Most often one of your salespeople brings you a sample. Some hi-tech knockoffs may need careful testing to establish that they are indeed knockoffs. For most simpler products, though, flaws are easy to spot.

And here's one tip: Counterfeiters hate to put either ® or ™ marks on products, because that blows their "innocent infringement" defense: if they knew the marks were protected, you're automatically entitled to triple damages. So register and mark your goods!

What Should You Do? When you find out someone's knocking off your goods, your first instinct might be to reach for the Winchester. Hold on! Remember:

Rule #1: *Don't Play Investigator*. That goes with—

Rule #2: *Don't Get Emotional*. The classic blunder is to call up the knockoff artist and yell threats. All that does is put him on his guard. As Bill Ellis says, "That automatically makes a hundred-dollar investigation into a three-thousand-dollar investigation."

That kind of blundering is the main danger, but it also raises the question:

How Dangerous Are Counterfeiters? To date, there's very little evidence of organized crime's role in counterfeiting. On the other hand, some of these people, as individuals, can be violent. Investigators are frequently threatened and take the threats seriously. We think you'd be wise to hire an investigator, both to do the job right and to keep yourself safe.

How Long Does an Investigation Take? Anywhere from less than a day to about three weeks, depending on a) how large and well-hidden the operation is, and b) your philosophy. Some people just want to bust the street vendors; others want to root out the whole organization.

William Steffin favors the more thorough job, which can, in theory, produce a more complete solution and a better chance of collecting damages. Bill Ellis seems to lean toward quick action to pressure the counterfeiters to move along; you don't collect big settlements, but you don't spend a lot of time and money on legal fees. Both say the strategy to use will depend on your situation.

Most counterfeiting organizations are extremely "shallow": behind the street vendors there might be one or at most two organizational levels. That's why investigations go so fast.

What Happens Next? Once your investigator has the facts, you (or better, your attorney) can get from the court a seizure order authorizing law enforcement agents to confiscate counterfeit goods. This order can be obtained without notifying the other side if your evidence is solid.

Before you swing into action, remember:

• *Location.* The courts won't give you a "roving" warrant to seize goods; you need a specific location. When you apply for it, remember that the federal marshals or local officers will usually need from twenty-four to forty-eight hours before they can act.

• *Transport.* The marshals or officers will not physically move the counterfeit goods for you. Bring trucks, dollies, movers—whatever you're going to need.

• *Documentation.* For safety's sake, you want a record of what you did on the premises. The smartest way is to videotape everything.

• *Certification.* You want somebody from your company there to certify that the goods taken are in fact counterfeit. Plan carefully; smoothness is everything.

What Does Action Cost? You have two kinds of costs: investigative and legal.

As a rule, counterfeiters don't fight back if all you want is to seize their goods. That can make the process quite cheap. The investigator's fees can be a couple of hundred dollars, especially if you sign on as a regular client.

For small businesses Mr. Ellis practices what he calls "tail-ending." It works this way: Suppose he raids a major counterfeiter on behalf of some big clients (say, Guess and Reebok). He seizes, maybe, 5,000 pairs of fake Guess jeans and 3,000 pairs of fake Reeboks. Guess and Reebok will split the cost of the raid—say, $10,000 each, if it was a three-week investigation followed by a raid involving a big team.

But over in the corner he finds five-hundred T-shirts with the forged logo of another client, good old BoolaBurger, Inc.

Mr. Ellis tells the counterfeiter, "I don't have a warrant for those T-shirts, but if you give them to me, I'll give you a receipt—and BoolaBurger won't press charges. Otherwise, I'll come back with another warrant, and I'll urge all three clients to press charges." Normally, the counterfeiter goes along. Then Mr. Ellis bills BoolaBurger for, say, thirty minutes of his time: maybe $200. That's "tail-ending," and for a small company, it can produce great results.

Legal costs are generally higher, normally between $2,000 and $5,000 if the counterfeiter gives in easily. You could spend up to $100,000, but only for a serious legal battle, where you expected a considerable recovery.

Generally an ongoing enforcement program for a small company will cost about $300 a month for just an investigator, plus perhaps $1,000 a month for occasional legal help.

Big tip. Spend the money early. If you hammer the first few counterfeiters who appear, word will spread and the crooks will move on to easier targets. Your enforcement costs will drop steadily.

What Are Your Legal Options? You'll have several choices in pursuing infringers and nearly all work well. You can sue in State or Federal court, depending on where your marks are registered. You can also have U.S. Customs seize goods being imported. And you can file criminal charges. Thanks to model laws created in California and now used in many states, counterfeiters generally get jail time for a second conviction. Your lawyer can help you decide what's best in each case.

What Long-Term Tactics Work? For any given infringement, you can take effective action. But fighting case after case gets expensive. What can you do on a long-term basis to keep your problems down?

1. Record your marks with U.S. Customs. You can get automatic enforcement help with imported knockoffs. Once you've secured your patents, trademarks, or copyrights, record them with Customs. That means filing: (1) a letter of information, explaining that you own mark(s), patent(s), or copyright(s), (2) a certificate of registration from the PTO or copyright office, (3) 5 copies of the certificate, for distribution to all Customs houses (that is, entry points), and (4) the filing fee. For details, contact your local Customs office or the U.S. Customs Service, Entry Licensing and Restricted Merchandise Branch, Room 2447, 1301 Constitution Avenue, N.W., Washington, D.C. 20229. Telephone: 1-202-566-5765.

Customs runs regular intellectual property seminars for its agents. There, representatives from trade associations talk about particular counterfeiting problems, so let your association know about any problems. (If you've signed with a major private-investigation firm, one of their investigators will sometimes be able to speak up specifically on your behalf and stress that you are enforcing your marks rigorously.)

And here's a tip from Customs: They have an elaborate letter-and-computer communications system. If they hear from an entrepreneur that he or she is being hit hard by counterfeiters, they'll put it on the network and redouble their efforts. So if you have a problem, tell them about it.

2. Follow through. Don't make this classic mistake:

Law enforcement seizes some counterfeits of your goods. The counterfeiter comes to you in tears, pleads ignorance, and offers to buy a license. You agree.

At that point you can kiss your enforcement program goodbye. Whatever they tell you, they'll never intercept another shipment for you, simply because they don't want to be used as your licensing agent. Law enforcement people are human. If they think you're going to throw their efforts away, they won't make the effort.

3. Design-in protection. Remember the idea of designing in useless bits or harmless errors as "markers." Then, don't take your ideas overseas, even for manufacturing bids, until you have all your intellectual property protection in place, including recording with Customs.

4. Spend money on a good "trim kit"—and have a separate manufacturer produce it. "Trim Kit" originally meant the fancy buttons, patches, or whatever added to clothing. Today it means the decorative add-ons to any product, even down to the packaging.

Anything you want to protect should have a trim kit complicated enough to be hard to copy, and the person who makes the main product should not be the one who makes the rest of the product. Don't simplify the counterfeiter's job.

5. Hire competent representation. Bill Ellis estimates that it takes five years' experience in the anticounterfeit field to qualify an investigator. Until recently, competent people could be found only in the big four counterfeiting states: California, Florida, New York, and Texas. Today they're frequently available elsewhere.

6. Don't encourage your manufacturers to rip you off. If you've hired someone to do your manufacturing, be especially careful about your reject policy. If you say that you won't accept more than 1 percent of defective goods and that they'll be stuck with all the rest, guess what will happen? You got it: They'll dump all the other rejects onto the illicit market. Even worse, they'll find out that means easy money and start making goods especially for the illicit market.

Always buy the defective goods from your manufacturers. You don't have to pay much—but get them. Then, to lower the defect rate, work with your manufacturers, not against them.

7. Don't use infringement suits to settle honest disputes with your licensees. If you fight with a licensee and unilaterally yank the license, don't immediately run to get him jailed for infringement if he keeps producing. If the courts rule the license is still valid, you'll get slammed in the countersuits.

8. Watch your own step! Remember that counterfeiting investigators are also hired to prove that the inventing companies have invalid patents or trademarks. Keep your paperwork up to date. Don't let the infringers hang you out to dry.

Summing Up Protecting your intellectual property isn't all that hard or all that expensive. Start early and be aggressive and you'll be fine.

59

Franchising, Part One: The Theory

The Power of Franchising

How BIG IS FRANCHISING? Today franchises produce more than $750 billion in annual U.S. sales; by the end of the decade, experts predict they will account for half of all American retail business.

Franchising is especially remarkable because it lets you take what you might not think of as "intellectual property"—a restaurant, a muffler repair shop, or a computer store—clone its submethods and trademarks, and sell them as a package.

It also has another, less philosophical advantage: Namely, franchisers can make a lot of money very quickly. Unfortunately, the very temptation to get hold of some of that money prompts people to go into franchising much too soon.

That leads us to:

The Great Rule of Franchising: Do Your Homework More precisely, you need to:

1. Recognize and organize the ideas you have to sell.

2. Polish them, so that they are reliable, teachable, and standardized.

3. Protect them, so they can be safely sold to others. This means getting all reasonable patents, trademarks, and copyrights, and protecting whatever else you can as trade secrets.

Take McDonald's, as one obvious example. Anyone buying one of their franchises gets, among other things: the famous trademarks (the Golden Arch is the best known); the recipes (trade secrets); patented equipment (like French fryers); copyrighted materials (from promotional materials to training manuals).

The buyer may just think he's buying a snazzy burger joint and a way to make money. But the quality of his investment is underwritten by all those various protectable bits of intellectual property—and by McDonald's ability to teach them to him.

The message? If you want people to pay money for your franchises, you have to be able to sell them a package of intellectual property they can't have for free.

Suppose you're traveling in the South Pacific, and, among many cultural riches, discover a wonderful fast food; it's like a delicious hamburger, only it has a fruit relish topping. By asking a few questions, you discover the patty is made from low-fat, low-cholesterol, and low-cost ingredients.

You get back to the States, and, with the magic recipes in hand, you make a few of these things—which you've dubbed "BoolaBurgers" after the town where you first saw them—and your friends are crazy about them. You invest a few dollars to open your first BoolaBurger joint, and pretty soon people are lining up for a block.

About two weeks after you open, one of these people hands you her card and says she'd like a BoolaBurger franchise. What do you do?

Well, presumably, you're going at least to consider cutting a deal. But what are you going to offer her that's worth more than what she'd get by just hiring a chemist to figure out what goes into a BoolaBurger?

Here are some possibilities:

Trade dress. "Trade Dress" normally means the way your products are packaged, but for a retail establishment it can also mean the way the establishment itself is "packaged"—that is, if the store's look is both unique and consistent for all the stores in the chain or franchise system.

Reduce this to a formula, to writing and drawings, perhaps beginning: "All BoolaBurger shops will have light wooden tables, dark red chairs, fake palm trees every ten feet, and lush jungle scenes painted on the walls."

The recipe. At the least it's a trade secret. As you know, "trade secret" definitions vary from state to state. Do whatever you can to see that yours is legally protected.

Can you patent the recipe? It's possible but not really likely. You'll have to show you've made some useful, nonobvious improvement over what existed on that South Seas island.

Trade name and mark. Try to protect the name and any appropriate symbols. Have a designer create, say, a palm-tree logo (it has to be stylized enough to be protectable).

Machinery. Have you made any "accidental" inventions—say, a relish-mashing tool—that might be patentable?

Copyrighted materials. At this stage, the best you might hope for is probably a good manual for training employees, but that might well be the basis for your manual for training future franchisees. (The manual can also be treated as a trade secret.) Eventually you'll have professional-grade advertising materials to copyright as well.

The more legal protection you have and the more work you've done to perfect your submethods and to package them in teachable form, the more likely you are to be able to get a prime price for each individual franchise.

We'll talk in the next chapter about the art and law of selling franchises. Right now let's talk about the pros and cons of franchising itself. After all, tempting as franchising is, it's not right for everyone.

Risks and Problems

If you move into franchising, you're taking on a whole new business. Where before you were selling hot dogs or mufflers or computers, today you're selling franchises.

Above all, remember that the law will generally assume you and your franchisees have what's called a "community of interests"; that means you cannot unreasonably expand your business at the expense of theirs. (Basically, you don't want to do that anyway. If the word gets out that you're stiffing your franchisees, the market for your franchises will dry up fast and you'll get sued—a lot.)

Honest franchisers generally find themselves in trouble over one of two issues: Either they're accused of selling so many franchises that they dilute the value of individual locations, or else they're accused of over-charging franchisees for mandatory supplies or services. You avoid the first problem by never opening a second store within a first store's "draw-ing radius," and the second by sticking close to industry norms and listening to franchisee complaints.*

Selling to Big Buyers Another set of problems comes from having too-powerful franchisees. Too often, in their early days, eager franchis-ers yield large areas to particular franchisees—most often either wealthy individuals or established corporations.

Big buyers will bring money and experience, but are likely to be hard to control. As a beginning franchiser, you're probably wise to limit both the size of territories and the number of locations one person or group can own. Otherwise, you're likely to find yourself in nasty struggles with these power blocks, and the end result is always expensive litigation.

A little caution will help you avoid the most common legal issues. But here's a tougher issue:

Giving Up Your Freedom Franchising your idea can open you up to all sorts of philosophical disputes with your franchisees. If you own all your outlets, you can largely do what you want. If your employees disagree with the idea of renaming your restaurant the Black Death Diner and selling fried bugs, you can ignore them (although, of course, ignor-ing employee feedback is usually bad business).

A franchisee, though, is virtually a partner. He or she has an equity investment in the operation and will probably fight for his or her views.

Many franchisers solve the problem by simply selling out and starting a new franchise whenever they think the old idea's become stale.

That's fine, but there's also a new approach to franchising meant to minimize franchiser/franchisee disputes. If you're willing to trade smaller profits for greater peace, then consider:

---

*In fact, recent court rulings have greatly limited a franchisor's right to make franchisees buy any supplies as part of the franchise deal.

The Unbundled Franchise In an unbundled franchise, you simply price each bit of intellectual property in your package separately and let prospective buyers buy what they feel they need.

There are two negatives to this. First, your revenue stream becomes unpredictable (except that you can expect it to decline over the years). Second, you're going to lose the uniformity across the system that has always been a hallmark of the best franchises.

In fact, most unbundled franchises seem to degenerate into providing franchisees just two services: business consulting and group purchasing. You can still make money providing those, but the revenues won't match building the next McDonald's or Midas empire.

Still, an unbundled franchise will probably minimize franchiser/franchisee disputes. If you want minimum trouble, it might be worth considering.

Franchising as Part of Your Growth Strategy Above all, don't think of franchising as an all-or-nothing strategy; in fact, most of the best franchisers also run stores of their own. That has several strong pluses. First, field data keep operations up to date; second, company-run stores should be highly profitable; and third, most potential franchisees want to know you believe in the business enough to engage in it yourself. (As long, of course, as you don't hog all the best locations.)

Consider Sbarro's, the Italian fast-food franchise that many people cite as one of the best-run companies in the entire restaurant field. As of mid-1991 there were 465 Sbarro's restaurants, with roughly four out of five of them company owned. Franchising, though, was growing in importance, especially overseas, where quick growth was needed.

Indeed, franchising is often a kind of accelerator pedal for successful companies that want or need to grow quickly without taking on a lot of debt.

That's the strategy Bandag, Inc. used in the early 1980s, when its major tire-recapping patents were running out and it needed to build a European presence fast. Pricing its franchises at $150,000 each, it moved fast to make itself what *Business Week* called "the McDonald's of re-treaders." Today Bandag has 20 percent of the European retread market, tying it with giant Michelin.

Franchising can work for much smaller companies as well. If you want to put your great idea on the map without burying yourself with debt, try franchising.

60

Franchising, Part Two: Selling Your Franchises

IN THIS CHAPTER, are some general facts about franchising and a closer look at one company whose approach to franchising seems particularly good.

The franchise is the Boll Weevil, a family-owned, family-style restaurant chain founded in San Diego in 1967. Actually a spin-off from a fancy steakhouse started in the 1940s, the chain grew (with zero debt) to twenty restaurants by 1989, when management decided to use franchising to produce faster but still debt-free growth.*

We spoke with Sean Richardson, Boll Weevil's president and grandson of the firm's founders. Certainly there's no one right way to franchise, but Boll Weevil has maintained a level of professionalism, and the general theory of franchising is well illustrated by the specific approaches Boll Weevil has taken.

Franchising—Who's Your Likely Buyer?

When franchising your business idea, even before you're ready to price it, you need to pay attention to—guess what?—your likely buyer.

There's no reason you can't design a franchise aimed at a tiny part of the population: If you want start a line of drive-in fusion research centers, more power to you. Still, most franchisers are going to be interested in the great middle portion of the market.

According to Francorp, an Illinois franchise consulting firm, the

---

*A minor tip on clever naming: The Southern-themed steakhouse was called the "Cotton Patch"; when the owners decided to open a hamburger joint next door to make use of all their steak trimmings, they named it "Boll Weevil." The Cotton Patch closed in the 1980s, but Boll Weevils are now at about forty units and growing fast.

median figures for American franchise buyers in 1990 looked something like this:

Annual income before buying franchise	$50,000.00
Net worth	$200,000.00
Age	40
Total initial investment	$98,000.00
Franchise fee	$20,000.00

In addition, while about 25 percent of these folks are refugees from big corporations, 60 percent didn't finish college, and nearly 15 percent are blue collar workers. Over 40 percent of all franchises are sold to husband-and-wife teams. (Source: Francorp, Inc. / *Business Week,* May 6, 1991)

What does that tell you?

Basically, your average franchise buyer is mature enough to have good judgment, is fairly prosperous but by no means rich, has worked for what he or she has, and expects to work for what follows.

Your buyer, in other words, is not likely to be looking for a handy tax shelter, or willing or able to overpay for a brand name. The majority, who are not college graduates, are going to favor clear, simple English without a lot of legalese or fancy prose.

(Boll Weevil, as you'll see, is almost perfectly targeted at the market: The firm requires applicants to have "a net worth of $200,000 and liquid assets of $100,000.)

The first question you have to ask is whether people with that kind of money to invest can make a living off what you propose to sell after they pay you royalties. If they can't, you don't have a franchisable idea. If they can, you probably have a solid franchising prospect.*

In that case, start thinking about—

Offering Your Franchise for Sale

To start franchising, you need to prepare at least four important documents:

---

*Again, a good franchise can be aimed at almost any market (remember Bandag's tire recapping businesses, which cost $150,000, and also required large capital investments from the franchisees). We're just talking about the average franchise.

- UFOC ("Uniform Franchising Offering Circular")
- Franchising agreement
- Operation manuals
- Brochures/promotional materials

We'll talk about each of those in detail shortly, but first let's ask:

Should You Use Consultants? Many first-time franchisers hire consultants to help. Do they pay?

Boll Weevil was unusual in using two sets of consultants. It started out with probably the best-known franchising group in the country, Francorp, but dropped them because it felt the services, while competent, were not sufficiently customized. Only once in six months did anyone from Francorp actually visit Boll Weevil. According to Sean Richardson, these large consulting groups are probably most helpful for people at the earliest stages of franchising.

Boll Weevil then was lucky enough to link up with John Gorman, one of the three founders of Taco Bell, who today consults with several new franchisers. Something of a legend in the field, Mr. Gorman charges franchisers only what he thinks they can afford, but he takes them on as clients only if their businesses interest him.

How Long Does It Take? The actual creation of the Boll Weevil franchise structure—UFOC, manuals, etc.—took roughly one year. Certainly some companies have done it faster, but that seems a reasonable time to allow.

How Much Does It Cost? Figures will vary, but Boll Weevil, which went first class (including two sets of consultants), estimates it spent about $120,000, legal fees included, to get to where it could offer the franchises to the public. (That doesn't count the twenty-plus years of learning by running the restaurants.)

Those are the basic parameters. Now let's look at the key documents:

Legal Disclosure: The "UFOC" While the federal government and most states all have their own rules governing franchise offerings, most of them now accept what's called the "Uniform Franchise Offering Circular" as the basic disclosure document—that is, the basic document you give people who are thinking about buying franchises.

You can get a free copy of the UFOC form from whoever regulates franchises in your state (usually the Department of Corporations). Here, in broad outline, is what it will ask you to provide:

• *Information about you and your fellow officers.* This is fairly detailed information: have you ever lost any relevant lawsuits, filed bankruptcy, been convicted of a crime? What's your employment history—do you have the ability to run a major franchise?

• *Description of the franchise.* This has to let a potential buyer know exactly what the business will do.

• *All fees.* Exactly what the buyer will be paying, both to buy the franchise initially and as ongoing royalties. Will there be monthly or quarterly fees, or will the royalties be on a strict percentage basis? Here, you'll also show any extraordinary fees, such as fees to allow the sale of the franchise to a third party.

• *Start-up investment.* Aside from fees, what will it cost your buyer to get the business itself up and running? How much for the building? For inventory? For training workers?

Obviously, for some of these things, especially real estate, you'll be able to give a range of values. But you must show that you understand the costs accurately.

• *Required purchases.* If your buyer is going to have to buy supplies or services from you, explain what they will be and what they'll cost.

• *Promised territories.* Are you granting an exclusive area to your franchisee? If so, define it, and also explain exactly what the franchisee must do to keep the rights to that territory: Run ads? Open a certain number of stores? Reach a particular sales volume?

• *Financing deals.* If you are offering financing to potential franchisees, you need to detail it here. Nothing, of course, requires you to offer such financing, but if you do, you must lay out the terms here.

• *Trademarks, patents, and copyrights.* The franchisee, of course, deserves to know you are the clear owner of any intellectual property involved in the business. So here you explain both your title to this property and your willingness to defend it on the franchisee's behalf.

• *Termination, sale, or renewal.* You must specify anything that would impact your franchisee's title to the franchise. Can he or she sell it to just anyone? Must he or she offer the franchise back to you first? If the franchise is for a term of years, what must be done to renew it, and on what terms? On what grounds can the franchise be flat-out canceled?

The UFOC mostly requires you just to provide the information a reasonable buyer would expect. Don't let it get you down. Clarity here and in the actual franchise agreement, which must be attached to the UFOC, will save you a lot of hassles later.

In addition, your application to register your franchise will probably require an audited financial statement, prepared by a recognized accounting firm. (We'd recommend using the biggest-name firm you can afford; it adds credibility.)

Your UFOC will be relatively easy. You and your lawyers really just fill in the blanks. We'd say the same thing for the actual franchise agreement: You decide the basic terms, such as franchise fee, royalty, and term (twenty years is probably the most common)—then you let your lawyers write the actual document.

But you'll need more creativity (and maybe a consultant or two) to put together the next document, which may be the toughest step in franchising:

Franchise Operators' Manual If there's one thing franchisers repeat over and over, it's that training is the hardest part of the job. As Sean Richardson puts it, "We're trying to teach everything we learned in twenty-two years in one six-week course."

Actually, the Boll Weevil course runs about six weeks in the company's training center, but that's six days a week, ten hours a day, and another month at the franchiser's own store. Still, here's the toughest part:

Your training program has to train not just managers but semi-independent businesspeople. You can always say that's not your job, but remember the Golden Rule Of Franchising: If they fail, you fail.

If you're not an experienced teacher, and especially if you don't have many years' experience training managers for your operations, spending money on consultants to help design your training program is a smart move.

Brochures: The Key First Step to Selling Now, with your agreement, training program, and UFOC in shape, you can begin thinking about selling franchises. The first step there is a comprehensive brochure, which should both inform prospective buyers and sell them on the idea of buying a franchise.

Just watch out for overselling—which is how many beginning franchisers get into trouble. They start a business, succeed quickly, and then, when they offer franchises, base their cost projections on too little information.

The way around the problem? Try offering prospective investors a range of values for costs and earnings. Here's a portion of the chart Boll Weevil uses:

TYPICAL BOLL WEEVIL RESTAURANT COSTS

	Low	*High*
Land Lease, Buildings and Construction	$12,000.00	$210,000.00
Utility security deposits	$1,700.00	$2,500.00
Equipment	$3,750.00	$150,000.00
Insurance	$3,000.00	$8,000.00
Franchise fee	$29,000.00	$29,000.00
. . . . and so on		

The range is tremendous, but at least it's honest. Just within California, for example, land costs can vary almost unbelievably, from the rural Central Valley to downtown San Francisco or Los Angeles.* Why put in an unrealistic figure, either too high or too low?

Giving a range of values protects you from fraud claims on the one hand and from discouraged buyers on the other. Just make it clear why you're offering such a range and that, once the prospective buyer is seriously interested, you will narrow down the projected costs and revenues for a specific location, until they are well-enough focused to take to a bank or other lender.

What Else Does the Brochure Tell a Buyer? Here's some of what the Boll Weevil "informational folder" contains:

• The folder itself: red-and-gold on the outside, inside decorated with draftsman-quality drawings of the restaurant's model interiors and exteriors.

• Glossy, full-color drawing of a model exterior.

• Copies of favorable articles about the chain.

• Eight indexed information sheets covering everything from the history of the franchise to its corporate staff and start-up support.

• A "Financial Fact Sheet" clearly itemizing the range of costs, from the franchise fee to the advertising fee.

---

*The wide range for equipment costs stems, of course, from the fact that equipment can be either leased or purchased.

• Return envelope, and business card of the president of the company.

• A financial disclosure form (clearly marked, "not a contract") for readers interested in further pursuing the purchase of a franchise.

• A slightly-over-one-page introductory letter, friendly in tone, which explains the various stages of the franchise purchase process.

In short, an effective blend of hard fact and soft sell. There's plenty of information and encouragement, but no potentially misleading figures of prospective income. The introductory letter explains that applicants who want to go further will be invited without obligation to visit (even to work briefly in) a company store, to see whether or not they like it. Only then will they be shown the UFOC, but the truth is, by then they'll probably know everything on it.*

One final point: If you read the Boll Weevil material in light of what you now know about intellectual property, you'd notice they've taken the right steps to protect their ideas; the text is sprinkled with references to "trademarked logos," "Confidential Training Manual," and the like. Whether you're buying or selling, that understanding of intellectual property is the clear sign of a pro.

Selling the Franchises: How Sweet It Can Be! If you've read this far, you're probably thinking that franchising is a giant pain in the neck: a year's work before you can sell anything, a lot of government regulations, and so on. But here's the payoff:

When Boll Weevil ran its first ad in the San Diego Union, over two thousand people responded in the first sixty days, and the first franchise sold within that time. Today, less than two years after start-of-sales, Boll Weevil has sold seventeen franchises (roughly twice the national average for the initial two years), and is adding one new franchise roughly every eight weeks.

Boll Weevil is purposely keeping its growth rate low, and will for another year, to learn how to manage expansion. Even so, seventeen

---

*Anyone seeking a Boll Weevil franchise has to go through six interviews, and three of those are specifically designed to discourage them from buying. By stressing all the negative points of franchising, these interviews do three positive things: weed out people who really would be unhappy as owners; protect the company from charges of misrepresentation; and use "negative selling" to help clinch deals. ("Negative selling" works on the assumption that the more you try to talk people out of doing something, the more eager they'll be to find reasons why they should do it. In other words, it's simple reverse psychology.

franchises mean $493,000 just in franchise fees. That doesn't count the real money, which comes from royalties. Figure that a well-run restaurant of the Boll Weevil type should easily do $1 million a year, and a reasonable estimate might be $850,000 a year in 5 percent royalties from the stores running thus far—again, a handsome return for what is now mostly the provision of consulting services to the up-and-running stores. Already you're looking at a great return on those $120,000 start-up costs.

And how many franchises can you sell? Well, John Gorman and his partners had nine hundred Taco Bells when they sold out to Pepsico.

There's huge money to be made in franchising your idea. But, having said that, let's add a few cautionary notes.

A Big Warning: Salespeople Don't let your salespeople undo all your good work. Sometimes, overenthusiastic salespeople start making claims, including income claims, which buyers will take as guarantees. And when the claims don't prove out, you get sued.

If humanly possible, you want to avoid what happened to West Coast Video, the nation's second-largest video chain. In 1991 the successful Philadelphia-based firm found itself being sued privately by several Illinois franchisees and by the Illinois State Attorney General for "making unregistered earnings claims, plus false and misleading disclosures regarding franchisees' costs and its own expertise." (*Wall Street Journal,* July 11, 1991)

West Coast Video, which has some five hundred franchisees, denies all charges, and the matter has not yet been heard by a court, so it's not fair to draw any conclusion, except this one—

Make absolutely certain that a) your written claims are provable, and b) your salespeople never go beyond what you've put in writing. You still can't eliminate the chance that somebody who fails with your franchise will blame you and file a suit, but you can reduce the chances they will win.

Sean Richardson says Boll Weevil uses "negative selling" in all its sales contacts; that is, they stress all the risks and hazards. Not only does that eliminate many legal risks, but, because people tend to trust you if you're honest, it helps complete many sales.

Expanding. We've already said that most franchisers are lucky to sell five franchises in each of the first two years. That's not entirely bad.

In fact, smart franchisers rarely want to grow too fast; they want to manage the growth. As you build infrastructure and improve your methods, you can pick up the pace.

The Boll Weevil method is to establish sales offices in a growth area, but to do the operational work from the home office. As stores come on line, operational people are added to the sales office. Once the selling is done (theoretically, after about two years), the sales staff is moved on to the next region, and the former sales office becomes purely an operations center.

Will You Have Problems? As of early 1992, with about two years of franchising under its belt, all but one of Boll Weevil's seventeen franchises had already turned profitable. The company had no major complaints. As Sean Richardson puts it, "When people are making money, problems are overlooked—and that's the key."

But here's one tip for fixing problems before they're serious. Boll Weevil's franchisees have their own organization. The parent company meets with that organization's top officers once a month, with all franchisees once a quarter. Complaints (if any) get heard and dealt with before they become serious.

Franchising—Your Ongoing Obligation If you're really out to build your fortune by franchising your ideas, you need to keep fresh ideas coming all the time.

If your franchisees fall behind in the race for market share, three things will happen, not necessarily in this order: Your royalty revenues from ongoing operations will dry up; interest in buying your new franchises will vanish; and your franchisees will start suing you for breach of your obligation to help them stay competitive.

In part, that means you need to spend money on R and D. But it also means this:

Just because you invented the franchise, please don't think you have a monopoly on ideas connected with it. One of the saddest developments is for the franchiser to begin rejecting franchisees' input. Ignoring their problems is bad; ignoring their creative ideas is perhaps even worse.

Ignore enough of your franchisees' ideas and one day you'll find they've sold the franchises to someone else and gone off to begin new franchises of their own. You'll have turned allies into competitors.

So listen to good ideas, from any source.

Summing Up Franchising can be the single best way of profiting from your business ideas. To make franchising work, though, you need to perfect your ideas—that is, reduce them to a workable, reproducible, protectable, and teachable format. Then you have to market the franchise, which puts you in yet another business. And finally, being a franchiser places you in a close, fiduciary relationship with anyone who buys one of your franchises.

61

Buying or Selling Ideas, and Finding Ideas to Invest In

THIS BOOK IS supposed to be about your great idea. But as a businessperson, you may well succeed simply by buying and developing other people's ideas.

In 1932, for example, two brothers, Earl and Charles Doolin, paid $500 for a Mexican restaurant's chip recipe. They started making the chips on their kitchen stove, and from that simple recipe built the Frito-Lay company.

Buying someone else's idea today is probably more complicated than it was in 1932, but with a little preparation you can still get very rich doing it. Buying an idea—what lawyers call "intellectual property"—is, in theory, no more complicated than buying any other property. To start, you want to be sure you're getting a clear title. In particular, you're looking at the following:

Origin of the Idea. Who created what you are buying? If it was a team, is the present owner willing to warrant there won't be future claims of ownership? You need to see any work contracts under which these co-inventors performed, as well as the original patent affidavits.

Subsequent claims. Has the idea/property been subsequently mortgaged, promised, or licensed to anyone else? (Watch for past deals that fell apart, before or after being formalized, and for any contracts, signed or otherwise, created in connection with them. Remember, people can sue over contracts that were never signed, if they can show they spent time or money in the reasonable expectation that those contracts were going to be signed.)

Types of registration and protection. Is the property properly patented/trademarked/copyrighted? Have proper notifications been put on all products? Have all the necessary fees (renewals, etc.) been paid to keep the protection fully active?

Quality of the protection. Make a judgment about the worth of the protection. Is the patent easily circumvented? Is the trademark the kind the courts will uphold?

Pending litigation. Is the present owner facing any big lawsuits? Obviously, patent or trademark suits are the major concern, but watch that there aren't any high-dollar-value lawsuits against the company as a whole, which might end up with the patents being seized as assets.

Other legal challenges. Is the present owner aware of any potentially infringing goods or services? Are the forms of legal protection, especially patents, nearing the end of lives? Remember, seventeen years is not a terribly long time in the life of a business.

Answering those questions means conducting an "I.P. Audit" of the sort discussed at the start of this section. We suggested then that a start-up company could conduct its own home-grown audit. You can also do that if you're buying a simple idea for little money, but if you're spending any significant amount, you'll probably want to use attorneys.

You may leave some of the questions for the auditing attorneys to handle, but many of them you can handle by yourself, and for nearly all, you can collect preliminary information and so shorten the time and cut the cost of the I.P. Audit.

What Do Audits Cost? The cost depends upon the complexity of the problem, and the cost of legal services in your part of the country. Still, the common services provided by good I.P. law firms tend to fall within these rough price guidelines:

Answering a specific set of questions: $1,000–$3,000
Training management to conduct its own ongoing audits: $2,500–$5,000
Auditing a single line of technology: $5,000–$10,000
Auditing a high-tech company: $100,000

Those prices are for parts of the country (New York, Los Angeles, Silicon Valley) where legal talent is highest-priced. You can probably knock about 20 percent off that for the same work performed in, say, the Midwest or the South. And don't hesitate to negotiate for a lower package price for services.

How Long Do They Take? Most law firms will tell you they can report on a small technology-based company in less than two weeks. Generally, that's true; but it often means "two weeks from when we can get started." Even the biggest intellectual property law firms aren't all that big. If you're looking for a high-tech acquisition, let your lawyers know early on, and find out their availability. A little scheduling will save you a lot of grief.

Pricing Intellectual Property How do you set a price for a piece of intellectual property? It's not easy, especially in an age when biotech companies with no products for sale are valued at hundreds of millions of dollars. Even more to the point, most deals are made with plenty of horse trading—that is, with much bluffing and guessing about each side's needs and strengths.

Still, let's say you're interested in buying the patent on a low-tech toy called a Widget. Widgets have been on the market for three years and now represent $1 million in annual sales. The company making them is netting $50,000 a year. It has the toys made under contract, so it doesn't own any factories: Its fixed assets (including company cars) are about $75,000. Its patents and trademarks look solid.

Now, you like Widgets, but you don't love them. How much do you offer?

The rule-of-thumb for buying a business is that you don't normally pay more than book value plus about 2.5 times net annual income. In the case of Widgets, Inc., that means:

$$75,000 + (2.5 \times \$50,000) = \$200,000$$

That's the top figure, usually reserved for companies with long track records and stable markets. Many investors wouldn't go over, say, $125,000 for Widgets, Inc. Still, your kids think Widgets are cute, and you think you can up profit margins by manufacturing them in your own plant.

You offer the company's owner $150,000. You think that's a fair offer, but you'll go up to $200,000 to clinch the deal.

She answers that a top producer of children's TV shows has been thinking seriously about creating a Widgets TV show. That'll mean $15,000 a week in fees for using the name, plus millions in fresh sales, more licensing deals . . . you name it.

In short, she's got dollar signs in her eyes, and won't sell for less than $1 million.

What happens now?

When You're Far Apart on Price In most businesses, when people want five times what you're willing to pay, you thank them politely and exit so fast you leave skid marks on their floor.

But with I.P. you have another option. You simply offer the seller participation in any future licensing arrangements for a limited time.

These limited-time royalties could represent a percentage of *all* licensing revenues you receive over, say, the next two or three years, or a percentage of all licensing deals initiated during the seller's time of ownership, or even "platform" payments. In a "platform," the seller gets say, a flat $25,000 if Widgets earns from $100,000 to 250,000 in licensing fees over the next few years; $50,000 if fees reach from $250,000 to $500,000; and so on. Straight percentages are simplest, of course, but stay flexible.

What percentage should you offer? First of all, remember that you should offer a percentage only of monies actually received by you; you don't want to find yourself paying royalties on monies you were promised but never received. Then—

A reasonable deal might be 10 percent of what you receive during the first three years.* In return, you should get not only the property, but a "non-compete" agreement, saying the seller won't go into business against you during the royalty period.

If your seller really believes she's on the verge of a fortune, she'll likely hang onto the business—as is her privilege. But if she only hopes a fortune awaits her, she may well take your terms. If so, get your attorneys to formalize the deal; if not, resume your search.

Never assume you have to make any given deal. There'll always be another opportunity along shortly.

If you do purchase intellectual property protected by patent, trademark, or copyright, be sure to register your purchase with either the PTO (for patents and trademarks) or the Copyright Office (for copyrighted materials, including computer software) within 90 days. Simply send a copy of the documents giving you ownership of the property, along with a cover letter clearly identifying the property, to the right office. Registration gives you important protection in case of bankruptcy of the original owner, and also makes it easier for you to resell the property, to borrow money against it, or to interest investors.

Other Places to Buy Ideas—Or Get Them for Free Buying ideas from the original creator is a reasonable approach. Since, however, everybody can always use one more idea, and since everybody likes a bargain, here are some ways you can get great deals on ideas:

---

* In fact, set your offer according to the advice of your legal counsel, and the going rate for the kind of property you're seeking.

Public domain ideas. Many great ideas are simply in the public domain: Either they were never protected, or their protection has expired, or they were created by the U.S. government, which makes much of its intellectual property available either for free or for relatively modest fees.

You cannot take something in the public domain and then copyright, trademark, or patent it. You can however, add to an existing product and protect what you've added. That's one reason old black-and-white movies are being colorized: The colorization gets its own new copyright, even if the black-and-white version remains in the public domain.

By the same token, anybody can get an old, unprotected edition of a literary classic, reset the type (or even photo-reproduce the original), and sell the resulting copies. If they wanted to protect their creation, though, they'd have to add new material: new art, say, or an introductory essay. The new material could itself be protected, even though the rest remains in the public domain.

An invention can likewise be protected even if its core is in the public domain. If, for example, you take a public domain computer program, refine its operation, improve the user interface, write a good manual, and package it creatively, you can probably protect the result as long as your application specifies clearly what is your original achievement, and what is derivative.

Where do you find technology? If you're looking for any interesting idea to commercialize, try approaching nearby universities. Those with significant research programs will probably have a licensing office, but the truth is, most such offices are extremely passive. If you want to hunt for exploitable ideas, try contacting individual labs first.

Normally, of course, you're looking for ideas that fit your particular strengths, needs, or interests. That means starting with a research center—and nobody runs more of those than the U.S. government.

That's why you should definitely know about the the National Technology Information Service, the central clearinghouse for licensable U.S. government research. NTIS can help you find, not only the latest federal technology available for license, but—

• *Government labs.* For entrepreneurs with ideas needing development, NTIS says it can help locate government facilities "willing to share their expertise, equipment, and sometimes even . . . facilities."

• *Big private companies.* Few people know this, but major companies often develop technologies they later decide not to commercialize, and so are willing to sell cheap or sometimes even give away. NTIS is beginning to offer access to this technology; one early contributor is Xerox. (Don't assume such technology is junk. In the early 1970s Xerox backed away from some computer research done at its famed Palo Alto Research Center. Two fellows named Wozniak and Jobs borrowed the ideas and created a gadget you may have heard of. It was called the Apple Macintosh.)

If you find an idea you'd like to license, the NTIS will help you get it, through the Office of Federal Patent Licensing, at its Center for the Utilization of Federal Technology (CUFT). Call CUFT at 1-703-487-4738 for information on cutting deals.

All these resources and many more are itemized in various NTIS publications, including the *Catalog of Government Inventions Available for Licensing*.

For details, contact NTIS at:

> National Technology Information Service
> 5285 Port Royal Road
> Springfield, Virginia 22181
> 1-703-321-8547

Even better, anybody with a computer and modem can just dial the NTIS's free Patent Licensing Bulletin Board and get the scoop on new opportunities weeks ahead of their print publication. Go on-line at:
1-703-487-4061
or call the NTIS Sales Desk at 1-703-487-4650, and ask for the *PLBB Users Manual*.

NTIS is itself going into the idea business, by joint-venturing with (mostly) small firms interested in commercializing its vast databases. They've already done more than a dozen deals, and say they can give a firm "go/no-go" answer in 90 days or less. They also seem to treat entrepreneurs kindly. Give them a try.

Using the Government: A Final Word All that's definitely to the good. Just remember what we were told by Dr. Stephen Gates, the refreshingly plainspoken organic chemist who heads CUFT:

• The Federal government has a vast amount of technical information, but it will be your job to convert it into marketable goods or services. Anybody looking for an off-the-shelf instant product is, in Dr. Gates's words, "in the wrong church." You're being offered valuable ideas that need to be commercialized—and that, Dr. Gates warns, can take "one hell of a lot of time and money."

• Be prepared to take the initiative. CUFT is not a consulting service and simply doesn't have the resources to help you figure out what you need. Go to them with a clear idea of what you want, and you can get a license in one afternoon. Show up just wondering if they can give you a hand with some vague problem, and they'll politely show you the door.

None of this is meant to discourage you. Federal labs have superb technical abilities, and are eager to see their work commercialized. Dr. Gates estimates CUFT cuts about a third of its deals with small businesses—as small as "the lone inventor in a garage." Indeed, all other things being equal, CUFT will favor a qualified small firm over a big one. And the licensing fees are certainly fair, running from a low of under 1 percent, to a high of over 5 percent (generally, for pharmaceuticals).

Realize that, despite much progress in a short time, federal labs are not commercial labs. You are the entrepreneur, so be ready to show the spirit.

Summing Up Investing in intellectual property is like any other investment: You evaluate the risk, calculate the property's value, and make an offer.

You now know how to organize, protect, promote, and even franchise your business ideas. You know how to negotiate for the sale or purchase of ideas. In short, you know plenty to send you roaring toward success.

Go get 'em!

62

Case Study: Sol Price and the Price Clubs

YOU'RE INTERESTED IN business ideas? How about this one? It's 1975, and a fifty-nine-year-old San Diego businessman named Sol Price comes to you with an idea for a completely new approach to retailing. He wants to build a warehouse-size building on the outskirts of town, fill it with merchandise for small business owners, and then charge them an annual fee to shop there. In return, he'll give them the lowest prices possible on every single thing he sells.

You know Sol Price was recently fired by the first company he built and that the buyer of that company is in a lot of trouble—but you also know Sol Price has a reputation for business genius and for the strictest personal integrity. He and his son are backing the new venture with a million dollars of their own money.

He wants you to put up $5,000 for one share in the venture.

Buy or pass?

Let's hope you said, "Buy"—because if you'd invested $5,000 in Sol Price's idea in 1975 and held onto it, by 1990 you'd have had an investment worth four million dollars.

Maybe you missed your shot at the Price Club, but how can you make your business idea work that well? Are there any rules? How, in short, did Sol Price do it?

The Accidental Retailer For someone who's received almost unbroken cheers for business creativity over the last fifteen years, Sol Price came to the game by a curiously roundabout route.

He started as an attorney. By all accounts, he was a splendid one, but in the prejudiced 1940s and 1950s, a Jewish attorney had no hope of representing big corporations, so his clients were mostly small business owners. Over time, though, he noticed two things. First, his clients increasingly sought his business, rather than his legal, advice. And second, he liked solving business problems.

More than a decade of solving other people's business problems left him surprisingly well-prepared to act when opportunity presented itself in a most unlikely fashion. An odd turn of events left his mother-in-law owning a rather nice but empty warehouse in the industrial part of town. What was she to do with it?

Two of Mr. Price's clients saw the building. To them, it looked just like that of a nonprofit outfit called Fedco, which sold merchandise at a discount to federal employees who joined as members.* They thought Fedco had an interesting business and suggested, perhaps half-jokingly, that Sol Price could probably do the same thing, only better.

A Borrowed Idea   Sol Price visited Fedco, liked its idea, and decided he could do it better. So he found eight investors each willing to put up $5,000, and his law firm added another $10,000. With that $50,000 they opened a for-profit company called "Fedmart," using Fedco's idea of selling discounted goods to a restricted group but aimed at a somewhat broader market.

Unfortunately, that broader market meant big trouble. Sometimes when you invent a better mousetrap the world doesn't beat a path to your doorstep—it just beats you over the head.

"The Business World Hates Change"   The creation of Fedmart proved the opening shot in a multiyear battle with the San Diego establishment. As the *New York Times* recalled in 1988: "Manufacturers and local merchants were outraged. . . . Newspapers refused to carry Fedmart's advertisements; the Better Business Bureau refused its application for membership."

Today, the discount department store seems commonplace and undramatic; it's the idea behind every Walmart or Target.†

How nasty was the fight?

In California, merchants have what's called an "automatic license" to sell bedding. Anyone can sell bedding, but if there's a complaint, an inspector can check to see if you're observing the relevant laws.

Shortly before Fedmart opened its doors, a state bedding inspector appeared. That was odd in itself, but odder still, this inspector didn't

---

*Fedco still operates successfully today, still a nonprofit membership store open to government employees.

†Indeed, in his autobiography, the late Sam Walton admitted quite frankly that he borrowed many of his best ideas from Sol Price.

have any bedding questions. He wanted to know where Fedmart was getting its money, who was running it—everything, in short, that could be useful to people who wanted to pressure Fedmart out of business.

Sol Price threw the inspector out of the store, told him his questions were baloney and he wasn't going to answer them—and then told him to "take his best shot": file suit, press charges, or whatever.

The inspector never called again. But for years the business community kept trying to freeze out the threatening new competitor. At one point Sol Price's own accountant headed the local Better Business Bureau—and Fedmart still couldn't get its membership approved.

With time, opposition dissolved, partly because discount retailing became commonplace nationwide, and largely, we suspect, because Fedmart worked unswervingly on what Sol Price calls "a fiduciary relationship" with the customer—that is, a relationship of special duty and moral obligation—and so won widespread support in the community.

Fired By the early 1970s Fedmart was a publicly held corporation, operating as far east as Texas and active in a wide range of businesses, but its stock had gone flat. In 1974, Price tried taking the company private again in a leveraged buyout, then dropped the idea when the SEC seemed likely to object.

Almost immediately, German retailer Hugo Mann made a bid for the company. As Sol Price recalls it, Fedmart management was "romanced" passionately: An infusion of German money would make all sorts of new ideas possible. Everything would be *wunderbar*. Between the romancing and a genuine feeling that, at least short-term, the buyout was the best deal for stockholders, Price agreed to sell.

"Within months, the romancing stopped. Then I was fired."*

The firing left Price, in his late fifties, moderately wealthy (the payout for his departure finally amounted to a little under $2 million), but with no career, when he was still in the prime of life.

What to do?

The Big Idea At an age when many people start thinking of retirement, Sol Price starting walking the streets of San Diego with his son, Robert, and talking with small businesspeople about their needs and wishes. Shortly, the key insight struck him.

Small businesses, in his view, "had every advantage over bigger ·

---

*Shortly after the firing the romance ended for Mann, too. With no understanding of the American scene, he soon ran Fedmart into the ground and then left the business.

ones" except one: They couldn't "buy right," that is, as cheaply as their big competitors. That was the recurring theme of his walking conversations. The person who could help small businesses buy goods as cheaply as the big ones did, would make a fortune.

There was the market—and it appeared to a man with both the vision to see it, and the practical experience to address it. Sol Price had spent over a decade as a lawyer advising small business owners. He knew their problems—and now he saw a solution.

What was needed was a store so big it would be essentially a vast warehouse, yet could move goods in and out at a pace previously almost unimaginable. The warehouse would be bare bones in style, built on cheap, out-of-the-way land, and stocked with everything for small businesses at rock-bottom prices. It would charge membership fees; take no credit cards; and run no ads, sales, or specials.

Making the Idea Work That, in broadest outline, was the Price Club idea. How well did it work?

Great—except for just one detail. A few months after opening, they were, in the words of the man who ought to know, "losing their butts."

The problem might have been any of a dozen things, but proved to be one of the last they suspected. There just weren't enough small businesses ready to try the new approach.

Once they found the problem, the solution was surprisingly simple: They just expanded membership judiciously, by creating a second tier of membership. People who didn't own small businesses could now join by paying a smaller fee, and in return receive a slightly lower discount on items they bought.

Expanded membership turned the trick—by the end of the next year Price Clubs were roaring, and they haven't stopped yet. Sales for 1991 neared $7 billion.

The average discount store sells annually about $175 worth of merchandise per square foot of floor space. The average office products superstore does about $300. And the average Price Club does $1,000 a square foot—and in much larger buildings. You get a quantum leap like that only with a truly new concept.

What were the principles that made the Price Club idea work? Here are five that seem important:

1. Master the details. Many analysts have called the Price Clubs the most important retailing idea of the past quarter century. What does Sol Price think about that?

"The idea counted for very little; the execution was almost everything."

What does Mr. Price mean by "execution"?

Well, let's say it's 1975 and you've got the idea for the Price Club. Good for you!

But now come the details. *Which* piece of undeveloped land? How exactly do you set those razor-thin markups? How do you persuade manufacturers to supply you when they're afraid of losing their regular outlets? Where do you find the quick-witted managers needed to run the new stores? Details matter in making any idea work, but in making a business idea work, they're decisive.

2. Keep creating ideas. The very fact that businesses live or die by the details means that you have an infinite demand for creative solutions to problems of every sort. In your early days, frankly, you'll probably find it easy to make changes, improvise, listen to others.

What Sol Price most remembers about the early Fedmart days is the spirit of brainstorming among all the partners. No idea, apparently, was too wild to be considered—from starting a bank, to naming house brands after well-liked employees. He and his management team took Fedmart into everything from construction to insurance.

But big companies ("like big nations") tend to ossify. As Sol Price puts it, "You have egos, and you have turf—and you have a system in which an idea can be an accusation: 'You [idiot], why didn't you think of that yourself?' " One of the great challenges of success is admitting you can do better—and so, fitting new ideas into a working system.

Today, Price Clubs are growing fast enough for people with ideas to rise quickly through the structure. More formally, the company operates Price Club Industries, which is meant to be its "entrepreneurial arm": developing new products and services for the stores to offer. Will that serve, or will the Price Club one day begin to slow down?

Only time will tell. The point for you is to keep your business as open as possible to new ideas every single day.

3. Keep the ideas focused. It's easy enough to say you should encourage creativity, but even good ideas have to be used wisely. It takes time to execute any idea, and that can take your focus off your Main Business Objective—what we've been calling your "dot." Yes, Sol Price recalls fondly the freewheeling early Fedmart days. Yet he now admits that many of those ventures, exciting as they may have been, really drew his focus away from his main business, and so, overall, hurt the business more than they helped it.

Today Mr. Price tries to focus his creativity more precisely. For example, one of the Price Club's earliest strengths was its real estate strategy: It bought out-of-the way land dirt cheap and then made it valuable by building its stores on it. Investing cash flow in fast-appreciating real estate, rather than reporting it as taxable earnings was a great way to build and preserve corporate wealth.

But by the late 1980s pressure was growing to build Price Clubs faster and faster. That took money—and borrowing money is expensive. Sol Price's solution was to create a REIT (real estate investment trust). The REIT will sell shares to raise money and then use the money to buy Price Club properties. The REIT will make money for its shareholders by renting the properties back to the Price Clubs, and perhaps, in the future, by selling the properties at a profit, or by co-developing new Price Club sites.

That means people unwilling to take the risks of buying stock can invest in the Price Club formula tangentially. Mr. Price went a step further, structuring the deal so REIT shareholders had preferential protection in case any of the properties got into trouble.

4. Behave ethically. Sounds obvious? Perhaps, but "Behave ethically" doesn't mean simply, or only, "Don't cheat people." Mostly it means, "Act according to your deepest beliefs—and your ideas will follow."

Nick Meyer had the most-watched movie in TV history when he decided to make an antinuclear war film, even though three previous directors had walked off the project and the experts told him the film would never be shown. A. P. Giannini founded the Bank of Italy as a bank for "the common man" after seeing his father murdered by a ranch hand over a one-dollar dispute—and deciding no one should ever be put in fear of his life over a dollar. Using that principle, the Bank of Italy— renamed the Bank of America—became the largest bank in the world.

Strong beliefs will help you focus what could otherwise be too-general creativity. When Sol Price, explaining why he didn't like credit cards, told the *New York Times,* "It's against my religion that people should go into debt to buy things," he was only partly playing with the English language. If you have a strong belief, let it guide your creativity. Otherwise, your heart and your head will always be at odds.*

5. Don't agonize about protecting your business idea. We've spent a

---

*Let's not be naïve about this. Behaving ethically is quite distinct from being a pushover. Business, especially, is about competition: You're there to win, or you shouldn't be there. But being tough, and being ethical, are by no means mutually exclusive.

lot of time talking about how you can protect your business's intellectual property: trade secrets, patents, trademarks, and the like. All that is extremely important, but the truth is that, even after you've taken all possible steps, people are always going to find a way to clone any successful business.

The Price Club already has at least five big-league competitors, plus a host of smaller clones. One of the big competitors is backed by Wal-Mart, the world's largest retailer, and a firm known for superb execution of other people's ideas. Another is run by a former Price Company executive.

That's a pretty daunting array. But Sol Price, who took on the entire business community of San Diego as a young attorney, who built one retail empire, lost it, and built another far larger, hasn't flinched yet.

When we asked him if he thought there should be something like a "business patent," protecting business ideas for a certain number of years, he answered with a story.

"When I ran Fedmart, many years ago, we had a competitor named Unimart, started by some of our ex-employees. One day, the fellow who put out our Fedmart newspaper came to me and complained, 'Mr. Price, every time I print something in the *Fedmart News,* two weeks later the same thing appears in the *Unimart News.* It's just not fair.'

"Well, I told him, 'That's the way the world runs—and when you get tired of running with it, you come and tell me, and I'll get someone who isn't tired.'"

"Two weeks later, the fellow quit."

And that was all Sol Price cared to say about the idea of protecting business intellectual property.

Good business ideas are meant to be used and improved, not held as private trusts. That's a philosophy Sol Price applies consistently. He got his start by improving someone else's retailing idea. Today he welcomes competitors to take their best shot with his great business idea. If they can use it to bring a better deal to the marketplace, they deserve the business.

(Of course, good luck to them in trying: Every single analyst's report we consulted on the Discount Warehouse industry ranked Price Clubs as the best-managed.)

That, in brief, is the Price philosophy. It built a $6.6-billion-a-year company in sixteen years, made many people fairly rich and several very rich indeed, and turned a major industry on its head.

Closing Words At the end of our interview Sol Price left us with a few lines that seemed to sum up much of his highly entrepreneurial view of creativity and of business in general:

"Ideas come from that irritation within you. When you get satisfied, sell out and go live on an island—because somebody else has something to give. And you don't have it anymore.

"You'd better get better every single day. Never mind the old saying, 'If it ain't broke, don't fix it.' If it ain't broke, *fix it*. Because if you don't, somebody else is going to fix it for you. And then they're going to fix you."

63

Remember Where You Came From

WE'VE WRITTEN THIS BOOK from our hearts as much as our heads: We believe that creativity, like freedom, lies at the core of the American experience and the American character. We also believe in free enterprise and the Constitutionally guaranteed right of people to profit from their creative endeavors.

Yet we'd be unfair if we did not acknowledge an equally honorable American tradition. It dates at least from Ben Franklin, (who refused to patent anything he invented, including the famous Franklin stove, American's first commercially successful invention), and Thomas Jefferson, whose creativity in everything from architecture and inventing, to literature and political philosophy probably ranks him as our country's only universal genius. Jefferson and Franklin held ideas to be the common property of all humankind—and felt their debt to those who came before them more than canceled their right to profit from what they themselves created.

That tradition continues today, in people like Berkeley professor Lofti Zadeh, who never made or sought a penny from the invention of "fuzzy logic," a mathematical innovation that led to several thousand industrial patents (mostly taken out by Japanese companies) in its first few years. It lives in Richard Stallman, considered by many to be the finest computer programmer alive, who not only gives away his own software but has fought for years to end the patenting and/or copyrighting of any software. Except for winning a "genius grant" from the MacArthur Foundation, he has yet to profit from programs in use by companies and research institutions worldwide.

We're certainly not urging you to donate your inventions whole cloth to the world at large, and obviously we'd never argue in favor of abolishing intellectual property rights. What you create is and should be yours alone, to dispose of as you see fit.

Yet we'd urge you to consider the views of Jefferson, Franklin, and others, at least to the degree of trying to pass along some of what you've gained, so as to help stimulate the community of ideas from which our common success stems.

What you do is up to you. Researching this book, we've met inventors who donated time to museums, films producers and directors who teach college courses and endow university fellowships, immensely wealthy business pioneers who underwrite entire university complexes or create their own philanthropies.

Herman Melville described our human condition as "a mutual, joint-stock world in all meridians, shipmate." We sail, or sink, together.

Maybe that's the greatest American idea of them all.

Appendix

Finding the Money for Your Great Idea

THROUGHOUT THIS BOOK, we've tried to provide basic tips about raising the money to turn your idea into reality—especially about the more exotic approaches, like royalty financing. In this brief appendix, though, we'd like to summarize the more traditional money sources.

Not every sort of great idea will require funding—or be eligible for it. First novels and screenplays, for example, generally develop as spare-time projects. Still, if you think you'll need to find money for your idea, here are some possibilities:

Grants

Realistically, grants are unlikely to be a primary resource for most idea projects—but they do occasionally work.

You need to show initiative in digging up grants, yet they are available in some surprising fields: while most are for artists, some are reserved for inventors and entrepreneurs. For example, the Department of Energy's Energy-Related Inventions Program (ERIP) provides grants averaging a hefty $83,000 to develop inventions which produce or conserve energy. Indeed, ERIP grants are available even for "inventions" still at the idea stage—a tremendous help for aspiring inventors.

Many sourcebooks can point you toward grants. Among the most encyclopedic (and most widely available in libraries) is the *Annual Register of Grant Support: A Directory of Funding Sources*. It emphasizes (as you would guess) grants and awards for academics and organizations—but also includes many grants open to all.

You might also be wise to contact any state or local business development organizations. They can often direct you either to grants or to cash-equivalent programs (like subsidized business incubators), which can be nearly as useful as good old money.

Microlenders

Microlending is a fairly new—and extremely promising—approach to helping small entrepreneurs launch new ventures. It began as a third-world program to make poor people self-sufficient by granting them business start-up loans as small as $50. Adapted to more-affluent American conditions, it has done beautifully here, with everyone from private nonprofits to the Small Business Administration (SBA) getting involved.

Here are the basics:

• Microlenders are especially interested in entrepreneurs who could not qualify for traditional loans: especially poor women and minorities.

• Loans begin as small as $500 and go up to around $25,000. The smaller loans are often available to first-time applicants quite easily; but you usually need to work with a given organization for a while, and to establish your credit history, before you can get the larger amounts.

• These are real loans, not charity. While the conditions for qualifying are non-traditional, you'll pay the same interest rates as you would for a traditional loan—and your repayments will be watched as closely.

• The apparent key to microlending's extremely big success rate is *peer support and review*. The most common form of this is to make anyone receiving a loan join a loan group with, normally, six to ten members. These members help and advise each other, arrange for group continuing education, and so on. They also make sure everyone stays current with his or her loan—especially since (with many microloan groups) as long as one member is delinquent, no other member can get any further loans. Peer pressure really works!

• While low-income people were the original targets of these loans, some programs now give about one-fourth of their loans to higher-income applicants. So don't automatically count yourself out by reason of income.

For more information, contact the umbrella organization for U.S. microlenders, the Association for Economic Opportunity, in Chicago: 1-312-661-1700. They can send you an information packet and the name of your nearest microlender.

Traditional Banks

One common lament of idea people—especially inventors and entrepreneurs—is that traditional lenders (banks and savings-and-loans) have almost no interest in backing ideas, inventions, or brand-new businesses. (Let's not even *talk* about their funding, say, your year off to write a screenplay or record an album!)

Traditional lenders loan money only against existing assets—or, at times, against assets (usually, real estate) to be purchased with the proceeds of the loan. For a business, that generally means they aren't interested in lending until you are shipping product and have significant accounts receivable.

That doesn't mean idea people should ignore traditional lenders. Indeed, it's plain smart for aspiring entrepreneurs to begin making bank contacts as early as possible. Find out (from other entrepreneurs, your attorney or CPA, or even newspaper accounts) which banks in your area have the best reputations for helping newer ventures. Move your checking account there and while you're setting it up, introduce yourself to the highest-ranking bankers you can reach. At this stage, it's largely social—but you'll probably find that once you're big enough for traditional funding, you'll get much better treatment from people who already consider you a friend. That's just common sense, of course, but you'd be amazed at how many people neglect it.

A few banks around the country are following the lead of California's Silicon Valley Bank, in offering early help for aspiring inventors and entrepreneurs. The services offered range from counseling to databases of lawyers, CPAs, and even available executives to serve as part-time corporate mentors. Ask what's available!

SBA-Backed Loans

The theory of SBA-backed loans for business is excellent: because the Federal government (through the Small Business Administration) guarantees these loans, banks are willing to loan at lower rates and for longer times.

In past years, though, the SBA loan process provoked bitter complaints for being slow, insanely burdened with paperwork, and unavailable to start-ups. Even the SBA admitted its programs had been largely reduced to helping established businesses buy real estate. Not exactly a bonanza for idea people.

In the early 90s, though, the SBA began trying to reverse that reputation with a variety of initiatives. Probably the most important of those was the "Low Documentation" (LowDoc) loan program, which began in July 1994.

Under LowDoc, entrepreneurs can borrow up to $100,000 for "soft cost" items (that is, non-machinery, non–real estate). More generally, the money can be used for a start-up, for expansion, or to buy a going business. Only applicants with essentially perfect credit are eligible—but they will find vastly reduced paperwork (a one-page form), a quick response (the target is a two-day turnaround), and yet loans at traditionally desirable SBA-backed rates, 2¾ percent above prime. For information, try your bank, the local SBA office, or the SBA at 1-800-827-5722.

Whether LowDoc will actually work, long-term, remains to be seen. Other SBA programs have sounded great in theory, then gradually succumbed to bureaucratic snafus. In its early execution, though, LowDoc has been impressive. Check it out!

Venture Capitalists

Venture capitalists invest money in your business (or sometimes, idea) at an early stage—generally, before you turn profitable. In exchange, you give them a percentage of the business, usually in the form of the right to buy stock before you go public. Accordingly, v.c.'s rarely make any money on their investment until the business goes public—at which point, through sale of their shares in your company, they can earn stunning returns. (Some highly successful venture capital investments can return $100 for every $1 invested.)

Venture capital is expensive: at the earliest stages, v.c.'s may expect as much as 75 percent of the business for their money. If a firm agrees to invest in you, they will quote you two numbers: a "commitment" (the amount they're willing to invest) and a "valuation" (what they think your business or idea is worth). The ratio of commitment to valuation tells you how much of the business they'll want in return: if they're investing, say, $2 million in a business they value at $3 million, they'll expect to get two-thirds of the business. Naturally, the earlier they enter a venture, the less they will assume it's worth and the larger a share of it they'll expect in return for a given investment. So, clearly, the longer you can carry the project on your own, the more of it you'll end up owning.

On the plus side, the best v.c.'s provide extremely valuable management help, credibility—*and* the money you need to grow quickly.

In general, venture capital is best suited to pretty sophisticated entrepreneurs and inventors. To approach v.c.'s with any reasonable chance of success, you should probably begin by sending a two- to three-page query letter, covering:

Referrals If your letter can begin by saying you have been recommended by a banker, attorney, or CPA known to the firm (or even better, one of the firm's existing clients), that will greatly improve your chances.

A "Vision" Statement No, nothing mystical—just a fairly temperate summary of what we've called your "dot," your ultimate business goal. You can present this as your "introductory" paragraph, but it needs to have a promotional element, something highlighting the big payoff for the money to be risked. Ideally, this paragraph (or two) will also cover a) the problem you're addressing and b) the size of your potential market, realistically estimated.

Your Competitive Advantage Venture capitalists don't invest in "me too" ideas; they're looking for the new products and services with the potential to win big. You need to show you have what one top venture capitalist calls your "unfair advantage"—something that's going to make your competitors (if any) wish they were in another line of work. Also make it clear how your competitive advantage will be protected from knockoffs: by trade secret, patents, and so on. Few people want to bet on an idea that can be stolen in the morning.

The State of Your Project Let them know—briefly—how far along in the project you are. Still planning? Testing prototypes? Shipping product? Also let them know, generally, how you'll use their money, if you get it. (Obviously, use some judgment here: if you're still at a very early stage, don't give away any valuable secrets!)

Your Management Team Venture capitalists almost never back individuals. If you don't have a team together, make it clear in your proposal that you'll accept help in assembling one. (You also summarize your own credentials here, of course.)

Organize the material any way you think reads well, but do try to cover those points. Obviously, there are exceptions to each of these points: if, for example, you've just patented a terrific invention, but have nothing else, many venture capitalists would be willing, and able, to help you launch the business.

If the firm is interested, they may write back requesting your business plan, or they may invite you in for a meeting. In either case, your business plan should be completed before you send your first query letter: you want to be ready to take the next step, if invited. You'll either mail in the plan if they request it, or use it as the basis of your presentation if they invite you in for a meeting. Both the plan and the presentation should cover the same things as any other traditional business plan: an analysis of the market, competition, main selling channels, and so on.

Two hints: Don't waste your money on any "packaging" services to give you a fancy-looking proposal: every v.c. we consulted said those packages carry no weight and are simply money thrown away. Also, try breaking your business plan into two segments: a "summary plan," running under ten pages, and a "supporting documents" packet, as long as necessary, with all the spread sheets, market analyses, etc.

"Seed stage" venture capitalists—which invest in ideas while they're still ideas—are not numerous, but they do exist. To find any sort of v.c., start with the latest annual *Pratt's Guide to Venture Capital Resources.* It breaks down v.c.'s by geographic region, then characterizes them according to the kinds of businesses which interest them, the amount they like to invest, and so on.

Well, that's the "horseback tour" of raising money for your great idea. Remember that new money sources are always appearing: try to ask every qualified person you meet (banker, CPA, attorney) what new approaches he or she recommends. Above all, though, the key is to understand at least three things:

1. The farther you can take the business on your own efforts and resources, the more of the final creation you're going to own. The sooner you begin selling off pieces of your idea, the less it's going to earn you.

2. The first step to keeping control of your idea is keeping your expenses to a minimum. If a garage was grand enough to launch Apple Computers and Hewlett-Packard, what are you doing with fancy offices?

3. Be flexible—try to put as much imagination into funding your business as you have into your great idea.

Finally, remember that it doesn't really take much money to launch a "great idea" business. In 1968, a young pharmacist named Jane Hirsh borrowed $500 from a friend to buy a machine for making chemical solutions to sell to hospital labs.

Ms. Hirsh made enough money selling those simple solutions that she was able to expand steadily over the next twenty-five years, gradually moving from hospital solutions into generic drugs. Indeed, she did so well that—

In 1993, she sold control of her company, Copley Pharmaceutical, to the German chemical giant A.G. Hoechst. Her share of the take? $148 million, the CEO and Chairman's jobs, and a mid-six-figure salary (plus bonuses) to stay on and run the business. She also kept 13 percent of the stock.

The point should be clear:

Money comes no higher than third. First, always, is the "dot." Then comes the plan to reach that dot at the lowest possible cost. Pick your dot—build your plan—and *then* go after the money.

You'll do great!

Recommended Reading

NEWSPAPERS CAN GIVE YOU a lot of information about innovation. Most major papers carry articles about interesting start-up companies and new inventions. The *New York Times* runs a Patents column on Mondays. The *Los Angeles Times* runs a first-rate occasional column by Michael Schrage called *Innovation*. The *Wall Street Journal* has weekly columns on both new technologies and (more surprisingly) design.

The trade papers do carry a reasonable amount of useful information, but people in the businesses warn that they often need to be taken with a large grain of salt—remember that a) they carry a lot of gossip, and b) even the best of them often lag behind events. As we've argued throughout, trend-spotting is hard to do from a distance, because by the time trends in the arts become well-enough established to be in the media, the deals for them have probably already been cut.

GOVERNMENT INFORMATION

A lot of books on copyright, patent, and trademark do little more than collect readily available Federal information and reprint it in convenient form. That's perfectly legal, of course; the Federal government rarely restricts copying of its materials. You may find those books a good investment simply because they save you the time and trouble of writing or calling the Federal government for information.

On the other hand, you might well prefer to get the information, including all the forms you'll need, straight from the source. If you live in or near a big city, contact the local outlet of the Government Printing Office. You can find it in the phone book, under the "U.S. Government" section. The GPO will generally be able to mail you the basic forms and pamphlets very quickly, usually in a couple of days. Costs are very modest.

What if you have more complicated questions?

The short way into the vast array of Federal agencies is to contact the:

> Federal Information Center
> P.O. Box 600
> Cumberland, MD 21502
> 1-301-722-9098

The F.I.C. can usually point you to the correct Federal agency for nearly any question, whether or not it has to do with intellectual property.

In addition to its Maryland number, the F.I.C. operates toll-free numbers in most states; check your local phone book under "Government Agencies—U.S. Government" for either the Federal Information Center or the General Services Administration. Beyond that, if you know generally what kinds of information you need, you can write or call the proper agency directly. For starters:

Copyrights If you have specific questions about copyrights, contact the:

> Copyright Office
> LM 455
> Library of Congress
> Washington, D.C. 20559

You can also speak with one of the office's copyright information specialists by calling: 1-202-707-3000.

Patents Correspondence with the Patent and Trademark Office goes to:

> Commissioner of Patents and Trademarks
> Washington, D.C. 20231

For pre-recorded general patent information, call 1-703-557-INFO, anytime. To speak with a live person, call 1-703-308-HELP during normal business hours.

The PTO receives approximately five million pieces of mail a year— or somewhere around nineteen thousand every working day. Try to be clear and concise in your questions, and always give full information when you refer to any existing documents.

The Office prefers that you write separate letters for each topic of inquiry. Thus, if you're asking for a copy of a patent, a PTO pamphlet, and a photostat of someone's patent assignment, you should write three separate, short letters, although they can all be placed in one envelope.

Reminder: Even if something goes wrong with your proceedings, keep your temper. PTO regulations require that applicants conduct themselves "with decorum and courtesy." The Office has the right to bounce any papers falling short of this standard—and it will!

Trademarks Again, most trademark regulation begins at the state level; as a starting point, you can contact your state's Secretary of State. To secure registration on a Federal level, you need to contact:

> The Commissioner of Patents and Trademarks
> Washington, D.C. 20231

For pre-recorded general trademark information, call 1-703-557-INFO, anytime. To speak with a live person, call 1-703-308-HELP during normal business hours.

Getting through to the PTO is generally difficult; If you have basic questions, you're probably wise to order *Basic Facts About Trademarks* from the Government Printing Office. It has not only the basic facts about applying, but the basic application forms.

If your application passes initial examination by the PTO, you'll be assigned a serial number. If you ever after have occasion to call the PTO, be sure to have the serial number ready; otherwise, you'll waste a lot of time.

GENERAL LEGAL HANDBOOKS

Playing your own lawyer is probably a mistake, but learning more about the law so you can work with your attorney is an excellent idea.

The legal literature on intellectual property is immense, and, unfortunately much of it is both highly specialized and (let's be frank) boring as heck.

Your best starting place may well be *Intellectual Property: Patents, Trademarks, and Copyright in a Nutshell.* The *nutshell* books (a series of dozens of titles) have been a standby for law students for years. The books are both technically accurate and (as legal texts go, anyway) highly readable.

MUSIC

Among the best legal handbooks for musicians is the *Musicians' Legal and Business Guide* (1991), published by Jerome Headlands Press and distributed nationally by Prentice-Hall. The earlier *Musicians' Manual,* published by the Beverly Hills Bar Association, covered many of the same concepts and still has value, but the *Legal and Business Guide* has important updates.

If you're looking for a guidebook to the business side of music, try *All You Need to Know about the Music Business* by Donald Passman, which was our favorite. Many people in the industry also recommend *This Business of Music,* which was also rated an "outstanding" reference book by the American Library Association, and its companion *More about This Business of Music,* both by Sidney Shemel and M. William Krasilovsky.

If you're ready to look for representation, Billboard's *International Talent and Touring Directory* and the *Recording Industry Source Book* both list agents, managers, and companies. *Billboard,* interestingly, lets you look up specific artists, then find out who represents them; that's useful if you want to locate reps sympathetic to your kind of music.

If you're looking for someone to record your music, try the Mix *Annual Directory of Recording Industry Facilities and Services.* It will give you names, addresses, and telephone numbers for everything from the small recording facilities to the major labels.

If you're interested in recording equipment of your own (and a somewhat less complete list of facilities), consider Billboard's *Annual Recording Equipment and Studio Directory.* Better still, get out and talk with people who are already running small facilities.

A final reminder: Music copyright protection begins at the time of fixation—which means you must have written the tune down, recorded it, or in some other fashion made it permanent if you want it to be protected.

Don't forget, though, that proving others infringed your copyright also means proving that they had access to the work, not just that their work sounds like yours and was done later.

BOOKS

Probably the most widely consulted handbooks for information about literary markets are: *LMP: The Literary Market Place* (which is something of a handbook for the publishing industry, listing publishers, agents, book manufacturers, and the like with bare information), and *Writer's Market,* a thick annual volume which is the book librarians will almost automatically hand you if you tell them you're looking for information on being a writer.

LMP lists plenty of hard facts—names, phone numbers, number of books published, and the like—but it's not in any real sense a "tip book" for beginning writers.

Writer's Market is an equally impressive listing of places to send your manuscripts. It also gives tips of perhaps variable quality (most of them stem from interviews scattered throughout the book) on how to succeed as a writer. You won't go wrong with either *LMP* or *Writer's Market*.

If you're just starting out, though, you might consider a less-well-known source: *Literary Agents of North America* is the most detailed source we've found for information on agents, and its Introduction, at only seven pages, is a gem of clarity and conciseness that neatly covers both the basics of modern publishing industry economics and the issues you should consider before signing with an agent.

As we've mentioned, you can establish the date you completed any literary or other work simply by mailing yourself a copy via registered mail and then, when it arrives, filing it unopened until you need to present it in court.

You can also arrange to have a copy filed with the copyright office of the Library of Congress or you can make use of the services of various professional organizations. For example, the Writers Guild of America, West (WGAW) will keep on file a copy of any screenplay for a period of ten years, for a fee of (presently) $20. If you ever get into a dispute, the WGA will testify in court that they received a copy from you on a specific date and kept it unaltered until the present. They will not, however, offer any testimony as to the work's similarity or lack of similarity to any other work. For that you'll need experts, and they charge a lot, usually at least $250 an hour.

VISUAL ARTS

A highly readable general guide to basic legal concerns for visual artists is the *Artist's Friendly Legal Guide,* written by four attorneys and published by Northern Light Press. Or try the free Visual Artists' Hotline run by the American Council for the Arts: 1-800-232-2789.

SCREEN AND TELEVISION WRITING

The two most useful books we know on screenwriting are *Selling Your Screenplay* by Cynthia Whitcomb (Crown, 1988), and *Screenwrit-*

ing: The Art, Craft, and Business of Film and Television Writing by Richard Walter (Plume, 1988). Beyond that, trust your own instincts: If a book seems likely to help you personally—that is, if you read a few pages and feel a surge of enthusiasm—it will almost certainly help you.

You probably don't want to buy books simply because they have a lot of technical-looking diagrams about "timing" scripts and such; most of that is just baloney. If you're on a really tight budget, just write for an application form for the Nicholl Fellowship contest; their one-page instruction sheet for applicants is an excellent guide to screenplay format.

For lists of Guild-signatory film and TV agents, and/or copies of the Guild's standard contracts, contact the:

> Writers Guild of America, West
> 8955 Beverly Boulevard
> Los Angeles, CA 90048
> 1-310-550-1000

Send a stamped, self-addressed envelope, plus $1.00 for the list of agents, or $15.00 for the contracts packet.

INVENTIONS

The United Inventors Association of the U.S.A. can refer you to your nearest nonprofit inventors' group, often a good place to start. Contact them at: 1-316-792-1375.

For information on invention marketing scams, try contacting the Inventors Awareness Group (IAG):

> IAG
> 171 Interstate Drive
> Ste. 6
> W. Springfield, MA 01089-4533
> 1-800-288-3938

IAG can also send you a very useful pamphlet on inventing basics.

You might also consider the Inventors Workshop International Education Foundation, at 1-818-340-4268. IWIEF began as an inventors' nonprofit almost twenty-five years ago. In recent years, they've become associated with a commercial venture, Eco Expo, which is a trade show for environmental products, but which still preserves some special activities for beginning inventors.

We stand by our advice that you should use a patent attorney to help protect your inventions. If, however, you feel you need to get a patent on your own, consider *Patent It Yourself* by David Pressman. It's not a simple book, or a short one, but it does an honest job of explaining the patent process.

LICENSING DEALS

Whether you're licensing a patent or franchise, here in the States or elsewhere in the world, one book you'll probably want to consider is *Licensing in Foreign and Domestic Operations,* originally by Lawrence Eckstrom, but now regularly revised by various experts. Published loose-leaf by legal publisher Clark Boardman Co., Ltd., it's a standard lawyer's reference; if you want to see model contracts, this is a natural place to start.

The Licensing Executives Society of the U.S. and Canada offers a pair of useful booklets. *The Basics of Licensing* covers both licensing and technology transfer; *Consultants and Brokers in Technology Transfer* lists LES members willing to provide a free one-hour consultation to people who want to license their inventions. Request either booklet from LES at 1-203-232-4825.

FOR BUSINESS IDEAS

We're bold enough to recommend another of our books to anyone starting a new business. *The New Small Business Survival Guide* (W. W. Norton, 1991) by Bob Coleman covers many business basics, such as raising money, choosing a corporate structure, and avoiding legal problems.

You can get a tremendous amount of free or low-cost information from the Small Business Administration. Consult your local phone book or contact their headquarters:

> The Small Business Administration
> 1441 L Street N.W.
> Washington, D.C. 20230
> 1-800-827-5722

You can also reach the SBA on-line at: 1-800-697-INFO.

And for help with government-backed loans, don't forget your local Certified Development Corporation.

You can learn a vast amount about any particular kind of business from trade associations or from trade shows. Probably the best guide to these is the *Encyclopedia of Associations,* published by Gale Research and available in many libraries.

Many idea-based businesses turn to exporting from their earliest days. With a fax machine, you can get free and useful information on foreign markets, trade shows, law, customs, and more. Start by calling: 1-800-USA-XPORT.

Using a menu they'll fax you, you can then request data on, say, toy markets in Ireland. Your phone company will charge you for the call which sends the information to your fax machine; but the information itself is free. (USA EXPORT makes its money selling your name to companies such as AT&T, which would want you as customer).

On a regular voice line, 1-800-USA-TRADE will connect you, toll-free, with a trade counselor at the Department of Commerce, who can guide you through government agencies available to help American exporters.

For questions about protecting your business ideas, one fine reference is the two-volume *Trademarks and Unfair Competition* by J. Thomas McCarthy. It's aimed at lawyers, but can help businesspeople, too.

GETTING LEGAL HELP

As we've explained, legal advice can be very expensive—but not getting it can be vastly more expensive.

Fortunately, people with ideas for the arts (whether screenplays, paintings, novels or anything else) can get assistance from a great number of state and local volunteer legal (and sometimes, accounting) professionals. The easiest way to contact these is simply to phone your local bar association, or else to check the phone book under "[State or City Name] Lawyers for the Arts." Most of these organizations will arrange for you to consult with an arts or entertainment lawyer for a greatly reduced fee. Usually, an hour's consultation will cost $35 or less; if the problem is more serious, you can work out a longer-term relationship at a rate you can probably afford.

One of the most active such groups in the country, especially helpful for questions about the music and film industries, is the:

> Committee for the Arts
> Beverly Hills Bar Association Barristers
> 300 South Beverly Drive, Suite 201
> Beverly Hills, CA 90212
> 1-310-553-6644

They publish a number of well-regarded legal guides to both music and the visual arts. On the East Coast, New York's Volunteer Lawyers for the Arts is the comparable group, but emphasizes the visual arts: 1-212-319-2787.

For advice with business contracts and the like, contact your local bar association. For sample contracts that will work in your state, try the publications of your state's CEB (Continuing Education for the Bar) association; but for any actual agreement, you're nearly always wise to consult an attorney.

Index

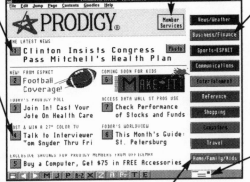